AAK9884

Tourism: A Gender Analysis

Tourism: A Gender Analysis

Edited by

Vivian Kinnaird and Derek Hall

JOHN WILEY & SONS

Chichester · New York · Brisbane · Toronto · Singapore

Copyright © the editors and contributors 1994

Published by John Wiley & Sons Ltd,
             Baffins Lane, Chichester,
             West Sussex PO19 1UD, England
             Telephone National Chichester (0243) 779777
                      International +44 243 779777

Other Wiley Editorial Offices

John Wiley & Sons, Inc., 605 Third Avenue,
New York, NY 10158–0012, USA

Jacaranda Wiley Ltd, 33 Park Road, Milton,
Queensland 4064, Australia

John Wiley & Sons (Canada) Ltd, 22 Worcester Road,
Rexdale, Ontario M9W 1L1, Canada

John Wiley & Sons (SEA) Pte Ltd, 37 Jalan Pemimpin #05–04,
Block B, Union Industrial Building, Singapore 2057

Library of Congress Cataloging-in-Publication Data

A catalog record for this book is available
from the Library of Congress.

British Library Cataloguing in Publication Data

A catalogue record for this book is available
from the British Library.

ISBN 0-471-94833-0

Typeset in 11/13 pt Palatino by Dorwyn Ltd, Rowlands Castle, Hants
Printed and bound in Great Britain by Bookcraft (Bath) Ltd, Avon

Contents

Contributors

Proinnsias Breathnach is Senior Lecturer in Geography at St Patrick's College, Maynooth, Ireland. His specialism is economic geography with particular reference to aspects of economic development.

Sarah Drea completed her MA thesis on the Organisation of Irish Tourism at the Department of Geography, St Patrick's College, Maynooth, in 1992. She is currently employed as co-ordinator of a research project under the EC RECITE programme in the Mid-west region of Ireland.

Tim Edensor is currently undertaking research on world tourism sites. He co-edited *Moving worlds* (Polygon Press, 1989).

Peggy Fairbairn-Dunlop is Senior Lecturer and Head of the Department of Agricultural Extension/Education at the University of the South Pacific, School of Agriculture, Alafua Campus, Western Samoa. She has undertaken substantial research and has published widely on tourism and development processes in the South Pacific.

Derek Hall is Reader in Geography and Development at the University of Sunderland, England. He has edited *Tourism and economic development in Eastern Europe and the Soviet Union* (Belhaven, 1991) and *Transport and economic development in the new Central and Eastern Europe* (Belhaven, 1993), and is the author of *Albania: development and change* (Pinter, 1994), together with a number of papers and book chapters on tourism in

Eastern Europe, Cuba, North Korea and sustainable tourism, some with Vivian Kinnaird.

C. Michael Hall is Senior Lecturer and Head of the Tourism Programme, University of Canberra, Australia. He is author of *Introduction to tourism in Australia: impacts, planning and development* (Longman Cheshire, 1991), *Hallmark tourist events: impacts, management and planning* (Belhaven, 1992), and *Wasteland to world heritage: preserving Australia's wilderness* (Melbourne University Press, 1992); co-editor of *Special interest tourism* (Belhaven, 1992) and of *Heritage management in New Zealand and Australia: interpretation, marketing and visitor management* (Oxford University Press, 1993); and has research interests in sustainable tourism, politics of tourism and leisure, event tourism, environmental history and heritage management.

Sinead Hennessy has worked on research projects in tourism development, and in both housing and office development. Her M.Phil (Exeter) concerned the employment of women in tourism-related industries in Cornwall. She is currently engaged in doctoral research relating to planning policy and inner-city housing in Dublin at the Department of Architecture, University of Manchester.

Marion Henry is a former teacher and currently a postgraduate student at the Department of Geography, St Patrick's College, Maynooth. She is conducting research on the local impact of tourism development in South-west Ireland.

Vivian Kinnaird is a Lecturer in Geography and Development at the University of Sunderland. Her research and teaching interests are in development studies, tourism and gender and development. She is co-editor with Janet Momsen of *Different places, different voices: gender and development in Africa, Asia and Latin America* (Routledge, 1993).

Uma Kothari is a Lecturer in Agricultural and Rural Development and Gender Issues in Development at the Institute for Development Policy and Management, University of Manchester. Her research experience has been in India and Central America.

Lila Leontidou, currently at the Department of Geography, King's College London, has been an Associate Professor at the Department of Geography and Regional Planning, National Technical University, Athens, where she has taught since 1986. She has also taught in Thessaloniki (1975–81), for short periods in universities in the USA, Spain and Italy, is a Senior Fellow at Johns Hopkins University, and is involved in several European research networks. She is the author of *The Mediterranean city in transition* (Cambridge University Press, 1990), as well as other books in Greek and articles in English, French, Italian and German.

Janet Henshall Momsen is Professor of Geography at the University of California, Davis. She has been working on Caribbean problems, specifically gender, agriculture and tourism, since 1963. She was Chair of the Society for Caribbean Studies, 1989–91, and has been Chair of the International Geographical Union Commission on Gender and Geography since 1988. She is author of *Women and development in the Third World* (Routledge, 1991), co-editor with Vivian Kinnaird of *Different places: different voices* (Routledge, 1993), co-editor of *Land and development in the Caribbean* (Macmillan, 1987), and editor of *Women and change in the Caribbean* (James Currey, 1993).

Mary O'Flaherty is a teacher and postgraduate student at the Department of Geography, St Patrick's College, Maynooth. She is conducting research on the development of recreational tourism in County Mayo, Ireland.

Preface

In attempting to fill a gap in the literature, our aim in this volume has been to draw on a range of contributors who could, both individually and collectively, stimulate debate on the gendered nature of tourism-related activities and processes. It appeared to us that the social construction of tourism was lacking a gendered component in the literature, and we have attempted to construct a framework within which a focus on the gendering of tourism could be articulated and explored. We acknowledge that this volume is only a beginning – it poses more questions than are answered. But we are confident in the knowledge that the debate will be taken up and elaborated.

We would like to thank our contributors for their participation in the debate and Neil Purvis for the artwork. A number of relatives, close friends and colleagues have sustained us through the evolution of this book. Not least, thanks are due to Iain Stevenson and Louise Metz at John Wiley for their support, good humour and efficient production.

Vivian Kinnaird, Derek Hall
Prudhoe and Newcastle upon Tyne, July 1993

Glossary of acronyms

CARICOM	Caribbean Common Market
CEC	Commission of the European Communities
CERT	Council for Education, Recruitment and Training (Ireland)
CTO	Caribbean Tourism Organisation
CTRC	Caribbean Tourism Research and Development Centre
CWIC	Caribbean and West Indies Chronicle
EC	European Community/European Commission
EKKE	National Centre of Social Research (Greece)
EOT	National Tourism Organisation (Greece)
ESYE	National Statistical Service of Greece
GDP	Gross domestic product
GNP	Gross national product
HMSO	Her Majesty's Stationery Office (UK)
KEPE	Centre of Planning and Economic Research, Athens
NCW	National Council of Women (Western Samoa)
OECD	Organisation for Economic Co-operation and Development
PATA	Pacific Area Tour Association
SIPTU	Services, Industrial, Professional and Technical Union (Ireland)
TAT	Tourism Authority of Thailand
TCSP	Tourism Council of the South Pacific
WSVA	Western Samoa Visitors Association

1
Tourism: gender perspectives

Vivian Kinnaird, Uma Kothari and Derek Hall

INTRODUCTION

Consideration of the economic, socio-cultural and environmental implications of tourism-related activity has a long tradition (Fox, 1977; Travis, 1982; Mathieson and Wall, 1982; Inskeep, 1987; Craik, 1991) and continues to be important in discussions of the 'impact' of tourism development (e.g. Williams, 1987). Specialisation in one or more of these general fields of inquiry has led to a deconstruction of analyses of the tourism process as a whole, in both the academic and policy-making literature. However, as the literature continues to focus on specialised areas of tourism development, for example, recent publications have highlighted 'special interest tourism' (Weiler and Hall, 1992), 'ecotourism' (Boo, 1991; Cater, 1991; Eber, 1992; Hall and Kinnaird, 1994), and 'alternative tourism' (see Wheeller, 1992), there is the risk of overlooking important themes that are common to the process of tourism development as a whole.

More recently, processes of tourism development have been theorised as important identifiers of social change (Smith, 1989; Urry, 1990; Shields, 1991; Chant, 1992; Harrison, 1992). Following from this, attempts have been made to reconstruct and re-interpret our analyses of tourism and tourism development, focusing on the social relations embodied in tourism practices and processes. In this book we seek to focus on issues of gender and gender relations as they form a part of wider social relations and social processes.

In this chapter we provide a selective review of the contemporary tourism literature and present some ideas for a conceptual framework with which to examine issues of gender relations and tourism processes. This framework is based on the recognition that tourism processes are gendered in their construction, presentation and consumption, and the form of this gendering is configured in different and diverse ways which are both temporally and spatially specific.

We begin with the recognition of the significance of tourism within the majority of world economies and as an important characteristic of modern consumer culture.

The significance of tourism

There is no doubt that tourism has, and continues to be, a focus for development. This is particularly significant in those regions of the world that are either suffering the social and economic hardship of de-industrialisation (e.g. Britain), or are seeking development options for foreign exchange earnings (through structural adjustment programmes, for example). The latter case includes many, if not all, of the developing countries, and the newly emerging former-communist regimes of central and eastern Europe (see Hall, 1991, 1992; Harrison, 1993). Consequently, the perceived importance of tourism for 'economic development' cannot be disputed. At the same time, statistical evidence depicts a remarkable increase in the number of international travellers from 25 million in 1950 to 425 million in 1990 (World Tourism Organisation, 1992). In addition, tourism is recognised as the world's fastest growing industry, representing seven per cent of all world exports (Harrison, 1992). These realisations indicate that the demand for international travel, linked to major indicators of lifestyle changes and opportunities among those most likely to participate in the international tourism market, will continue to expand. Therefore, tourism is, and will continue to be, a significant strategy for capital accumulation. Tourism is seen as a 'soft' means of promoting development: it is attractive because it faces fewer constraints than alternative forms of economic development. There is an absence of market protectionism; technological and human resource demands are low (it is service-oriented and, for the most part, requires low-skilled labour), and it appears to have fewer environmental and infrastructural constraints than would heavy manufacturing or agricultural development (Hitchcock *et al.*, 1993).

In addition to developments in the international tourism market, domestic/national tourism in many countries is also increasing. This is partly due to the prevalence of increased leisure time and wealth creation, but also to the encouragement of tourist-related development in regions seeking to restructure their economies. As Edensor and Kothari point out (Chapter 8), in Britain the heritage industry occupies an increasingly central role in local and national strategies for economic growth and development. Regions attempt to present and promote a unique tourism image based largely on their 'heritage'. Attractions such as Wigan Pier, Beamish Museum and the Ironbridge Gorge are popular tourist destinations where visitors can gaze on the industrial past and experience a bygone English industrial heritage. A similar image is presented by former industrial centres such as Manchester, Bradford and Tyne and Wear (Buckley and Witt, 1985). South Tyneside, a borough of Tyne and Wear, is actively promoting the industrial heritage of the River Tyne, encouraging tourism as a strategy for economic diversification and urban regeneration (Wyatt, 1991).

Despite its significance for economic development, issues of social change as affected by, and interacting with, the adoption of tourism as a strategy for development, especially in developing countries and regions, appears to have been marginalised in the literature. A review of the major issues within academic and policy-oriented 'development studies' reveals a dearth of the social articulations of tourism-related development (notable exceptions include Britton, 1991; Harrison, 1992; Smith, 1989; Brown, 1992; Selwyn, 1992). At the same time however, considerable effort is spent carefully analysing agents of social change. These analyses are driven by the search for 'appropriate development' strategies and training, and broad considerations of the social, cultural and economic relationships that occur within 'development' (as witnessed, for example, by the huge literature on, and attention paid to, the 'gender and development' approach to development planning). We would argue that tourism and its projected growth into the next century deserves similar attention. An analysis of tourism-related activity is an important conceptual and methodological tool for the understanding of social relations and individual and group behaviour. Development approaches, strategies and practices which are aware of gender bias in the development process are now recognised as necessary for successful 'development' (see Elson, 1991).

Furthermore, an analysis of tourist practices tells us a great deal about issues of identity, nationhood and representation. Tourism-related activity is one of a number of 'projects of representation' (see Katz, 1992) which are undertaken through the perceptions and motivations of the tourist in relation to the nature and articulation of the tourism 'product' as defined by host societies in conjunction with a myriad of marketing agents. Therefore, tourism development and the types of tourism-related activity present in a particular place, is a two-way process that is dependent upon the social relations present in both host and guest societies. Tourism-related activity is, therefore, a lens through which we can identify a 'space of betweenness' which is necessary in order to build political and intellectual practice as well as points of reference in our analysis (see Katz, 1992, p. 506). As academics and consultants we must position ourselves as observers and participants in the processes of tourism development and build individual perceptions and understandings of social relations into our analyses of tourism-related activities.

Outline of chapter

This chapter is divided into three main parts. First we examine theoretical and conceptual issues. Secondly, we outline various definitions of tourism and offer a critique of these approaches. Finally, we review the major debates and approaches within the literature and suggest a conceptual lens through which the chapters of this book can be read.

WHY GENDER AND TOURISM? A CONCEPTUAL FOCUS

Conceptually, we are focusing on three principal issues which we consider crucial to an understanding of tourism processes. First, tourism is a process that is constructed out of gendered societies and therefore all aspects of tourism-related development and activity embody gender relations. Secondly, gender relations both inform, and are informed, socially, in a number of diverse and complex ways. Economic, political, social, cultural and environmental relations are all part of the process of tourism development. These are articulated and configured in various ways and change over time: as such, tourism cannot be analysed as a separate sphere of economic, social, environmental or cultural life in any society. Although tourism involves these different spheres, it is not separate from them, but rather engages all of them as processes of change, and conceptually cuts across and emerges out of their inter-relatedness.

Thirdly, since tourism-related activity has become an important process of development, the social, economic and political relations which result are part of overall issues of power and control. These power relations can be articulated through race, class or gender. Although all of these power relations are significant, for the purposes of this book we are focusing on gender and therefore ask several questions: how are gender relations constructed within tourism? How do they change over time? What are the implications for wider issues of inequality and control?

Broader issues of the hierarchical social and economic characteristics of capital accumulation allow us to begin to answer these questions. Many sociological and anthropological analyses of the process of tourism development highlight the inherent power relations that embody touristic activity and the tourism product within the context of international tourism. Nash (1989) views international tourism as a form of imperialism with the 'metropolitan centres' maintaining control over the nature of tourism and its development.

> It is this power over touristic and related development abroad that makes a metropolitan centre imperialistic and tourism a form of imperialism. (Nash, 1989, p. 39)

Nash cites the examples of the North American vacationer who demands American fast food, hot running water and the use of English language as a familiar imperialistic image. De Kadt (1979) stressed the importance of macro-economic policy making, linked to colonialism and the political economy of North–South domination, for understanding the local implications of international tourism development. Similarly, Britton (1982) discussed the development of tourism in the South Pacific region, suggesting it had followed the course of 'core' domination over the 'periphery' and providing empirical evidence to support his claims (see also Hoivik and Heiberg, 1980). Tourism in the South Pacific is controlled by foreign investment, destinations are re-created by metropolitan advertisers, and eventually tourism development serves foreign interests over the interests of the local. This pattern of control over tourism as an industry leads some to comment on the 'underdevelopment' of the poor and the 'development' of the rich that tourism brings (see Selwyn, 1992; Kincaid, 1988). Tourism can, therefore, be seen as a mechanism for the incorporation of developing countries into an essentially exploitative global economic system (Antrobus, 1990).

Thus, international processes of tourism development have been perceived as part of economic and political power relations within a political economy perspective of global development and underdevelopment. As Selwyn (1992) states, however, the difficulties of this approach lie in being able to refer to economic and political systems at both the global and the local level. Articulating the concepts of international economic and political power relations explains many of the relationships that emerge within international tourism. However power relations also exist within national tourism and are focused much more acutely at the local level where issues of race, class and gender can be analysed as significant political power relations.

We agree with other commentators (Selwyn, de Kadt, Nash, Britton, Kincaid) that tourism processes involve some notions of power and control. An interesting and necessary step forward in this argument is to realise that tourism involves processes which are constructed out of complex and varied social realities and relations that are often hierarchical and unequal. All parts of the process embody different social relations of which gender relations are one element. Whether we examine divisions of labour within the tourism process, the social construction of sites in the landscape and as part of 'heritage', how societies construct the cultural 'Other',[1] or the realities of the 'tourist' and the 'host', it is necessary that we examine issues of relationships, differences and inequalities in terms of gender relations.[2] This allows us to concentrate on women's and men's differential experiences, construction and consumption of tourism.[3] How does tourism articulate gender relations and how do gender relations inform and articulate the form of different tourism processes?

As we shall see from the case studies in this book, women and men are involved differently within tourism processes, and, as a result, the relationships, consequences and the eventual configuration of the tourism experience for hosts and guests is gender specific. The differential effects of tourism as a strategy for development are evident in our conceptualisation and analyses of the implications of touristic activity. In addition, the way in which all societies, whether host or guest, embody a changing set of gender perceptions, stereotypes and relations, and articulate these as part of their individual notions of 'reality', has implications for the marketing of tourism and for the motivations of guests to visit or of hosts to entertain. For example, the advent of sex-tourism, which has become widely discussed within the socio-cultural 'impact' literature is overtly concerned with male/female (or male/male) host/guest encounters. This form of touristic activity has flourished within societies which have a particular set of patriarchal gender/power relations that are steeped in historical traditions and interact with the modernisation and globalisation of their economies and societies (Mackie, 1988; Lee, 1991; Chapter 7 in this volume). Mackie (1988) views prostitution in South-east Asia and the popularity of sex-tours, especially among Japanese male tourists, as an economic power relation that reflects a long history of class, gender and race in the region. According to Kikue (1979), South Korea's notoriety as a destination for Japanese sex-tourists is partially due to Japan's former colonisation of South Korea and the racist overtones this implies. Racism, it is argued, also explains why Japanese women are ambivalent regarding the engagement of Japanese men in sex-tourism, finding it more acceptable if their husbands pursue foreign rather than Japanese prostitutes (Lee, 1991; see also Cohen, 1971, 1982).

The significance of tourism and tourism-related activity as both a form of economic development and a social phenomenon of contemporary life cannot be disputed. Yet, as we shall see in the next section, narrow definitions of tourism and theoretical frameworks constructed to examine it often ignore the inter-related nature of different societal constructs, thereby overlooking the wider power relations that are inherent in the process of tourism development and tourism-related activity. Tourism processes articulate and are constructed out of these social and power relations. This is not to say that processes of tourism always reinforce gender differences and inequalities. However, all processes are constructed out of different social relations and these inevitably embody power, inequality and control. All processes are dynamic and use gender relations. What, therefore, does tourism development mean for women and men in different societies?

DEFINING TOURISM

A variety of definitions for tourism and tourism activity exist within the literature that are specific to the particular analysis under consideration. We would argue that differing definitions reflect differing perceptions and understandings of tourism processes. Generally, we can identify two broad approaches. The first reflects the traditional attempt to quantify people's movement across space in order to take part in tourism-related activity. The aim of these analyses is to try to capture movements of tourists, in order to quantify the economic, social or, more recently, environmental impacts of tourism. Accounting for the provision of tourism infrastructure, the employment of thousands of people and the 'multiplier' effect of this type of economic activity is important for the assessment of development potential (see Archer, 1982; Mathieson and Wall, 1982). The second trend emerges from sociological and anthropological perspectives and seeks to broaden our understanding of the social relations inherent in processes of tourism development. Tourism is thus seen as a social phenomenon (Hovel and Feuerstein, 1992). However, in both cases there is a need to differentiate between international and domestic tourism to provide adequate, encompassing definitions of both.

Quantifying tourism-related activity

International tourism can be traditionally characterised and identified using statistical data that can be collected from ports of entry. In 1934, the League of Nations defined an international tourist as a person who visits a country other than his/her own for at least 24 hours (Selwyn, 1992). This is a definition echoed by the World Tourism Organisation. 'Excursionists' visit a place other than their own home for a period of less than 24 hours and have been studied in attempts to quantify domestic tourism. These definitions are extremely broad (Harrison, 1992) and problems of data compatibility between places are evident. However, in both international and domestic tourism, the reasons for visits are usually recreation or business, although family and educational visits are often included and are very important motivations for domestic tourism (Hall, 1991).

In the face of these broad generalisations, Smith (1989) offers a series of tourist typologies in search of a definition of the tourist 'role' and the tourist's potential for integration with the host community. An argument centred around the 'effects of tourist numbers' contrasts the economically non-lucrative, but culturally non-disruptive 'explorer' who adapts to the host's cultural norms with the economically lucrative (for some) charter holiday-maker arriving in vast numbers, demanding all the comforts of home and remaining separate from the local social environment (what Sampson, 1968, refers to as the 'cruise liner effect'). Yet, despite these definitions (see also Cohen, 1974; Hamilton-Smith, 1987), there is a perceived need to provide a simple blanket definition of tourism and the tourist in order to make cost/benefit analyses straightforward and replicable for tourism development planning.

There are limitations to this quest for straightforward, statistical definitions. First, contemporary movements of people between countries encompass many whose primary reason for visiting another country is other than what is usually perceived as tourist activity. Those who move to work as temporary labourers or who are refugees are not associated with tourism (Ward, 1975a, 1975b; Salt, 1981, 1985; Castles and Kosack, 1985; King, 1990; Estrada-Claudio, 1992). Ironically, guest workers may travel to other countries or regions to work in the tourism industry but do not constitute tourists themselves (Poulsen, 1977; Lever, 1987).

Secondly, domestic tourism accounts for a substantial proportion of tourist activity. Historically, the seaside resorts along the Channel, North Sea and Irish Sea coasts of Britain, France, Belgium and the Netherlands existed on the strength of domestic tourism. The annual pilgrimage to the seaside, especially among the urban working class, supported a well-established tourism sector in coastal communities (see Williams and Shaw, 1988). In North America, domestic tourism is statistically enhanced by the vast distances which the tourist can travel and remain a 'domestic tourist'. Many other countries would appear to be experiencing an increase in domestic tourism. In India, for example, domestic tourism is becoming increasingly popular as more leisure time and greater discretionary income (for some) become part of an Indian industrial economy (Smith, 1989). A huge domestic tourism sector is also developing in China, Taiwan and Korea.

Thirdly, these narrow definitions also limit our wider understanding of other processes occurring within tourism development which are integral to tourism-related activity, such as the relationships between individuals, the social relations that are constructed out of these, and the perception of the cultural 'Other'. Consequently, for our purposes these definitions abstract tourism from wider processes of change and more importantly from the articulation and construction of differences and hierarchies between people. Simple statistical accounts treat individuals as merely being involved in spatial movement. Tourists are therefore not seen as people who embody social relations and their positions and roles as wider agents of social change are ignored. There is a tendency therefore to view tourism as an unproblematic and apolitical activity and one that is beyond a political critique.

Finally, on a broader conceptual note, limitations arise in attempts to theorise tourism in order to understand fully its significance in contemporary economies and 'its role in creating the materiality and social meaning of places' (Britton, 1991, p. 452). Describing travel flows and the various impacts of tourism infrastructure and tourist arrivals may be important, but it does not establish well-grounded theory, nor does it enable us to conceptualise tourism within broader geographical or sociological debates (see Britton, 1991; Urry, 1991).

Tourism as social interaction

Tourism is also seen as involving a wide variety of human activities, behavioural patterns and motivations which are situated within socially specific contexts. Smith (1989) defines a tourist as a leisured individual who 'voluntarily visits a place away from home for the purpose of experiencing a change' (Smith, 1989, p. 1). Urry (1990, 1991) defines tourism-related activity as a composition of a number of interacting characteristics that encompass both international and domestic tourism. First, tourism is part of leisure activity which, from a sociological perspective, is viewed in relation to concepts of 'work' and 'home'. As such, tourism activity is opposite to work and is

> one manifestation of how work and leisure are organised as separate and regulated spheres of social practice. (Urry, 1990, p. 3)

Graburn (1989) provides a similar definition suggesting that tourism is part of the process of re-creation necessary to renew us for the everyday world of work and home. Rojek (1985) argues that tourism, as a subset of leisure, is dependent on 'free-time' and therefore as shorter work weeks and longer holiday entitlements are increasing for some, the growth of tourism-related activity is inevitable. As part of leisure time, tourism, therefore, enables individuals to spend a period of time in a new place or places (Urry, 1990, p. 3).

Secondly, tourists search for the unique and therefore in most tourism activity, there is a clear distinction between the ordinary on the one hand and the extraordinary on the other. For Urry (1991, p. 49) tourism arises out of this contrast. Graburn goes further by suggesting that different forms of tourism are associated with particular hierarchies of rank and prestige which demonstrate the variety of experiences and perspectives of the individual ranging along the continuum of the ordinary/extraordinary:

Although the outward rationale for tourism has as many variations as there are tourists, the basic motivation seems to be the human need for recreation. Tourism is one manifestation of the fulfilment of this need – one that, because of the more affluent economic status of the developed world, is enabling many people to see 'how the other half lives'. (Graburn, 1989, p. 36)

The contrast between the developed and developing worlds is obvious and one that is part of the power relationships that are evident in international tourism. This type of analysis attempts to examine the social relations of the tourist focused on the different class positions of those who could be tourists and those who are only in a position to serve the tourist. This assumes a social and economic differentiation between the tourist and the host which is based on differing levels of disposable income and leisure time. A parallel distinction can be drawn within domestic tourism. However, here the distinctions are often blurred and sometimes reversed. Much tourism in Britain, for example, is based around visits to national sites of heritage and royalty. Here, differentiation between the tourist and the host is clearly evident, albeit in an obverse way to that indicated by Graburn. Similar examples can be found in Hollywood tours of movie stars' homes and day trips from Barbados to the Grenadines to gaze at the holiday retreats of the world's wealthy elite.

Thirdly, the tourism industry draws upon a variety of signs, symbols, daydreams and fantasies through which it promotes the tourism product while simultaneously paying attention to the ever-changing nature of these elements:

People seek to experience in reality the pleasurable dramas that have already emerged in their daydreams, but reality always turns out to be deeply disappointing and so consumers are continually turning to new products or places to visit. (Urry, 1991, pp. 51–2)

The tourism industry is in the business of selling these daydreams and the culture of consumerism, which characterises contemporary tourism packages, provides various experiences, signs and symbols and encourages the search for novelty (Britton, 1991). For the individual as tourist, participation in the consumption of the tourism product satisfies a number of desires ranging from the fantasy of living a particular lifestyle and confirmation of social status to an invigoration of the body and spirit and a confirmation or challenge of attitudes (Featherstone, 1990; Britton, 1991).

MacCannell (1976) emphasises the 'mythical' quality of tourist perceptions which is constructed with the help of tourism marketing agents (Uzzell, 1984; Dann, 1981; Selwyn, 1993). Tourist brochures help to construct the myths and fantasies that are characteristic of certain key ideological features of Western culture which include representations of men and women which associate action, power and ownership with the former and passivity, availability and being owned with the latter (Selwyn, 1992, p. 355). Similarly, Dann (1981) emphasises the power of tourists that underlies the function of the tourist brochure. Hosts are represented as passive and willing to fulfil the myths and fantasies of the tourists' desires.

Tourism involves a wide variety of economic, social and environmental considerations as part of the tourism product, and emphases placed on each yield differing analyses and development strategies. Whether international or domestic, tourism is characterised by the lack of a tangible 'consumer product' (Lanfont, 1980). Rather, it is a combination of services (accommodation, catering, transport), culture, particular geographical features, which provide different activity spaces, and other intangibles such as atmosphere and hospitality (Lanfont, 1980). In addition, tourism is consumed at the point of 'existence' and involves more than the material; it is cultural; it involves gazing upon and the 'selling' of 'otherness' and the unique (see Urry, 1990; Canan and Hennessey, 1989; Byrne Swain, 1990). It is this uniqueness that best characterises and defines the nature of tourism and tourist activity which changes over time. Tourism therefore involves the purchase of the particular social relations and characteristics of the host and hence

> the service is infused with the particular social characteristics of gender, class, race, generation, education and so on. (Urry, 1991, p. 50)

Discussions of tourism through sociological constructs has advantages for our purposes. These interpretations move us on from simple definitions of tourism to examine the constructions of different tourists' realities and the process in which they become engaged. Using Urry's conceptualisation, for example, it is possible to gain a clearer understanding of the processes of tourism and the social relations that it embodies. However, at the same time Urry (among others) does not deal with gender issues in any substantial way, and it is this area which, we argue, requires particular attention.

The nature of the definitions offered by Urry, Lanfont, Dann, Uzzell, Britton and Selwyn allow us to comment from a gendered point of view. The notion that tourist-related activity becomes a sphere of social practice characterised as 'modern' and 'bound up with major transformations of paid work' (Urry, 1990, p. 3), leads us to ask some fundamental questions about work (both paid and unpaid) and the implications of this sphere of activity for both hosts and guests. For hosts, issues of employment opportunity and the control of wage employment creation are gendered. As we shall see, the types of work available within the tourism industry are often gender specific and are based on Western perceived notions of the sexual division of labour. For guests, it is interesting to examine what type of 'work' comprises that sphere of activity that provides the motivations to seek leisured tourist pursuits. Are we considering both paid and unpaid work as seen in modern Western society? If so, then perceptions of work are inherently gender differentiated, especially when women's and men's paid and unpaid work commitments are considered. As Britton (1991) suggests, the distinction between work and non-work is more clearly defined for men than it is for women. Women's work within the home is less distinguishable from their 'leisure time'. Thus, the huge increase in the demand for self-catering tourist accommodation, both domestically and internationally, leads one to question the gender imbalance in an assessment of tourism as 'escaping work'. A similar argument may hold true for escaping the familiar confines of home.

Yet, a more important critique can be made of the signs and symbols, myths and fantasies that the tourism industry uses to both market tourist destinations and to reinforce the general perceptions we have about the world. Who are tourism professionals catering for? Signs and symbols, myths and fantasies are often male oriented (Enloe, 1989). Women and sexual imagery are used to portray the 'exotic' nature of a destination, the airline that will take you there and, in some cases, the main reason for the visit (Antrobus, 1990) (such as the overt advertising of sex-tourism in Thailand). Furthermore, as Urry (1990) suggests, the signs and symbols used in tourism promotion are part of a broader understanding of the world in general, thus tourism has a much longer-term impact on our knowledge and perception of the world than the short-term periods of travel may imply (see Selwyn, 1992). Tourism development and the marketing of tourist-related activities have the potential to reinforce stereo-typed roles for women and men as witnessed by the sexual division of labour, the concern for a 'nation of busboys' without the corresponding concern for a 'nation of chambermaids',[4] the promotion of Asian women as 'passive' traditionalists who are not influenced by the feminist ideals of Western women and therefore make better companions,[5] and the expectation that women will provide that traditional 'otherness' that is sought by the ever-discerning tourist.

DEBATES AND APPROACHES: GENDER CONSIDERATIONS

We have stressed that specific processes of tourism development are constructed out of gendered societies and therefore economic, social, cultural and environmental change is expressed in complex and varied ways. Individual case study analyses of the process of tourism development usually focus on one of these sub-concerns of tourism and tourism-related activity. We argue that each articulates particular sets of gender relations which provide a common thread through which to interpret the literature.

Economic development

Although there is considerable disagreement regarding the economic implications of the process of tourism development, there is a recognition of tourism as an important contributor to gross national product, foreign exchange earnings, employment generation and for urban and regional regeneration. A review of the literature covering all aspects of the economic debate is beyond the scope of this chapter. However, for our purposes, a focus on the significance of employment creation within the process of tourism development has important gender considerations. The actual employment generating effects of tourism are hotly debated. It is difficult to account accurately for the employment creation effect of tourism because it cuts across many sectors of the economy. Furthermore, employment is seen as being of both a direct (in accommodation or tourism facilities) and indirect nature (arising from secondary tourism provision or in work resulting from the general increased spending power within the 'host' area) (see Archer, 1982; Mathieson and Wall, 1982). However, it is widely accepted that employment opportunities do arise from tourism development. It is the quality, and type of work activities available, the differential access of men and women to these employment opportunities, the seasonality of employment and the existing and new gender divisions of labour generated which are important for development. Recent studies (Bagguley, 1990; Rees and Fielder, 1992; Chapters 2 and 3 in this book; Levy and Lerch, 1991; Monk and Alexander, 1986) have shown that in many tourism development areas employment opportunities have been confined to unskilled, low paid work, such as kitchen staff, chambermaids, 'entertainers' and retail clerks. In addition, calls for the 'flexibility' of service as envisaged by a new' dynamic tourism (see Poon, 1989, 1990) that can easily respond to changes in demand further complicates employment structuring.

As with all other forms of employment, these areas of 'tourism work' both reinforce and often transform gender divisions of labour. A gender focus within the hotel and catering industry in Britain raises interesting conceptual issues. Gender stereotyping is evident and sex segregation at different levels of employment activity is apparent. Women work as counter and kitchen staff, domestics and cleaners, while men work as porters and stewards. Over 50 per cent of men employed in the industry are in a professional, managerial or supervisory occupation (Crompton and Sanderson, 1990). Women are recruited into work which is deemed to represent their traditional domestic responsibilities for which they will be inherently skilled (Rees and Fielder, 1992).

Similar arguments are echoed in case studies focusing elsewhere. In a survey of tourism workers in Barbados, Levy and Lerch (1991) found women to be employed in less stable, lower paid and lower status work. However, in the developing world, where the transformation from agriculture to manufacturing and service industry employment is often viewed positively, these problems of inequality are rarely expressed, particularly when they are focused on women. Early advocates of tourism as a strategy for modernisation viewed tourism employment as a positive way of integrating underprivileged subgroups into the mainstream economy (Levy and Lerch, 1991). Low skilled jobs were viewed as good opportunities for women and ethnic minorities (Jafari, 1973). However, these notions merely echo stereotyped sexist and racist social ideologies and reinforce the social stratification systems present (de Kadt, 1979). They also create overt gender and ethnic divisions of labour within the tourism industry (Britton, 1991). In many developing countries where tourists are white and those serving tourists are black, the nature of the service may be interpreted as servility and seen in the context of colonial history (see Perez, 1973–4 for a discussion of the Caribbean).

Reinforcement of the gender divisions of labour are not always interpreted pessimistically, however. In Greece, women had wage-earning opportunities through the development of tourism co-operatives (Chapter 7 in this volume; Castelberg-Koulma, 1991). The work had enabled women to gain more independence and move their traditional domestic labour into the public domain. In such cases, changing gender relations are evident as women work and earn publicly and gain an element of financial autonomy. This is so despite the fact that the nature of the work does not appear to threaten prevailing gender roles and can be accommodated within the prevailing sexual division of labour. Similar arguments are made for Ireland by Breathnach *et al.* in Chapter 3, for Cornwall by Hennessy in Chapter 2, for Barbados by Levy and Lerch (1991), for Mexico by Chant (1992) and for the Caribbean by Price (1988).

Access to tourism-related employment is overtly gender biased. There is overwhelming evidence from the literature that the majority of jobs, especially those of low skill and wage, are occupied by women. However, it is important to emphasise that prevailing social norms regarding 'women's work' have underpinned and allowed this to take place. It seems that Western perceptions of women's role have also permeated transnational tourism organisations and diverse cultures. At the same time, the significance of new work opportunities for changing gender relations appears to be relatively unexplored.

Socio-cultural change

The implications of the movement of large masses of people from one place to another carrying differing sets of motivations, preconceptions and desires to 'find something new', have a profound influence on all social and cultural aspects of both the host and guest societies. Traditionally, the tourism literature has generated considerable debate over the social and cultural 'impacts' of the process of tourism development. Here, we look at three particular areas: the commoditisation of culture, changing value systems, and changing family structure, all of which have central gender considerations.

Commoditisation of culture

Processes of tourism development and tourism-related activity are paradoxical in their demand for the traditional/modern. As a process for development, tourism is providing a strategy for economic and social change that has been widely debated within the framework of modernisation (see Harrison, 1992). However, in the quest for the unique, the tourist often searches for the traditional, the 'Other'. Thus, somewhere in the changes that are occurring within the process of tourism development, there is a requirement for the maintenance of tradition and the need to sell, or commoditise, those traditions as 'otherness'. Discussions of tourism's relationship with authenticity and the changing nature of the meaning of cultural arts and traditions are well documented (Cohen, 1983, 1988). Yet, more recent comments suggest that an analysis of the impacts of commoditisation on those involved in the production of ethnic art depicts an understanding of how issues of gender, class and ethnicity intertwine (Swain, 1993).

It is clear that the ways in which individual societies deal with the commercialisation of their culture are profoundly gendered.

Swain (1989, 1993) suggests gender roles have shaped the development of tourism among the Kuna of Panama and the Sani of Yunnan, China. Among the Kuna, women produce *mola* artwork, a traditional fabric handicraft, and maintain a 'marketable image of ethnicity'. Men produce and maintain the political forum through which the community interacts with tourists' interests. However, the position and relative power of women and men are interdependent for the success of indigenous tourism enterprises. This is partly due to the fact that tourism grew out of the *mola* trade and sewing *molas* is women's work. Although women sell *molas* in local markets, its wholesaling in urban centres is men's work. However, with the further development of tourism among the Kuna and their integration with the rest of Panamanian society and economy, changes in gender roles are evolving. In China, the government promotes ethnic tourism using exotic images of Sani women who are frequently seen wearing traditional ethnic dress. Yet, some Sani women are also involved in the production of ethnic handicrafts and the marketing of them in the towns and cities near by. Many Sani men are employed in providing tourism services and support women's home craft production. The active involvement of both men and women in both Kuna and Sani tourism development is evident, yet Swain (1993, p. 40) suggests that although women in both societies have gained some measure of economic independence and empowerment through tourism enterprises, they remain 'exoticized female images of the other, with little real power in their distinct state societies'.

Women and men play different roles in the selling of their traditions and culture. Whether it is *molas* in Panama, dances in Bali (McKean, 1989; Picard, 1990), Amish quilts in Pennsylvania (Boynton, 1986) or *tapa* in Western Samoa (Chapter 6 in this volume), gender relations and roles are an important element of authenticity and tradition and change dramatically to the demands of the process of tourism development.

Changing value systems

It is argued that host/guest relations lead to an exchange of values whereby locals take on the values of tourists and reciprocally, tourists identify with their hosts. The extent to which these exchanges take place depends on the nature of the interaction between host and guest. This is further dependent upon the type of tourist, the form of individual tourist-related activity and the degree to which the host can interact with tourists, based on the underlying ideology of the host regime and its structuring of the tourism industry. Some argue that the interaction of tourists with host societies allows a demonstration effect that is the cultural equivalent of commoditisation (see Harrison, 1992, p. 30).

However, some form of interaction does occur and the ways in which changing value systems are gendered are significant. Chant's (1992) analysis of women in Puerto Vallarta, Mexico, suggested that women's changing perceptions of themselves and their potential position as individuals were affected by their interaction with women tourists who displayed characteristics of autonomy and self-reliance. In Greece, Castelberg-Koulma (1991, p. 198) identifies the importance of Greek women's involvement in tourism-related activity through the establishment of co-operatives as an important breakthrough toward overthrowing the stereotyped picture of the

> Greek woman . . . portrayed as an old crone, dressed in black, in an underdeveloped rural setting

set against the sexualised object of the Western female tourist.

> These male gazing images attempt to reflect the dominant scene, to the detriment of both Greek and foreign women. (Castelberg-Koulma, 1991, p. 198)

Castelberg-Koulma (1991, p. 210) concludes that not only does the formation of women's co-operatives give Greek women a position within the process of tourism development, but they are also 'a new form of encounter between hostess and guest'.

Perhaps the most widely discussed aspect of tourism-related activity which affects societal value systems is sex-tourism (Chapter 7 in this volume; also see Cohen, 1971, 1982; Kikue, 1979; Davidson, 1985; Mackie, 1988; Lee, 1991; C.M. Hall, 1992). Some portray the effects of sex-tourism as the most significant 'social impact' of the process of tourism development (e.g. Hovel and Feuerstein, 1992). The breakdown of traditional family arrangements, morality and social structure is partially blamed on the questionable relationships that emerge from the sex-tourism industry. However, included within sex-tourism is a wide variety of relationships (Harrison, 1992), and sex plays a role in many different kinds of tourism; among some hosts this type of interaction with tourists can bring possibilities for increased income and status (see Cohen, 1971).

Family change

Changing gender relations are articulated through tourism's interaction with families and changing family structure. Studies report on a variety of inter-relationships and processes of change that tourism and particular family structures create when they interact. This varies according to the extent and type of tourism as well as the 'traditional' family structure (Harrison, 1992).

Case studies depict the spatial specificity of the nature of the family's interaction with the process of tourism development. In the Caribbean, Antrobus (1990) argues a gender-aware focus within analyses of the process of tourism development reminds us that women's interaction with tourism has a more profound mediating and determining effect on the experience of the family than does that of men, due to women's powerful position in the family. Here, she raises issues of family breakdown due to changes in the division of labour, economic power (particularly since men are in higher paying employment) and the sexual tensions that can emerge within the household unit with the increasing number of males involved in escort or sex-tourism services.

In other studies, changes in family structure and the power of family members reflect a 'modernisation' of the family unit. In Crete, Kousis (1984) found that due to mass tourism, rural family structure was changed at a number of levels, reflecting more widespread control of decision-making among family members and the possibility of increased autonomy for women. Although she found little change in the rates of marriage, family size had been reduced and there was less dependence on land. In Mexico, Chant (1992) found incidences of female-headed households more dominant in areas of readily available tourism employment. Here, women found economic autonomy and therefore the ability to control their own family environment. Brown (1992) and Peake (1989) discuss the changing role of young men within the traditional family structure of the Gambia and among the Swahili of Kenya, respectively. Young men gain greater family status and economic autonomy through their interaction with tourists. For Brown (1992) young men act as 'culture brokers' between their families and tourists. Visits to family villages enhance the tourist's authentic Gambian holiday experience, while at the same time offering economic benefits to the young men and their families, often long after the tourist has returned home. Similarly, Peake (1989) found young men gained employment both formally and informally in Kenya's tourism industry through which the power structure of their families changed dramatically. Employment opportunities for young men removed power from the traditional elder men in their families and thereby influenced the political structure and status system of the community (Harrison, 1992).

The environment

The environmental consequences of the process of tourism development have long been an important focal point within the tourism literature, particularly as strategies of sustainable development and general environmental concerns have become widely discussed. Latterly, sustainable tourism and eco-tourism have become declared goals of the tourism industry (WTTERC, 1993). This has come about particularly as a result of the critique of mass tourism's destruction of the environment (see Boo, 1991; Eber, 1992). The 'greening' of tourism appears often to have been adopted as a marketing and public relations ploy rather than a genuine response to perceived needs.

Yet, tourism's interface with the environment is more than just the way in which the environment is used or abused by tourists and tourism. Societies' appreciation for the environment is socially constructed both temporally and spatially and the way in which we 'see' the environment is based on the changing economic, social and geographical organisation of tourism (Urry, 1992). For example, Western society's appreciation for landscape in the nineteenth century was an historically specific social and cultural construction of the external world as defined through 'scenery', 'views' and 'panoramas' (Green, 1990; Urry, 1992). More recently, similar hegemonic arguments can be made for the need to protect the environment. The consumption of particular types of tourism experience includes the importance of visual consumption (Urry, 1992), thereby imploring individuals to preserve those environments considered aesthetically pleasing or valuable for specific tourism-related pursuits. Thus, protection of the environment, from a tourism perspective, does not necessarily have anything to do with protection for the sake of broader environmental ethics and global responsibilities, but rather for the marketing and selfish individual tourist consumption of environmental diversity and aesthetic.

The way in which individuals 'view' different environments is, therefore, a result of the social construction of their beliefs and experiences. Issues relating to the gendered nature of these constructions of environmental values from a tourism perspective do not appear in the literature. Research which deconstructs environmental values along gender, class and race differences would provide a valuable contribution to an understanding of the significance of the environment within processes of tourism development.

However, we can extend the argument to depict other areas of social interaction within 'valued environments' which have a more obvious gender articulation. The attraction of rural spaces, as exemplified by the value placed on national parks and the aesthetics of the 'countryside', has increased tourism's significance in otherwise economically marginalised, rural areas. The economies of such areas are characterised by small-scale, flexible enterprises that are based on family labour and, often, patriarchal relations (Britton, 1991). Changes in the balance of power with respect to family decision-making and an emphasis on the informal, rather than formal, economy has important implications for gender relations (Mackenzie, 1988; Britton, 1991).

CONSTRUCTING THEORETICAL FRAMEWORKS: THEMES TO TAKE FORWARD

The case studies in this book focus on the specificity of tourism-related activity and development in different parts of the world.

They contribute to an understanding of the variety of gender perspectives that have been outlined in this introduction and, therefore, can be conceptually understood through the gender-aware framework which we have emphasised here:

1. Tourism-related activities and processes involved in tourism development are constructed out of gendered societies. Consequently, the articulation of masculine and feminine identities by both host and guest societies are important components of the types of tourism taking place and the maintenance of the economic and political agenda of the international tourism industry (see Enloe, 1989).
2. Gender relations both inform, and are informed by, the specificities of the social practices of all societies. Therefore, economic, social, cultural, political and environmental aspects of tourism interact with the gendered nature of these societies and the way in which gender relations are defined and redefined over time.
3. Discussions of gender and gender relations are about power and control. Gender relations are political relations at the household, community and societal levels. Tourism's identification as an industry based on the economic, political or social power relations between nations or groups of people creates a meaningful extension to the politics of gender relations. Tourism revolves around social interaction and social articulations of motivations, desires, traditions and perceptions, all of which are gendered.

The contributions by Hennessy (Chapter 2) and Breathnach *et al.* (Chapter 3) focus on employment and the way in which tourism-dependent economies and societies in Cornwall, England and the west of Ireland, respectively, are gendered in their inclusion of women in the tourism-related labour force. Issues of employment opportunities, in both historical and contemporary contexts, ghettoise women in work in a way that is seen to be an extension of domestic activity, especially in relation to their involvement in the provision of bed and breakfast accommodation. Under forces of economic restructuring within the broader economies of Britain and Ireland, both studies find tourism a somewhat weak alternative to other forms of economic development. Utilising tourism as a strategy for development (and the gender division of labour it reinforces) creates a situation in which women, otherwise marginalised in the workforce, are very much part of prevailing capital and patriarchal structures (see Hennessy, Chapter 2).

In Chapters 4, 5, and 6, each author discusses a number of interacting factors which comment on gender and gender relations within their specific contexts. In Chapter 4, Leontidou discusses a number of gender-related issues which are articulated at the boundaries between work and leisure, between spatial areas, between individuals' experience in the tourism labour force and between hosts and guests within the social context of Greece. She echoes many of the concerns of other researchers regarding the changing social relations resulting from tourism: the ethical problems arising from the differing roles of men and women and their respective interaction with tourists. Until recently, men have had much greater interaction with tourists in both their employment in tourist-oriented services and their more intimate relationships with foreign women. At the same time, Greek women have experienced isolation from tourists, especially women tourists. However, with the promotion of 'alternative' tourism, particularly in interior, rural areas, a changing focus on the roles of women and men in the process of tourism development is evident. Values placed on the environment and the establishment of agro-tourist co-operatives give women new power and control.

In Chapter 5, Momsen raises the themes of family and social values within a framework which depicts the significance of the tourism industry and its implications for work in the Caribbean. Here, high rates of unemployment have been a characteristic of the region for several decades and the promotion of tourism has, to some, been seen as a panacea for development, particularly in the small islands of the Leeward and Windward chains. However, social tensions among hosts and between hosts and guests have arisen. Increased incomes among tourism service workers have led to a redistribution of authority within the family, often resulting in tensions in gender relations. The involvement of both men and women in sex-tourism adds to this tension, especially when their respective positions within this form of tourism-related activity are considered. For women, involvement in sex tourism is motivated by income generation which results in improved family welfare. Men's motivations are based on their desire to exercise sexual power over foreign women and, perhaps, forge a relationship that allows them to leave the islands altogether.

Tourism has a long tradition in many Caribbean countries and as the international tourism industry seeks to offer new, exciting holidays, some countries are experiencing the economic uncertainty that tourism can bring. A decline in tourism receipts has led to further unemployment and a general public dissatisfaction with the value of tourism development, a situation recently experienced in Barbados.

In Western Samoa, Fairbairn-Dunlop (Chapter 6) again successfully ties together several of the strands we have been discussing here. The articulation of tourism development through cultural and traditional practices which are gender-specific has meant that both women and men participate fully in the process. As in many of the studies reviewed earlier, Western Samoan tourism depicts the commoditisation of traditional Samoan beliefs and practices. Women, who have well-defined rights and resources under customary law, are able to take advantage of the tourism industry. Their experience of it is controlled by the prevailing ideological articulation of gender roles and relations and the sexual division of labour. Case studies of women's tourism enterprises exemplify the point. They reinforce the argument that for both men and women in Western Samoan society, the widespread fear that tourism will undermine traditional Samoan customs is paramount. Consequently, this fear is the largest attitudinal factor affecting the way in which the tourism industry in Western Samoa is configured.

Michael Hall (Chapter 7) provides an overview of the sex tourism industry in South-east Asia, focusing on the way in which it is articulated in different societies. He argues that sex tourism can only be understood within a framework which heeds careful attention to the varieties of structural inequality which occur within the region. The complex hierarchies and power relations, based on gender and institutionalised racism, are important components. These inequalities are exacerbated by the host/guest relationships that result and which, he argues, can only continue to perpetuate current unequal gender relations.

Both Chapters 8 and 9 are somewhat of a departure from the other chapters in the volume. In 'The masculinisation of Stirling's heritage', Edensor and Kothari illustrate the ways in which tourism-related activity and the promotion of tourism through an appreciation of heritage and nationalistic pride is configured exclusively by one (which is not necessarily the only) interpretation of national heritage. They show through an analysis of several sites of historical significance in Stirling, Scotland, the way in which the presentation of 'Scottishness' is defined through white, heterosexual, male values which valorise battle heroes and warriors. The place (and space) for Scottish women, ethnic minorities and homosexuals in this articulation of heritage is questioned.

In Chapter 9, we highlight recent writings in both academic and popular literature of the nature and significance of women travellers in both historical and contemporary contexts. A proliferation of literature has appeared on the women travellers of the Victorian and Edwardian periods which comments on their motivations, their feminisms and their position within the all male exploration clubs of the times. The women's dialogue with Western imperialism and their 'view' of the world depict interesting insights into other cultures while at the same time commenting on the hierarchical positioning of the white male explorer over the white female traveller.

All of the chapters in this book focus on gender perspectives of processes of tourism development which are articulated through the social practices of host and guest societies. Unless we understand the gendered complexities of tourism, and the power relations they involve, then we will fail to recognise the reinforcement and construction of new power relations that are emerging out of tourism processes. With tourism representing one of the largest sectors in international and national trade, it is essential that we reformulate our focus to identify associated societal change and what it means for women and men.

NOTES

1   Explanations regarding the concept of 'the Other' have arisen out of feminist, anthropological and, more recently, post-modern interpreta-

tions of societal and individual difference. Feminist theory has discussed the way in which women are constructed as 'non-men' in mainstream social science theoretical debates. Women are therefore categorised as 'Other'. Similarly, articulations of the differences between societies or social groups can allow the dominant voice to classify 'the Other'.

2   These issues can also be explored through an examination of power relations articulated through race, class and sexuality.

3   This does not mean that the different experiences of 'women' and 'men' create homogeneous experiences for each group. Intra-gender differences are very important and often indicate the varying ways in which different women and different men experience social practices.

4   Enloe (1989) explains this point: 'Nationalist leaders who have become alarmed at the tourism-dependent policies imposed by foreign bankers and their own governments have been reluctant to rally around the symbol of the oppressed chambermaid. Men in nationalist movements may find it easier to be roused to anger by the vision of a machete-swinging man transformed into a tray-carrying waiter in a white resort – he is a man who has had his masculine pride stolen from him. Caribbean nationalists have complained that their government's pro-tourism policies have turned their society into a "nation of bus-boys". "Nation of chambermaids" doesn't seem to have the same mobilizing ring in their ears. After all, a woman who has traded work as an unpaid agricultural worker for work as a hotel cleaner hasn't lost any of her femininity' (Enloe, 1989, p. 34).

5   South-east Asian women are portrayed in this way in both the sex-tourism industry and the mail-order bride business in an attempt to appeal to Western men who are discouraged by Western women's so-called empowerment. Davidson (1985, p. 18) exemplifies this with a German advertisement that stated 'Asian women are without desire for emancipation, but full of warm sensuality and the softness of velvet'.

REFERENCES

Antrobus, P., 1990, Gender issues in tourism, Paper presented to the CTRC. Conference on Tourism and Socio-cultural Change in the Caribbean, June 25–28.

Archer, B.H., 1982, The value of multipliers and their policy implications, *Tourism Management*, **3**: 236–41.

Bagguley, P., 1990, Gender and labour flexibility in hotel and catering, *Services Industries Journal*, **10**: 737–47.

Boo, E., 1991, *Ecotourism: the potentials and pitfalls*, World Wildlife Fund, Washington, D.C., 2 vols.

Boynton, L., 1986, The effects of tourism on Amish quilting design, *Annals of Tourism Research*, **13**(3): 451–65.

Britton, S., 1982, The political economy of tourism in the Third World, *Annals of Tourism Research*, **9**: 331–8.

Britton, S., 1991, Tourism, capital and place: towards a critical geography of tourism, *Environment and Planning D: Society and Space*, **9**: 451–78.

Brown, N., 1992, Beachboys as culture brokers in Bakau Town, The Gambia, *Community Development Journal*, **27**(4): 361–70.

Buckley, P.J., Witt, S.F., 1985, Tourism in difficult areas: case studies of Bradford, Bristol, Glasgow and Hamm, *Tourism Management*, **6**; 205–13.

Byrne Swain, M., 1990, Commoditizing ethnicity in Southwest China, *Cultural Survival Quarterly*, **14**(1): 26–9.

Canan, P., Hennessey, M., 1989, The growth machine, tourism and the selling of culture, *Sociological Perspectives*, **32**(2): 227–43.

Castelberg-Koulma, M., 1991, Greek women and tourism: women's co-operatives as an alternative form of organisation, in Redclift, N., Sinclair, M.T. (eds), *Working Women*, Routledge, London, pp. 197–212.

Castles, S., Kosack, G., 1985, *Immigrant workers and class structure in Western Europe*, Oxford University Press, Oxford.

Cater, E., 1991, *Sustainable tourism in the Third World: problems and prospects*, University of Reading, Department of Geography, Discussion Paper 3, Reading.

Chant, S., 1992, Tourism in Latin America: perspectives from Mexico and Costa Rica, in Harrison, D. (ed.), *Tourism and the less developed countries*, Belhaven, London, pp. 85–101.

Cohen, E., 1971, Arab boys and tourist girls in a mixed Jewish–Arab community, *International Journal of Comparative Sociology*, **12**(4): 217–33.

Cohen, E., 1974, Who is a tourist? *Sociological Review*, **22**(4): 527–53.

Cohen, E., 1982, Thai girls and farang men, *Annals of Tourism Research*, **9**(3): 403–28.

Cohen, E., 1983, The dynamics of commercialized arts: the Meo and Yeo of Northern Thailand, *Journal of the National Research Council of Thailand*, **15**: 1–34.

Cohen, E., 1988, Authenticity and commoditization in tourism, *Annals of Tourism Research*, **15**: 371–86.

Craik, J., 1991, *Resorting to tourism: cultural policies for tourist development in Australia*, Allen and Unwin, North Sydney.

Crompton, R., Sanderson, K., 1990, *Gendered jobs and social change*, Unwin Hyman, London.

Dann, G., 1981, Tourism motivation: an appraisal, *Annals of Tourism Research*, **8**(2): 187–219.

Davidson, D., 1985, Women in Thailand, *Canadian Women Studies*, **16**(1): 16–19.

de Kadt, E., 1979, *Tourism: passport to development*, Oxford University Press, Oxford.

Eber, S., 1992, *Beyond the green horizon*, World Wide Fund for Nature, London.

Elson, D., 1991, *Male bias in the development process*, Manchester University Press, Manchester.

Enloe, C., 1989, *Bananas, beaches and bases: making feminist sense of international politics*, Pandora, London.

Estrada-Claudio, S., 1992, Unequal exchanges – international tourism and overseas employment, *Community Development Journal*, **27**(4): 402–10.

Featherstone, M., 1990, Perspectives on consumer culture, *Sociology*, **24**(1): 5–22.

Fox, M., 1977, The social impact of tourism – a challenge to researchers and planners, in Finney, B., Watson, K. (eds), *A new kind of sugar: tourism in the Pacific*, Center for South Pacific Studies, University of Santa Cruz, Santa Cruz, California, pp. 27–47.

Graburn, N., 1989, Tourism: the sacred journey, in Smith, V. (ed.), *Hosts and guests: an anthropology of tourism*, University of Pennsylvania Press, Philadelphia, 2nd edition, pp. 21–36.

Green, N., 1990, *The spectacle of nature*, Manchester University Press, Manchester.

Hall, C.M., 1992, Sex-tourism in South-East Asia, in Harrison, D. (ed.), *Tourism and the less developed countries*, Belhaven, London, pp. 64–74.

Hall, D.R. (ed.), 1991, *Tourism and economic development in Eastern Europe and the Soviet Union*, Belhaven, London.

Hall, D.R., 1992, The challenges of international tourism in Eastern Europe, *Tourism Management*, **13**(1): 41–4.

Hall, D., Kinnaird, V., 1994, Ecotourism in Eastern Europe, in Cater, E. (ed.), *Ecotourism: the sustainable alternative?* Belhaven, London.

Hamilton-Smith, E., 1987, Four kinds of tourism, *Annals of Tourism Research*, **14**(3): 332–44.

Harrison, D. (ed.), 1992, *Tourism and the less developed countries*, Belhaven, London.

Harrison, D., 1993, Bulgarian tourism, a state of uncertainty, *Annals of Tourism Research*, **20**(3): 519–34.

Hitchcock, M., King, V., Parnwell, M., 1993, Tourism in South-East Asia: introduction, in Hitchcock, M., King, V., Parnwell, M. (eds), *Tourism in South-East Asia*, Routledge, London, pp. 1–31.

Hoivik, T., Heiberg, T., 1980, Centre–periphery tourism and self-reliance, *International Social Science Journal*, **32**(1): 69–98.

Hovel, H., Feuerstein, M.–T., 1992, After the carnival: tourism and community development, *Community Development Journal*, **27**(4): 335–52.

Inskeep, E., 1987, Environmental planning for tourism, *Annals of Tourism Research*, **14**(1): 118–35.

Jafari, J., 1973, The role of tourism on socio-economic transformation of developing countries, unpublished Master's thesis, Cornell University.

Katz, C., 1992, All the world is staged: intellectuals and the projects of ethnography, *Environment and Planning D: Society and Space*, **10**: 495–510.

Kikue, T., 1979, Kisaeng tourism, in ISIS, *Tourism and prostitution, ISIS International Bulletin*, **13**: 23–5.

Kincaid, J., 1988, *A small place*, Virago, London.

King, R., 1990, The social and economic geography of labour migration: from guestworkers to immigrants, in Pinder, D. (ed.), *Western Europe: challenges and changes*, Belhaven, London and New York, pp. 162–78.

Kinnaird, V., Wyatt, E., Hall, D., 1994, Tourism and social change: some gender considerations, in Cooper, C. (ed.), *Progress in tourism, recreation and hospitality management*, Vol. 6, Belhaven, London.

Kousis, M., 1984, Tourism as an agent of social change in a rural Cretan community, unpublished PhD thesis, University of Michigan, Ann Arbor.

Lanfont, M.–F., 1980, Tourism in the process of internationalisation, *International Social Science Journal*, **32**(1): 14–43.

Lee, W., 1991, Prostitution and tourism in South-East Asia, in Redclift, N., Sinclair, M.T. (eds), *Working Women*, Routledge, London, pp. 79–103.

Lever, A., 1987, Spanish tourism migrants: the case of Lloret de Mar, *Annals of Tourism Research*, **14**(4): 449-70.

Levy, D., Lerch, P., 1991, Tourism as a factor in development: implications for gender and work in Barbados, *Gender and Society*, **5**(1): 67–85.

MacCannell, D., 1976, *The tourist: a new theory of the leisure class*, Schocken Books, New York.

McKean, P.F., 1989, Towards a theoretical analysis of tourism: economic dualism and cultural involution in Bali, in Smith, V. (ed.), *Hosts and guests: an anthropology of tourism*, University of Pennsylvania Press, Philadelphia, 2nd edition, pp. 119–38.

Mackenzie, S., 1988, The politics of restructuring: gender and environment in deindustrialised areas of Canada, paper presented to the International Geographical Congress, Sydney, Aus, August.

Mackie, V., 1988, Division of labour: multinational sex in Asia, in McCormack, G., Sugimoto, Y. (eds), *The Japanese trajectory: modernisation and beyond*, Cambridge University Press, Cambridge, pp. 218–32.

Mathieson, A., Wall, G., 1982, *Tourism: economic, environmental and social impacts*, Longman, London.

Monk, J., Alexander, C., 1986, Freeport fallout: gender, employment and migration on Margarita Island, *Annals of Tourism Research*, **13**: 393–413.

Nash, D., 1989, Tourism as a form of imperialism, in Smith, V. (ed.), *Hosts and guests: an anthropology of tourism*, University of Pennsylvania Press, Philadelphia, 2nd edition, pp. 37–52.

Peake, R., 1989, Swahili stratification and tourism in Malindi Old Town, Kenya, *Africa*, **59**(2): 209–20.

Perez, L.A., 1973–4, Aspects of underdevelopment: tourism in the West Indies, *Science and Society*, **37**(4): 473–80.

Picard, M., 1990, 'Cultural tourism' in Bali: cultural performances as tourist attractions, *Indonesia*, **49**: 37–74.

Poon, A., 1989, Competitive strategies for 'new tourism', in Cooper, C. (ed.), *Progress in tourism, recreation and hospitality management*, Vol. 2, Belhaven, London, pp. 91–102.

Poon, A., 1990, Flexible specialisation and small size: the case of Caribbean tourism, *World Development*, **18**(1): 109–23.

Poulson, T.M., 1977, Migration on the Adriatic coast: some processes associated with the development of tourism, in Kostanick, H.L. (ed.), *Population and migration trends in Eastern Europe*, Westview, Boulder, Colorado, pp. 197–215.

Price, S., 1988, *Behind the planters back*, Macmillan, London and Basingstoke.

Rees, G., Fielder, S., 1992, The services economy, subcontracting and the new employment relations: contract catering and cleaning, *Employment and Society*, **6**(3): 347–68.

Rojek, C., 1985, *Capitalism and leisure theory*, Tavistock Publications, Andover, Hants.

Salt, J., 1981, International labour migration in Western Europe: a geographical review, in Kritz, M.M., Keely, C.B., Tomasi, S.M. (eds), *Global trends in migration*, Center for Migration Studies, New York, pp. 133–57.

Salt, J., 1985, Europe's foreign labour migrants in transition, *Geography*, **70**: 151–8.

Sampson, A., 1968, *The new Europeans*, Hodder and Stoughton, London.

Selwyn, T., 1992, Tourism, society and development, *Community Development Journal*, **27**(4): 353–60.

Selwyn, T., 1993, Peter Pan in South-East Asia: a view from the brochures, in Hitchcock, M., King, V., Parnwell, M. (eds), *Tourism in South-East Asia*, Routledge, London, pp. 117–37.

Shields, R., 1991, *Places on the margin: alternative geographies of modernity*, Routledge, London.

Smith, V., 1989, Introduction, in Smith, V. (ed.), *Hosts and guests: an anthropology of tourism*, University of Pennsylvania Press, Philadelphia, 2nd edition, pp. 1–17.

Swain, M., 1989, Gender roles in indigenous tourism: Kuna mola, Kuna yala and cultural survival, in Smith, V. (ed.), *Hosts and guests: an anthropology of tourism*, 2nd edn, University of Pennsylvania Press, Philadelphia, pp. 83–104.

Swain, M.B., 1993, Women producers of ethnic arts, *Annals of Tourism Research*, **20**(1): 32–51.

Travis, A.S., 1982, Managing the environmental and cultural aspects of tourism and leisure development, *Tourism Management*, **3**: 256–62.

Urry, J., 1990, *The tourist gaze: leisure and travel in contemporary societies*, Sage, London.

Urry, J., 1991, The sociology of tourism, in Cooper, C. (ed.), *Progress in tourism, recreation and hospitality management*, Vol. 3, Belhaven, London, pp. 48–57.

Urry, J., 1992, The tourist gaze and the environment, *Theory, Culture and Society*, **9**: 1–26.

Uzzell, D., 1984, An alternative structuralist approach to the psychology of tourism marketing, *Annals of Tourism Research*, **11**(1): 79–99.

Ward, S., 1975a, European capitalism's reserve army, *Monthly Review*, **27**(6): 17–32.

Ward, S., 1975b, European migrant labour: a myth of development, *Monthly Review*, **27**(7): 24–38.

Weiler, B., Hall, C.M. (eds), 1992, *Special interest tourism*, Belhaven, London.

Wheeller, B., 1992, Alternative tourism – a deceptive ploy, in Cooper, C. (ed.), *Progress in tourism, recreation and hospitality management*, Vol. 4, Belhaven, London, pp. 140–5.

Williams, A., Shaw, G. (eds), 1988, *Tourism and economic development: Western European experiences*, Belhaven, London.

Williams, P.W., 1987, Evaluating environmental impact and physical carrying capacity in tourism, in Ritchie, J.B.R., Goeldner, C.R. (eds), *Travel, tourism and hospitality research: a handbook for managers and researchers*, John Wiley, New York, pp. 385–96.

World Tourism Organisation, 1992, *Tourism trends*, WTO, Madrid.

WTTERC (World Travel and Tourism Environment Research Centre), 1993, *Travel and tourism: environment and development*, WTTERC, Oxford.

Wyatt, E., 1991, Tourism development in South Tyneside: its role in economic regeneration, unpublished dissertation, Geography Section, University of Sunderland, Sunderland.

2
Female employment in tourism development in South-west England

Sinead Hennessy

INTRODUCTION

There are studies which examine the economic significance of tourism, some of which provide estimates of the numbers employed within tourism at national, regional or local levels. There is, however, little research which addresses the conditions of employment in tourism. While existing studies provide quantitative data, few studies provide qualitative assessments of the nature of tourism-related employment. Given that considerable emphasis is placed on tourism as a generator of employment, it is clear that consideration should be given to the nature of such employment. This chapter presents the findings of a study of the conditions of employment for women in tourism-related industries in Looe, Cornwall, South-west England, carried out in 1986.

Looe, which is situated on the south-east coast of Cornwall, was chosen as a study area principally because its economy is heavily dependent on tourism (Hennessy *et al.*, 1986, pp. 6–7). The number of people staying in Looe increases considerably during the tourism season. In the 1981 census the resident population of the area was shown to be roughly 4,300. In 1988, however, there was tourist accommodation of approximately 5,200 bed spaces. Economically, the town reflects the domination of the tourism industry. There are a considerable number of business establishments catering primarily for tourists in the form of, for example, leisure facilities, gift shops, restaurants and cafes. The closure of establishments during winter months lends the town a different character outside the tourist season. Research has shown that establishments in all sectors in Looe were found to have a relative dependence on tourism (Hennessy *et al.*, 1986, p. 25). This dependence was assessed in terms of seasonal effects as measured in relation to (a) the closure of businesses, (b) occupancy of tourist accommodation, (c) rates of turnover in catering and retail establishments, and (d) levels of production in local industry.

THE ECONOMY OF CORNWALL

The economy of Cornwall is heavily dependent on the tourism industry. While estimates of tourism-related employment reflect the difficulties involved in assessing the impact of tourism on jobs, employment in tourism in Cornwall is shown to have increased from around 13,000 in 1961 to approximately 20,000 jobs in 1973; and this estimate excludes seasonal employment (Cornwall County Council, 1976, p. 12).

Whereas women made up roughly 40 per cent of the workforce in tourism in 1961, the share of female employment increased to 48 per cent in 1973. In the mid-1970s, one in five working women and one in ten working men in Cornwall were employed in tourism. Men and women were also shown to be disproportionately distributed within individual sectors of employment. Male employment predominated in agriculture, construction, and in skilled services such as motor repairs. Female employment was predominant in retail distribution, hotels and catering. This implies that female labour predominates in those sectors of the Cornish economy which are tourism-related.

A recent study suggests that, while there has been an overall real decrease in tourism-related employment in Cornwall, there has been an increase in tourism-related jobs in certain sectors (Shaw *et al.*, 1987, p. 18). Employment in tourism in 1984 is estimated to have amounted to roughly 18,000 jobs. In the period 1981–84, employment in hotels and catering, which provides the greatest number of tourism-related jobs, increased by over 8 per cent. Employment in the retail sector increased by 9.5 per cent over the same period. It is also shown that women predominate in tourism-related employment in Cornwall and that employment is mainly part-time with seasonal fluctuations. However, the nature of employment varies between individual sectors to reflect their relative dependence on tourism. Industrial establishments have the lowest proportion of part-time employees (19%) and public houses the highest proportion (78%). In this respect it is also interesting that the industrial sector also has relatively few women workers (28%), whereas retail establishments employ the highest proportion of women (77%). In terms of fluctuations in employment levels, seasonal employment in Cornwall is most extensive in the accommodation sector, restaurants, cafes and public houses. As will be shown below, data relating to the nature of employment in Cornwall reflect that of tourism-related employment in Looe.

In terms of recent changes in tourism-related employment, Cornwall may have been particularly affected by the stagnation in the domestic tourist market. Other areas of Britain are drawing a relatively greater share of the domestic market, mainly through the development of new or 'specialist' forms of tourism (Williams and Shaw, 1988, pp. 81–103). While the number of overseas visitors to Britain has increased, Cornwall attracts a relatively small share of tourists from abroad. Moreover, due to its peripheral location Cornwall is not well placed to take advantage of the growing 'short-break' holiday market. At the same time, while there has been a relative decline in the number of visitors to Cornwall, tourists staying in self-catering accommodation have shown a significant increase. This trend has major implications for the local labour force in tourism and for women in tourism-related employment.

Although tourism is a relatively labour-intensive industry, it is to be expected that the forms of capital involved in tourism will follow the same 'logic' as other forms of capital; that is, there will be a drive to reduce labour costs and enhance competitiveness. The drive to reduce labour content and labour costs may be evidenced by a tendency to pay relatively low wages, to employ part-time or seasonal labour, or develop a pool of workers within the 'informal economy'. Thus, for example, in terms of the rise of self-catering accommodation it might be noted that full-time employment accounted for 53 per cent of employees in serviced accommodation in Cornwall and only 33 per cent of employees in self-catering accommodation (Shaw *et al.*, 1987, p. 95). In addition, some hotel groups (for example, Rio Stakis) have created new 'multi-role' employment grades as a way of increasing the flexibility of the workforce. At the same time, the decline in hotels or serviced accommodation, and the allied increase in self-catering accommodation, represent a switch from forms of capital dependent on relatively high levels of labour to forms of capital employing relatively fewer workers. It is suggested that if the trend towards self-catering accommodation continues, the growth in the numbers of tourists will outstrip the growth in jobs in the tourism industry (Cornwall County Council, 1986, p. 8).

Future changes in the nature of employment in tourism will follow from structural changes within the tourism industry. With respect to new forms of tourism, such as theme parks, 'wet weather' facilities or wildlife centres, importance might be given to the extent to which these may create secure, full-time or skilled employment as opposed to seasonal, part-time, low-paid or unskilled employment. Moreover, there is the question of whether new forms of employment will absorb mainly young, generally low-paid workers, and the capacity of new jobs to provide secure employment and incomes sufficient to support families or households. Allied to all of these issues is the question of female employment and the role of women as a source of relatively cheap, casual or disposable labour. In this respect the labour force in new forms of tourism in Cornwall is typical of tourism development generally in that it consists mainly of female employees of whom a significant proportion are part-time (Shaw *et al.*, 1987, p. 149).

It might also be noted that, notwithstanding the role of female labour in tourism, Cornwall has a relatively low level of female employment. This is said to be due to a combination of factors such as lack of opportunity, high rates of unemployment, difficulties of location and transport and, paradoxically, the availability of alternative seasonal employment in tourism. It is argued that the availability of seasonal employment dissuades women from seeking year-round employment. However, the relatively low rate of economic activity for women in Cornwall may be deceptive in that, historically, women are said to have worked unofficially in agriculture (on family farms) and in tourism, for example, where they provide bed and breakfast. Moreover, the extent of female labour in the 'black economy' is not known.

The conditions of labour in Cornwall mean that, like male workers, many women have not been employed under conditions which provide a basis for unionisation. The structure of the economy in Cornwall, together with the availability of seasonal work, result in both a relatively low activity rate for women within the general economy and in low wages (Massey, 1984, p. 225). Moreover, while seasonal work results in low annual wages, where it supplements household incomes it may also cause primary wages to be maintained at relatively low levels.

The relatively fragmented structure of capital in tourism in Cornwall is such that locally based large-scale capital and State ownership are relatively insignificant. Manufacturing industry in Cornwall declined during the 1950s, and in the mid-1960s Cornwall experienced a remarkable in-migration of firms and people. Two-thirds of the firms were branch plants of larger establishments and a significant proportion of the employees taken on by new firms were women. At the same time, there was a migration to Cornwall of 'small entrepreneurs', whose individual capacity to generate employment was relatively low. Moreover, small-scale manufacturing industry in Cornwall was not generally growth oriented (Perry, 1979, pp. 19–20). It may be that some business owners attracted to Cornwall for environmental reasons have little incentive to expand businesses. There is evidence to suggest that some entrepreneurs in tourism are not generally ambitious. Moreover, it is argued that, in Cornwall, locally based small-scale capitalists might seek to discourage the establishment of industries or businesses employing a significant workforce in order to avoid an escalation in the demand for labour and increased wage levels.

THE LABOUR FORCE IN LOOE

Given that the economy of Looe is heavily dependent on tourism there is a high incidence in the general labour force of part-time, seasonal work and female employment. While there are differences in the conditions of employment within different sectors of the economy of Looe, about two-thirds of a general sample of employees were shown to be working part-time (Hennessy *et al.*, 1986, p. 19). As might be expected, the proportion of part-time employment was lowest in the industrial sector and highest in self-catering accommodation. In addition, most categories of business in Looe were found to follow a seasonal pattern with some retail and industrial establishments experiencing less fluctuation in levels of employment throughout the year.

Women accounted for 39 per cent of the total labour force in Britain in 1981; however, in Looe women constituted roughly three-quarters of the workforce of a sample of businesses (Mallier and Rosser, 1987, p. 20; Hennessy *et al.*, 1986, p. 19). While roughly two-thirds of a sample of all employees surveyed in Looe were found to be working part-time, it is known that nationally women, and especially married women, are more likely than men to take up part-time jobs (Mallier and Rosser, 1987, p. 136).

The high proportion of women workers in the tourism industry in Looe may result from a number of factors. Regardless of whether labour is part-time or seasonal, the nature of occupations in the tourism industry in Looe is such that more women than men are likely to be employed. The predominance of women in tourism reflects the greater role of women in the service sector as a whole (Mallier and Rosser, 1987, p. 44). In addition, women in Looe are likely to be restricted to locally available employment, perhaps because of the low density of urban development in the area, poor public transport and lack of access to the 'family' car (Massey, 1984, p. 225). Moreover, levels of pay may be insufficient to cover the additional transport costs of long-distance commuting.

Given that the local economy in Looe is relatively dependent on tourism, this does not mean that there is a homogeneous form of labour and a homogeneous form of capital. While many workers hold employment which is dependent on tourism, the degree of dependence varies significantly between business establishments. For example, employment within establishments providing accommodation may be entirely dependent on tourism, while some retail and service outlets might be relatively dependent on tourism, where dependence is measured, for example, in terms of fluctuations in turnover and numbers of staff employed. The relative dependence on tourism of any specific job may be difficult to measure in that it may be calculated in terms of both the immediate income to a firm which flows from tourism and the sum of effects which follow from tourism-related expenditure within a wider economic context. While the degree to which specific forms of employment are dependent on tourism may be difficult to measure accurately, the conditions under which employees negotiate with employers may vary significantly. For example, with respect to wage negotiations, employees may work for a national or international company where wage levels and conditions of employment are established at a national level; alternatively, employees may be said to operate within a local labour market within which the conditions of employment are established on a personal and local level, as for example, where employment in a bank in Looe is compared with employment in a local guesthouse. However, it may also be evident where employment in a local hotel is compared with employment in a hotel held by a national or multinational company.

WOMEN'S TOURISM-RELATED EMPLOYMENT IN LOOE

Questionnaire surveys were administered to 125 women working in Looe at the height of the tourism season in August 1986. These women represent a random sample of women in tourism-related employment in Looe. The women surveyed in Looe were asked to relate not only the details of their employment but also details of their age, marital status, motherhood, and their roles as wage earners within the household. Thus, the study considered both the conditions of women within the economy and within the home. Moreover, the ambitions of the women were examined, together with their educational and vocational qualifications, in order to test the suitability of their employment to their ambitions.

It is interesting that the task of surveying women in tourism in itself exposes some of the conditions of their employment. For example, women were interviewed at home where they might be unrestricted in their responses to questions concerning conditions of work. Moreover employers who provide the poorest conditions of employment, or who employ workers within the 'black economy', might have been less likely to co-operate with a survey undertaken at work. While workers in the 'black economy' do not pay national insurance contributions or income tax, the employers of those workers also fail to pay the employers' national insurance contributions or to register employees with the Inland Revenue.

Economic relations and conditions of employment

It is widely held that employment in tourism is socially classified as unskilled. Shop work, waitressing, cleaning and bar work were shown to be the most common forms of employment undertaken by women in tourism-related employment in Looe. In Looe, the women surveyed worked predominantly in retailing (30 per cent), restaurants and cafes (25 per cent) and hotels and guesthouses (15 per cent). Only 12 per cent of the women held skilled employment. However, a significant proportion of women had skills they did not use at work – even where women had more than one job. Of 125 women surveyed in Looe, ten had two jobs and one woman had three jobs.

The majority of the women (58 per cent) surveyed in Looe were in part-time employment. Young women (aged 16–25) were shown to be more likely than relatively older women to work full-time. Married and divorced or separated women were more likely (than single women) to be in part-time employment which may relate to their duties as mothers. The responsibilities of working mothers with relatively young children were reflected in the low proportion of women working full-time. Of the 34 women with one child or more aged 14 years or under, only seven (20 per cent) were in full-time employment. In addition, because the proportions of full-time and part-time employment vary within individual sectors, women who are dependent on part-time work will be drawn into particular sectors of the economy. For example, women might be drawn into employment in public houses where jobs are predominantly part-time.

Seasonality is an important characteristic of tourism-related employment. In an analysis of employment in Looe, jobs were broken down in terms of seasonal employment where the duration of employment is 1–24 weeks per year, short-term jobs (25–40 weeks per year) and annual employment (41–52 weeks per year). Given these definitions, roughly two-thirds of the women surveyed were in seasonal or short-term employment. If seasonal, short-term and annual employment is broken down in terms of individual sectors, it is shown that retail establishments provide a high proportion of annual jobs, while restaurants and cafes account for the greatest number of seasonal jobs.

The degree to which seasonal or short-term employment meets the needs of women in Looe is likely to vary with regard to marital status and whether women have children. The majority of women had a preference for annual employment, albeit on a part-time basis. Therefore, while seasonal or short-term employment draws a lower total (annual) income than year-round employment, it may also provide employment at a time which is inconvenient for women with school-going children. An examination of the interrelationships between full-time and part-time employment, and seasonal, short-term and annual employment shows that seasonal, part-time employment is the commonest form of employment for the women surveyed. However, where employment is annual, it is more likely to be full-time.

Given the relatively poor conditions of employment for women in Looe, whereby employment is largely unskilled, seasonal or part-time, the extent to which employees were found to return to employers year after year was remarkable. With respect to the main employment of 125 women surveyed, 6 per cent had worked for the same employer for 11–26 years (or seasons in the case of seasonal employees), while 15 per cent had worked for their employer for 6–10 years or seasons. Another 40 per cent of respondents had worked for their employer for 2–5 years or seasons.

In examining the conditions of employment for women attention must be given to sickness benefit, pensions and other employment benefits. National insurance contributions are payable by both employers and employees if earnings of employees are above the lower earnings limit. Payment of national insurance contributions confers eligibility for state benefits such as sick pay, unemployment benefit, maternity allowance and in some cases retirement pensions. Only 45 per cent of the women surveyed in Looe were making national insurance contributions. In the restaurants and cafes, and hotels and guesthouses sectors, approximately two-thirds of the employees were not making national insurance contributions. However, roughly half the employees in the retail sector were paying national insurance, perhaps reflecting the greater number of full-time employees in this sector. While the majority of part-time employees (76%) surveyed were not making national insurance contributions, almost half these were in seasonal employment. It is possible that the earnings of some of the women who were not making national insurance contributions were below the lower earnings limit, however others may have been part of the 'black economy' and did not pay national insurance or tax although eligible to do so. Some measure of the 'informal economy' in Looe may be gained from the fact that, of a sample of women who gave details of pay, 60 per cent were evading national insurance contributions. There may also be a tendency for some employers to take on a number of part-time workers whose earnings fall below the lower limit in order to avoid payment of the employer's national insurance contribution.

Only 18 per cent of the women surveyed in Looe were found to receive sick pay benefits through an employer's scheme. Moreover, only 7 per cent of these women were contributing to an employer's retirement pension scheme which would provide a pension other than a state pension.

The incidence of trade union membership among women surveyed was remarkably low. Only 4 per cent of the women surveyed were members of trade unions. It is known that on a national level women are less likely than men to join trade unions, although the proportion of women is increasing. With respect to Looe, however, where employment is part-time and within small-scale industries, employees are less likely to be unionised.

The levels of pay of the women covered by the study were conditioned both by the fact that they are women and by their geographical location as workers in Cornwall. While the average hourly earnings of women are generally lower than men, levels of pay in the south-west region, and particularly in Cornwall, are relatively low in relation to other regions of England (Trade Union Research Unit, 1985, Appendix Table 3; Robinson and Wallace, 1984, p. 6). Of the women surveyed in 1986, 76 per cent earned between £1.20 and £2.00 per hour. There was a relatively wide spread of rates of pay within individual industrial sectors with the lowest rates of pay in retail establishments, restaurants and cafes.

Social conditions and women employed in Looe

The women covered by the study did not constitute a homogeneous social group but varied with respect to factors such as vocational skills, education and class. However, there is a predominance of younger women in tourism-related employment in Looe and roughly three-quarters of the women surveyed were aged 16–35 years, although roughly two-thirds were either married or divorced and 57 per cent had one or more children. Both the age profile and the number of married respondents may indicate that tourism-related employment in Looe provides supplementary incomes within the households of married women and for younger women living with parents.

Younger married women surveyed may not have completed their families, and may take up employment in Looe between periods given over to childbirth and rearing infants. Given the number of respondents with children, importance must be given to the manner in which women combine their roles as mothers and employees. In order to determine the importance of the women as wage earners, they were asked if they viewed themselves as the main 'breadwinner' within their respective households. More than one-third saw themselves as the main 'breadwinner', although the majority of those aged 16–20 did not.

Employment opportunities and satisfaction

In the light of evidence that the employment held by the women in Looe is largely unskilled, consideration was given to the correlation between qualifications, skills and the nature of tourism-related employment. Attention was also given to the availability of childcare and to the ambitions of women in relation to the timing and availability of employment. In short, the conditions which women require, or would prefer, were compared with the actual conditions of employment provided in Looe.

No formal educational qualifications were held by 44 per cent of the women, although 38 per cent held CSE or 'O' level qualifications. Of the total workforce in the south-west in 1985, 31 per cent had no educational qualification, and 24 per cent held CSE or 'O' level qualifications (South-West TUC, 1985, pp. 2–7). Therefore, the tourism industry in Looe might be said to absorb relatively high proportions of employees with no educational qualifications.

It is interesting that the position of the women in Looe alters if the focus in placed on skills rather than educational attainments. In order to determine whether the women in Looe were capable of taking up alternative employment, they were asked if there were any jobs requiring skills (other than those relating to their present job) which they could do. Almost one-third had vocational skills attained through vocational training which were 'higher' than the level of skills used in their present employment and were thus skilled workers in unskilled employment. However, because the economy of Looe is dominated by the tourism industry, it is unlikely that these women could obtain jobs locally which would utilise their skills. Furthermore, given the nature of the women's employment, there is little evidence that women were likely to secure further vocational training in their present employment. As already stated, only 12 per cent of the women were in skilled employment.

Access to childcare facilities is an important factor in relation to the capacity of women to take up paid employment in that it affects not only the time women are available for work, but also the levels of pay which must be achieved to pay for childcare. It is clear that the mothers of younger children covered by this study provided care for their children mainly within the family and that husbands and parents (or parents-in-law) were mainly responsible for childcare. The capacity of the husbands of working mothers to care for children reflects the general nature of employment in Looe. Moreover, employment such as cleaning, bar work and waitressing may be undertaken outside the working hours of husbands. Professional childminders played an insignificant role in the care of the children of working mothers and were used by only two of the mothers in the study. After the family, the next most frequent form of childcare was an informal arrangement with friends and neighbours. Given the low rates of pay for women in Looe, it is unlikely that wages could cover the cost of professional childcare. Thus, it may be that those women who are unable to obtain childcare through family or friends are prevented from entering the labour market.

The degree to which the flexibility of working hours in the tourism industry accommodates the needs of working women with children should not be over-estimated. That the peak in the tourism season during July and August coincides with children's school holidays is likely to present difficulties for some women.

CONCLUSIONS

The study undertaken in Looe provides a number of insights into the nature of women's employment in tourism. The women covered by the study were relatively young and the majority were married or divorced with one or more children. Many of the women clearly provided supplementary household incomes whether as young women living with parents or as married women. While further research is necessary to determine accurately the importance of women's incomes as a proportion of household incomes, the majority of the women surveyed did not see themselves as principal 'breadwinners' within their households. Moreover, the view that tourism-related employment for women provides supplementary household incomes was further confirmed by evidence of the low levels of pay achieved by women.

The occupations of the women in tourism-related employment in Looe were generally low-skilled. The most common forms of employment undertaken by the women surveyed were shop work, waitressing, cleaning and bar work. The principal establishments providing employment for the women were retailers, cafes, hotels and guesthouses. While much of the women's employment was part-time, seasonal or short-term, some women were found to have retained jobs for a number of years while others returned to employers for successive seasons.

Roughly half the women surveyed were born in Cornwall. In contrast, a study of tourism establishments in Cornwall shows that 84 per cent of the owners or managers of those establishments were in-migrants to Cornwall (Shaw et al., 1987). Broadly, it may be argued that tourism-related establishments in Looe are largely owned (or managed) by in-migrants while a significant proportion of the female workforce is indigenous. This points to a scarcity of local entrepreneurs or locally available capital within Looe. Further research might show that local women were relatively disadvantaged by the capacity of in-migrants to raise investment capital through the sale of residential property outside Cornwall. Moreover, the inflation of property prices in Looe, through the importation of capital by in-migrants, might be shown to inhibit locals seeking either to establish or invest in businesses or enter property markets.

The degree to which the conditions of tourism-related employment in Looe coincide with the needs and preferences of the women surveyed was shown to vary. Part-time employment appears to be an integral part of the tourism industry in Looe, although some of the women who wanted part-time employment were working full-time and vice versa. For employers, part-time employment is preferable because it is cost effective where jobs involve 'anti-social' hours or where there are peak periods of demand throughout the day. Part-time employment is welcomed by many women, if it coincides with school hours, or is available in the evenings or at weekends when husbands are available for childcare. Women in tourism-related employment in Looe who were mothers of young children were generally found to provide childcare through husbands and grandparents.

The supply of part-time employment for the women surveyed roughly equated with the proportion of women who expressed preferences for part-time employment. In contrast, however, if employment is considered annually (whether full-time or part-time) it is shown that, while roughly 62 per cent of the women surveyed were in seasonal or short-term employment, the majority (80%) expressed preferences for year-round employment. While some women working in tourism in Looe were dissatisfied with seasonal and short-term employment, such practices are to the advantage of employers who may take up and dispose of workers in accordance with annual fluctuations in consumer demand. Thus, it may be argued that women in tourism-related employment in Looe provide a form of flexible and disposable labour. In this respect, it has been argued that married women may play an important role in the provision of flexible and disposable labour (Beechey, 1978, pp. 190–1). On becoming unemployed or redundant, married women often remain invisible in terms of official unemployment statistics. Small-scale capital and 'patriarchal' structures may be seen to work together in Looe where women are taken on and let go as seasonal and short-term employees in the tourism industry. The disposability of workers in Looe is compounded by the existence of the 'black economy', which means that women workers are excluded from the legislative protection afforded by the State and the collective power of trade unions.

Disposable workers, some of whom are working in the 'informal economy', are likely to be in a poor bargaining position in terms of conditions of employment. Thus, as might be expected, conditions of employment for the women surveyed in tourism-related employment in Looe were relatively poor. It may be argued, for example, that the employment of the women surveyed was characterised by a relative lack of security. While some women in seasonal employment did return to employers for successive seasons, seasonal employees have no guarantee that they will be re-employed. The re-employment of seasonal workers might be said to provide employers with experienced workers, while employers incur minimal labour costs. Furthermore, it is characteristic of the small scale of the tourism industry in Cornwall that many establishments are family-run and a significant number of women may be employed in these enterprises. Much of the labour of these women is likely to remain unrecognised officially. As with the employment of women in the 'black economy', little is known of the nature and conditions of the employment of women within family-run operations.

In terms of educational qualifications and vocational skills, there is evidence of under-achievement among women in tourism-related employment in Looe. Roughly 42 per cent of the women surveyed held 'O' levels or higher qualifications. Almost one-third of the women had vocational skills they were not using in their present (largely unskilled) employment. Furthermore, those women who had skills, expressed ambitions to find employment where their skills could be used.

Nationally, there exists evidence of a degree of under-achievement among women. The Women and Employment Survey (Robinson and Wallace, 1984) shows that some women who were educated to 'A' level standard had taken up semi-skilled occupation on entering the labour market (Dex, 1987, p. 123). At the same time, it is shown that some women experience considerable downward occupational mobility in their working lives. Periods of disruption in women's working lives, caused by childbirth or moves because of husband's employment, were generally found to result in downward occupational mobility; notably, where women took part-time jobs after childbirth. If the initial under-achievement of women is shown to work together with subsequent downward occupational mobility, the combined effect results in a considerable waste of human resources.

Conditions of employment in the tourism industry in Looe may be considered within the context of the tourism market in Britain and abroad. In that Looe as a tourist destination is in competition not only with the rest of Britain but with overseas resorts, there is a relationship between, for example, wage levels in Looe and wage levels in tourism resorts in Spain or Portugal. Thus, it may be argued that capitalists in Looe may have a limited capacity to provide better conditions of employment for workers. The small scale and character of capital in Looe has a significance for the workforce. Doubts may be raised as to whether the owners or managers of establishments, many of whom have migrated to Cornwall, will create significant numbers of new jobs (Perry, 1979, pp. 19–20). Furthermore, while it has been shown that capital in Looe is small-scale, establishments have a high turnover of ownership and an associated high rate of closures (Hennessy *et al.*, 1986, p. 26). This may suggest that capital in Looe operates on relatively small profit margins. However, if small-scale or low-profit tourism establishments have a limited capacity to provide adequate conditions of employment for workers, this limited capacity should be recognised where tourism is promoted as a generator of employment.

REFERENCES

Beechey, V., 1978, Women and production: a critical analysis of some sociological theories of women's work, in Kuhn, A., Wolpe, A. (eds), *Feminism and materialism*, Routledge and Kegan Paul, London.

Cornwall County Council, 1976, *The holiday industry*, Cornwall County Council, Truro.

Cornwall County Council, 1986, *Cornwall County structure plan first alteration, discussion paper: tourism*, Cornwall County Council, Truro.

Dex, S., 1987, *Women's occupational mobility: a lifetime perspective*, Macmillan, Basingstoke.

Hennessy, S., Shaw, G., Williams, A., 1986, *The role of tourism in local economies: a pilot study of Looe, Cornwall*, University of Exeter, Exeter.

Mallier, A.T., Rosser, M.J., 1987, *Women and the economy: a comparative study of Britain and the USA*, Macmillan, London.

Massey, D., 1984, *Spatial divisions of labour: social structures and the geography of production*, Macmillan, London.

Perry, R., 1979, *A summary of studies of the Cornish economy based on surveys carried out 1974–1978*, Cornwall Industrial Development Association, Truro.

Robinson, O., Wallace, J., 1984, *Part-time employment and sex discrimination legislation in Great Britain*, Department of Employment, London.

Shaw, G., Williams, A., Greenwood, J., 1987, *Tourism and the economy of Cornwall*, University of Exeter, Exeter.

South-West TUC, 1985, *Low pay in the south-west*, South-West TUC, Bristol.

Trade Union Research Unit, 1985, *Patterns of trade union development 1966–1984*, Ruskin College, Oxford.

Williams, A., Shaw, G., 1988, Tourism: candyfloss industry or job generator?, *Town Planning Review*, **59**: 81–103.

3
Gender in Irish tourism employment

Proinnsias Breathnach,
Marion Henry, Sarah Drea and
Mary O'Flaherty

INTRODUCTION

This chapter is concerned with some of the gender dimensions of the Irish tourism industry. A brief outline of the industry and its recent development is presented initially. In the absence of data on the gender characteristics of tourists themselves, the chapter focuses on those working in the tourism industry in Ireland, set in the context of the position of women in the Irish workforce in general. A number of aspects of employment in tourism, including skill levels, part-time and seasonal work, segmentation, flexibility and trade union membership are examined from a gender perspective. There follows a case study of the nature of employment in the bed and breakfast business. The chapter concludes with some observations on the implications for economic development in Ireland of the strong emphasis currently being placed on tourism by the Irish government.

TOURISM IN THE REPUBLIC OF IRELAND

Traditionally, the Republic of Ireland was heavily dependent on its agricultural sector, which accounted for over three-fifths of all employment at the time independence from the United Kingdom was achieved in 1922. Continued out-migration from agriculture allied to an energetic programme of industrialisation (especially after 1960) produced a sharp reduction in the farm sector's share of the workforce and a corresponding growth in the share of manufacturing and, in particular, urban-based services. However, recurring recession and growing levels of unemployment in the 1980s spurred the government to seek out new areas for economic development. In particular, tourism was targeted as a key vehicle for economic growth owing to its strong performance in the international economy.

One dimension of this, an 'Operational Programme' for tourism, was devised for the period 1989–93 with substantial financial support from the structural funds of the European Community (Ó Cinnéide and Walsh, 1991). This programme provided for a total investment in the tourism sector of some IR£300 millions over the period of the plan. The programme envisaged a doubling of incoming tourist numbers to 4.2 million, an increase in tourism revenues of IR£500 millions (about 75 per cent), and the creation of 25,000 additional tourism-related jobs (an increase of one-third). These were very ambitious targets, given that global tourism had been growing at an average rate of only five per cent in recent years (Henry, 1992).

The first two years of the Operational Programme *did* produce vigorous growth in tourist numbers and revenue, and particularly in investment (Tansey Webster and Associates, 1991; Dunne, 1992). However, there was a slight decline in numbers in 1991, due principally to a slump in the North American market (attributed mainly to the impact of the Gulf War), although aggregate revenue continued to expand.

Overall, tourism (domestic and overseas) accounted for about seven per cent of both GNP and total employment in Ireland in 1990. However, in the period 1985–90, tourism contributed 37 per cent of the net employment growth in the economy (Tansey Webster and Associates, 1991). Tourism also makes a very important contribution to the Irish balance of payments, accounting for seven per cent of total exports of goods and services in 1990 (Central Statistics Office, 1991b), and, perhaps more importantly, over half the overall net current account surplus in that year (Tansey Webster and Associates, 1991).

Great Britain has always been by far the most important source area of overseas tourists visiting Ireland; in this context, the 'ethnic market' consisting of Irish emigrants and their descendants has been of paramount importance. However, over the last thirty years, while the British market has continued to grow in absolute terms, its share of the overall market has shrunk, as other source areas have grown even more rapidly (Table 3.1). Up to the late 1970s, the North American market was the main growth area, with the ethnic market again being of key importance in this case. However, since then, the most rapid growth has come from Continental Europe, which now accounts for one-quarter of the total, compared with 58 per cent for Great Britain and 14 per cent for North America.

The proportionate shares of total tourist numbers accounted for by the different source areas are not matched by their shares of revenue generated. In 1990, Great Britain accounted for only just over 40 per cent of revenue (compared with 58 per cent of visitors), due mainly to the fact that visitors from this source tend to stay with relatives and friends rather than in commercial accommodation. Continental Europe contributed one-third of total revenue and North America one-fifth. Northern Ireland is not included in Table 3.1 as it is treated separately in the accounts published by Bord Fáilte (the Irish Tourist Board): in

Table 3.1 *Trends in overseas tourism to the Republic of Ireland, 1960–90*

Source area	1960 No. ('000)	1960 %	1970 No. ('000)	1970 %	1980 No. ('000)	1980 %	1990 No. ('000)	1990 %
Great Britain	827	87.9	1,061	72.7	1,068	61.7	1,785	57.7
North America	69	7.3	258	17.7	260	15.0	443	14.3
Continental Europe	25	2.7	110	7.5	336	19.4	744	24.0
Other	20	2.1	30	2.1	67	3.9	124	4.0
Total	941	100.0	1,459	100.0	1,731	100.0	3,096	100.0

Source: Bord Fáilte, various.

1990, it accounted for 16 per cent of all out-of-state tourists, but just 8 per cent of tourism revenue (Bord Fáilte, 1991).

Visiting relatives and friends remains the single most important reason for tourists to come to Ireland: in 1990, 46 per cent of surveyed overseas visitors gave this as the purpose of their visit. Another 19 per cent came to Ireland for business purposes (business travel being included in Ireland's tourism accounts). For those coming to Ireland purely on holiday, the Department of Tourism and Transport has identified the main attractions as being an attractive physical environment conducive to a wide range of recreational and leisure pursuits, the friendliness of the people, a strong folk and cultural tradition, and a distinctive archaeological heritage (Ó Cinnéide and Walsh, 1991).

Irish tourism has an important regional dimension, in that tourists are attracted disproportionately to the more rural and remote western part of the country, where incomes are generally below the national average (Table 3.2). Table 3.2 shows that the western regions, with below-average incomes, attract above-average levels of tourism revenue, with the result that tourism makes a much greater contribution to personal incomes in these regions than it does in other regions.

Given the emphasis being placed by the Irish government on tourism as a means of income and employment expansion, and the resultant growing importance of the industry in the national

Table 3.2 *Regional distribution of income from tourism in the Republic of Ireland, 1990*

Region	Share of tourism income (%)	Share of population (%)	Per capita income index*	Tourism revenue as % of total personal income
East	29.8	40.9	112	3.7
Midlands	7.2	10.2	86	4.7
South-east	9.6	10.9	90	5.6
South-west	22.1	15.1	99	8.4
Mid-west	9.7	8.8	95	6.6
West	12.8	8.3	87	10.1
North-west	8.7	5.9	85	9.9

Sources: Central Statistics Office (1991a); Tansey Webster and Associates (1991).
* Ireland = 100

economy, there has been a surprising dearth of critical analysis of the implications of tourism development. Such literature as has been generated by the academic and consultant communities has tended to focus on such topics as overseas marketing strategies, the organisation of the tourism industry, and future investment needs (e.g. Price Waterhouse, 1987; Quinn, 1989). Such issues as the nature of the employment provided by the tourism industry and the social, cultural and environmental impacts of tourism development have been largely ignored (but see Deegan and Dineen, 1991), despite the emergence of a substantial literature on these issues elsewhere (Henry, 1992). In particular, tourism has managed, thus far, to escape the growing concern with gender issues which has developed in Ireland in recent years. This chapter seeks to rectify this situation by exploring in some detail the gender dimensions of the way in which the Irish tourism industry operates. Two such dimensions immediately offer themselves for consideration: first, the gender characteristics of tourists themselves and, secondly, the gender characteristics of those providing the tourism 'product'. Each of these is considered in turn.

GENDER CHARACTERISTICS OF TOURISTS

Scott and Godley (1992) have posed the question: 'Are leisure worlds generally segmented along the lines of gender identification?' This seems an obvious question, yet one which appears to have been largely – if not entirely – ignored in the extensive literature on segmentation in tourism marketing. Thus Quinn (1989, pp. 126–7), for example, in reviewing tourism marketing, states that:

> The most frequently used market segmentation criteria fall into either of two categories: socio-economic, e.g. based on income level, age grouping, educational standard, occupation, family size, etc.; or product-related, based on the type of product purchased, the frequency of purchase, etc.

While gender may well be subsumed under the catch-all 'etc.' at the end of this list, it clearly did not present itself to the writer as a criterion of particular importance.

Similarly, a recent paper by Bord Fáilte's senior market research executive argues that a successful marketing strategy must address market segmentation by 'visitor type, socio-demographics and life-style' (Maher, 1992, p. 5.1). The paper then presents information on a number of tourist surveys which break down tourists by region of origin, education, age, income level, family demographic structure, and social class, but with no mention at all of gender. This despite the fact that Bord Fáilte *does* normally include a question on gender identification in its tourist surveys.

Conventionally, gender studies argue that, where no allowance is made for gender differences in social research, this is because of a gender bias which subsumes female behaviour into that of the dominant male pattern. However, in the case of tourism, it may be that the underlying assumption is that tourists travel as couples or family groups with shared aspirations and objectives. But, as highlighted in a feature article in the *Irish Times* (20 April, 1992), conflict rather than unity of purpose is quite common on family holidays. Indeed, one psychiatrist quoted in this feature regarded family holidays as a common cause of marriage breakdown, with disagreements over preferred activities being an important contributory factor.

In the absence, therefore, of appropriate survey data on the gender dimension of tourist behaviour, it is impossible to carry our exploration of this dimension further, except to argue that there is a clear need to incorporate gender differences into tourism marketing research and to develop marketing and service strategies with a view to catering specifically for such differences.

WOMEN IN THE IRISH LABOUR FORCE

There is, by contrast, a considerable volume of information concerning the role of women in Irish tourism employment. However, in order to place our examination of this information in context, it is appropriate to review, initially, the role of women in the Irish labour force in general.

The modernisation of the Irish economy and of Irish society in the twentieth century has not, as elsewhere, been accompanied by a sharp rise in female participation in the paid labour force. In

1987, Ireland's female labour force participation rate (the proportion of the female population aged 15–64 in the labour force) was the lowest of the 22 OECD countries, at 37.5 per cent (in the majority of cases the rate was above 50 per cent, and exceeded 70 per cent in the case of the four Nordic countries). There was only a marginal increase in the rate over the previous 20 years, during which time Ireland was surpassed by Italy, Spain, Greece, and Portugal (Callender, 1990). This low participation rate means that women comprise a relatively small proportion of the total labour force (30.9 per cent in 1987, up from just a quarter in 1971).

To a significant extent, the low level of involvement by Irish women in paid labour may be attributed to a lack of labour market pressures, in that the Irish economy has portrayed a chronic historical inability to provide adequate employment for its population. This is reflected in high levels of emigration (since independence was achieved in 1922, over one million people have emigrated from a country which, in 1991, had a total population of just 3.5 million) and, more recently, very high unemployment levels (currently of the order of 20 per cent).

More importantly, in the past Irish women have been excluded from the labour force by a range of legislative measures, including a discriminatory social welfare system and obligatory retirement on marriage for female public servants. However, a series of laws establishing formal equality for women workers was enacted in the 1970s (arising directly from EC membership in 1973), while equality of treatment under the social welfare code was gradually extended in the 1980s. The slow growth in women's employment in response to these measures has been due partly to prolonged recession since the early 1980s and high levels of income tax, even for those on low pay. At the same time, it is clear that many women remain outside the paid workforce due to traditional social and cultural value systems, strongly championed by the Irish Roman Catholic church, which emphasises a family-centred role for Irish women (O'Dowd, 1987). This is classically reflected in the Irish constitution, enacted in 1937, which specifically states that the place of women is in the home and seeks to 'ensure that mothers shall not be obliged by economic necessity to engage in labour to the neglect of their duties in the home' (*Constitution of Ireland*, nd, p. 138).

Predictably, those women who *are* engaged in paid work are heavily concentrated in the services sector, which accounted for 77 per cent of all women workers in 1987, compared with 57 per cent of total employment (Blackwell, 1989). Women account for 44 per cent of service workers compared with just one-third of all paid workers. Women represent 30 per cent of manufacturing workers, a proportion that has been growing slowly, albeit due mainly to contraction in male employment in the sector. While women have figured prominently in the branch plants of foreign (mainly electronics) firms which have been a central element in national industrial policy since 1960, employment growth in this sector has been largely offset by secular decline in the textiles and clothing industries, where female manufacturing employment was traditionally concentrated (Breathnach, 1993).

In the services sector, women are particularly strongly represented in personal services (mainly hotels and restaurants), professional services (teaching and nursing), financial and business services, and the lower echelons of the civil service. They are poorly represented in wholesale distribution, transportation, and the security forces. This, of course, is typical of advanced economies.

As elsewhere, the labour market options available to Irish women are greatly circumscribed by the stereotyping of an educational system which steers women away from technical and skilled manual occupations and towards a narrow range of service occupations. This bias is, of course, further enhanced by the predispositions of recruiting agents. The resultant constriction of employment opportunities inevitably means that many Irish women must either accept poorly paid unskilled work or opt out of the workforce altogether.

Although, at 7.1 per cent of the total workforce in 1987, part-time employment in Ireland is less common than in other advanced economies (Dineen, 1989), it is, as elsewhere, dominated by women workers (70 per cent of the total). Part-time work frequently suits married women (who make up one-half of all part-time workers) in particular; thus, survey evidence shows that the majority of Irish part-time workers opt voluntarily for this form of employment (Dineen, 1989), although the level of involuntary part-time work is growing.

Women also constitute a majority (55 per cent) of temporary workers, who make up 8.5 per cent of the overall Irish workforce. However, in this case the great – and growing – majority are in temporary employment because of an inability to find permanent jobs (although older women in particular are more inclined to opt for temporary work by choice). Particular reference has been made here to both part-time and temporary employment, not only because of the fact that they are dominated by women workers, but also – as shall be seen – because of their significance in the tourism industry.

WOMEN'S EMPLOYMENT IN IRISH TOURISM

Because of its highly heterogeneous nature and the fact that it overlaps with many other economic activities, tourism employment is not easily quantifiable. However, in the case of Ireland, detailed surveys carried out by the Council for Education, Recruitment and Training (CERT), the national tourism training agency, provide an excellent database for analysing the structure of employment in the industry (CERT, 1987, 1988, 1991).*

In 1987, an estimated 57,000 people were engaged directly in providing tourism services; however, because many of these were employed part-time, or were simultaneously providing services to non-tourists (retailing, catering, etc.), this figure converts to 38,500 full-time equivalents (CERT, 1987). This figure accords well with other estimates of employment in the industry (Tansey Webster and Associates, 1991). When one includes indirect employment (supplying goods and services to the industry) and further employment induced by the multiplier effects of tourist expenditure, total tourism-related employment for that year rises to 63,000, representing about 6 per cent of total employment and 10 per cent of service employment.

Table 3.3 gives a breakdown of tourism employment by subsector and gender. While the CERT surveys provide much detail on the gender division of labour in most areas of tourism employment, it is not complete. It has therefore been necessary to estimate the gender division for some sub-sectors from other sources. The proportions given in the table therefore should be regarded as roughly approximate rather than precise.

Table 3.3 Employment structure of the Irish tourism industry, 1987[1]

Sub-sector	As % of total employment	Women as % of sub-sector
Accommodation	49	70
Catering	11	38
Transport	16	18[2]
Tour operators	6	76
Administration[3]	5	44[4]
Leisure/recreation	6	50
Retailing	8[5]	40[6]
Total	100	54

Notes:
1 Unless otherwise stated, all data derived from CERT (1987).
2 Based on national gender division for transport sector (Blackwell, 1989).
3 Refers to public servants involved in tourism administration.
4 Based on overall gender division in civil service (Blackwell, 1989).
5 Refers to full-time equivalents.
6 Based on national gender division in retailing (Blackwell, 1989).
All figures are rounded.

Table 3.3 shows that, in 1987, women accounted for some 54 per cent of all those employed in Irish tourism. This is significantly in excess of the proportion of women in services generally (44 per cent), and almost twice the proportion of women in the overall workforce (31 per cent). If one excludes the male-intensive transport sub-sector (mainly involved in bringing tourists into the country), women account for 60 per cent of tourism employment. For accommodation, which accounts for one-half of tourism employment, the proportion rises to 70 per cent.

Women's employment in the hotel sector

It is clear, therefore, that tourism is an atypical sector in the Irish economy, in that it is characterised by a predominantly female workforce. In order to explain this, a closer examination will be carried out of the accommodation sub-sector, in which women workers are particularly prominent. This examination is based on a detailed survey carried out by CERT (1988) of employment in hotels and guesthouses (hereafter simply the 'hotel sector'), which account for the great bulk of employment in the sub-

Table 3.4   Structure of employment in the Irish hotel sector, 1988

Employment category	As % of all employment	Women as % of category
Full-time permanent	52.1	59.2
Part-time permanent	12.5	79.4
Full-time seasonal	13.6	73.5
Part-time seasonal	2.4	88.2
Casual	19.4	n/a
Total	100.0	66.0*

Sources: CERT (1988); authors' additional calculations.
* Excluding casual.

sector. The hotel sector is particularly oriented to the tourism industry, with 80 per cent of employment being tourism-related (CERT, 1987).

Table 3.4 provides a breakdown of employment in the hotel sector into different employment categories, and gives the female proportion of employment in each category. Just over one-half of all employment is full-time permanent, with a further one-eighth being permanent but part-time. The remaining one-third of jobs are seasonal (both full-time and part-time) or casual.

Excluding casual workers (for whom no gender breakdown is available) women comprise two-thirds of all employment in hotels – over twice the overall female participation rate in paid employment in the country. However, the female proportion is lower for full-time permanent jobs (59 per cent) and higher for all the other categories: part-time permanent (79 per cent); full-time seasonal (74 per cent); and part-time seasonal (88 per cent). This employment structure is very similar to that noted by Bagguley (1990) for the British hotel and catering sector.

The domination of part-time and temporary employment by women is, as noted previously, a common feature of advanced Western economies. The fact that these employment categories constitute such a large proportion of total employment in the hotel sector – almost a half compared to just 16 per cent in the national workforce – therefore goes a long way to explaining the disproportionate representation of women workers in the sector. However, the fact remains that women are also disproportionately represented among full-time permanent workers in the sector.

The second key explanatory factor in accounting for the high level of female employment in the hotel sector is the low level of skill required of the sector's workforce: less than one-third of all workers may be regarded as skilled in the sense of having received at least some formal training. Even among full-time permanent workers, only a minority (44 per cent) have any formal training. Skill levels are particularly low (only one-seventh of all workers having had formal training) among part-time, seasonal and casual workers, the great majority of whom are women.

In all work categories, men are more likely to be skilled than women; and the higher the skill level of an occupational category, the more likely it is that it is full-time, permanent and male. Of managerial positions (eight per cent of all employment in the sector), 90 per cent are full-time permanent and three-quarters are formally trained, but only 40 per cent are held by women. By contrast, less than half (44 per cent) of unskilled 'accommodation assistants' (chamber maids) (nine per cent of all jobs) are full-time permanent, and all are women. Similarly, over 90 per cent of waiters/waitresses (21 per cent of all hotel employment) are women, and less than 30 per cent of jobs in this category are full-time permanent.

Gender segmentation in the hotel sector

There is considerable variation in female representation as between the different 'departments' of the hotel sector. Women are particularly prominent in the accommodation (99 per cent of all workers) and restaurant and banquet (86 per cent) departments, but only comprise a minority in management (40 per cent) and the bar and nightclub (48 per cent) departments. The remaining departments, kitchen (61 per cent) and reception and general (57 per cent) occupy intermediate positions.

Within departments, there is also a high level of gender segmentation by occupation. Of kitchen staff, the vast majority of head chefs (skilled) and porters (unskilled) are men, while almost all kitchen assistants and wash-ups (both unskilled) are women. While restaurant and banquet staff are predominantly female, head waiters/waitresses are mainly men. In the reception and general department, those working as receptionists or in accounts are almost entirely women, while porters, doorpersons and maintenance workers are almost all male. In management, of 161 managing directors and general managers, only one is a woman.

However, there are some occupational categories where segmentation is not so apparent. Almost one-half of chefs (other than head chefs) and barpersons are women (although in the latter case, women are much less likely to be full-time permanent). And, while there are virtually no female managing directors or general managers, of those with the simple grade of 'manager', 44 per cent are women, with the proportion rising to 49 per cent for assistant/duty managers and exactly one-half for trainee managers. This could mean improving opportunities for women to progress to top management positions in future years. Alternatively, it could simply mean that women gradually get squeezed out as they move up the managerial ladder. Hicks' (1990) findings would tend to support the latter interpretation.

Flexibility in hotel employment

While much attention has been devoted in recent times to growing (imposed) flexibility of the workforce (especially in the manufacturing sector) in advanced economies (Atkinson, 1985; Gertler, 1988; Schoenberger, 1988), labour flexibility is a long-established feature of the hotel sector. In Britain, while functional flexibility emerged in the 1960s in response to labour shortages, it tended to be superseded in the 1970s by increasing numerical flexibility, mainly in the form of part-time and seasonal work (Bagguley, 1990). While part-time work is more conducive to functional specialisation than flexibility, it has many attractions for employers. These include the ability to adapt to daily and weekly fluctuations in customer demand and the ability to avoid social insurance contributions, holiday and sick pay, etc., for part-time workers. The fact that part-time and temporary workers are more difficult to organise by trade unions is also seen as beneficial by many employers. There is also the fact, noted earlier, that part-time and seasonal work is also attractive in particular to many women (especially married) workers.

According to Bagguley (1990), in Britain, functional flexibility is particularly common among management staff in full-time jobs. In Ireland, CERT (1988) found a very high – and growing – level of functional flexibility outside management grades, with 73 per cent of hotels and 88 per cent of guesthouses reporting flexible practices in non-management grades. The main area of functional flexibility involves movement between bar, restaurant and receptionist work. As the latter two categories are overwhelmingly female in content, it can be concluded that most functionally flexible workers in the hotel sector are women. The same applies, of course, to numerically flexible workers.

CERT (1988) also found that functional flexibility is particularly concentrated among non-Grade A hotels. To a certain extent this is due to greater scope for functional specialisation in the larger Grade A establishments. However, it is also noteworthy that trade unions are strongly established in the Grade A sector, but are almost entirely absent from the lower hotel grades. Irish hotel workers are mainly organised by the Services, Industrial, Professional and Technical Union (SIPTU), the dominant union for general workers. SIPTU has negotiation agreements with 54 Grade A hotels representing three-quarters of all rooms in the Grade A sector (SIPTU, 1991). However, less than half the hotel rooms in Ireland are of Grade A standard, and trade unions are almost entirely absent from the other grades, where functional and numerical flexibility are particularly prominent.

Regional distribution of hotel employment

CERT (1988) also provides information on the regional distribution of hotel employment. Table 3.5 relates each region's share of hotel employment to its share of total employment. A ratio of greater than one in the right-hand column indicates a disproportionate concentration of hotel employment in a region. The table shows that hotel employment is particularly strongly concentrated in the western half of the country. This corroborates the findings by Tansey Webster and Associates (1991), noted earlier, that tourism makes a disproportionate contribution to personal incomes in western regions. This is undoubtedly significant, in that these are the most underdeveloped regions in the country, with below-average incomes and inferior employment oppor-

Table 3.5   Regional distribution of Irish hotel employment, 1988

Region	% of Irish total		
	Hotel employment (1988)	Total employment (1986)	Ratio
East	29.0	43.7	0.66
Midlands	5.5	8.8	0.62
South-east	10.9	10.4	1.05
South-west	21.8	14.7	1.48
Mid-west	11.4	8.9	1.28
West	12.1	8.1	1.50
North-west	9.4	5.4	1.74

Sources: CERT (1988); Central Statistics Office (1989).

tunities compared with the east of the country. Of particular relevance in this context is the fact that, in the past, employment opportunities for women tended to be relatively poorer for women in the west (Gillmor, 1985). Tourism, with its disproportionate tendency to provide work for women, therefore contributes in an important way to expanding work opportunities for the female labour force in this part of the country.

On the other hand, given the unskilled and frequently part-time or seasonal nature of employment in the hotel sector, it is clear that the disproportionate concentration of this employment in the west does not augur well for the prospects of closing the average income gap with the east, where high-quality service employment is heavily concentrated. Hotel employment, therefore, does provide a considerable level of employment in areas where job opportunities of any kind are in short supply, but at the cost of exacerbating inter-regional income disparities.

Women's employment in other tourism sectors

CERT (1991) provides detailed information on employment in a wide range of tourist-related activities outside the accommodation, catering and access transport sectors. Most of the activities in question (referred to hereinafter as the 'miscellaneous tourism' sector) relate to leisure and recreation, but some other activities, such as internal transport and other tourist support services, are included. In employment terms, the most important activities involved are golf, craft centres, car hire, language centres and historic houses. Most of these activities also cater for non-tourists (such as golf, theatres), so that not all the jobs involved can be attributed to tourism. However, from CERT (1987) we can estimate that around 60 per cent of the employment concerned is tourism-dependent. This in turn amounts to almost 20 per cent of all direct employment in tourism in Ireland in 1990.

Data on the gender make-up of employment is available for sub-sectors accounting for three-quarters of all employment in the miscellaneous tourism sector. It is from these sub-sectors that Table 3.6 has been compiled. A comparison between Tables 3.4 and 3.6 shows that the nature of employment in the miscellaneous tourism sector is rather similar to that in the hotel sector. CERT (1991) does not provide for a 'casual' employment sector, but a comparison of the two tables suggests that such jobs are mainly subsumed into the 'part-time seasonal' category in the miscellaneous tourism sector. Thus, in both the hotel and miscellaneous sectors, about one-half of all jobs are full-time permanent, with a further 35–40 per cent in the seasonal/casual category.

Just over half of all the employment in the miscellaneous sector is taken by women. This participation rate, while considerably less than that for the hotel sector (66 per cent), is nevertheless in excess of the female participation rate in services employment in general (44 per cent), and considerably in excess

Table 3.6 *Structure of employment in the Irish miscellaneous tourism sector, 1991*

Employment category	As % of total employment	Women as % of category
Full-time permanent	49.9	48.0
Part-time permanent	10.4	54.9
Full-time seasonal	22.1	55.8
Part-time seasonal	17.5	38.0
Total	100.0	52.3

Sources: CERT (1991); authors' additional calculations.

of the proportion of women in the overall workforce (31 per cent). As with the hotel sector, women are under-represented in the full-time permanent category and over-represented in the part-time/seasonal categories; however, the divergences from the overall average female participation rate are not as marked as in hotel employment, where women are overwhelmingly dominant in the latter categories.

Of the 40 separate activities covered in the CERT survey, just seven account for almost 60 per cent of all employment. While the survey does not provide the detailed and systematic analysis of skill levels contained in the CERT (1987) survey of the hotel sector, some general indications can be gleaned from the report. Thus, only one-quarter of employment in caravan/camping sites is full-time permanent, and two-thirds of this is male, whereas two-thirds of seasonal employment is female. Most jobs in this activity are unskilled.

By contrast, over four-fifths of employment in car hire is full-time permanent, and this is mostly male. This coincides with a high level of good-quality employment in sales, maintenance and administration. Golf courses portray an even division between full-time permanent and other forms of employment, but in both cases, some two-thirds of employment is male. In historic houses, the bulk of employment is either part-time or seasonal, with over 80 per cent of seasonal workers being female, compared with one-half of those who are full-time permanent.

Irish language courses provide almost entirely seasonal employment, most of which provides supplementary income for teachers and those providing accommodation (both largely female). Language centres (mainly involved in teaching English to continental Europeans) provide a sizeable amount of full-time permanent employment (about two-fifths of the total), although the majority of jobs are seasonal. Teachers are the main occupational group involved, and these, in turn, are mainly women.

Craft production is something of an exception to the general pattern of women primarily being involved in either seasonal or unskilled (or both) forms of employment in this sector. The great bulk (70 per cent) of employment in this activity is full-time permanent, a high proportion is skilled (almost one-third are craft workers), yet women predominate (70 per cent of all workers).

Overall, however, it is clear that the general pattern of employment in the miscellaneous tourism sector replicates that of the hotel sector, with women being disproportionately represented in the sector's workforce in comparison with other sectors outside tourism, and that this is particularly the case with part-time and seasonal work, which itself is much more common throughout the tourism industry than it is in the economy generally.

Women and the provision of bed and breakfast accommodation

One sector of the tourism industry which is almost exclusively dominated by women is the bed and breakfast (B&B) sector. In 1991 there were over 3,200 premises involved in this business which had been approved by Bord Fáilte; this was an increase of almost 40 per cent on the number reported by CERT (1987) for 1985. Using the ratios contained in CERT (1987), these 3,200 establishments would have represented 7,500 jobs, 70 per cent of them seasonal, and 90 per cent female, converting to 3,330 full-time equivalents. Over half of these premises are located in the seven west coast counties stretching from Kerry to Donegal.

However, for each approved B&B establishment, it is estimated that there are three unapproved operations (Ó Cinnéide and Walsh, 1991), which suggests that, in all, there are up to 13,000 B&B premises in the country. It is unlikely that the unapproved operations provide a similar level of employment to their approved counterparts, in which investment levels are generally higher. Nevertheless, it seems reasonable to suggest that, overall, the B&B sector provides employment for upwards of 20,000 people (mostly women), or about 9,000 full-time equivalents.

An exploratory survey of 35 B&B establishments was carried out by the authors in early 1992 in the Killarney area in the south-west of Ireland in order to examine a number of themes concerning the nature of employment in the sector. Killarney, with a population of about 10,000, is Ireland's leading tourist resort, based on the internationally renowned lake and mountain scenery in the vicinity. The town has 28 hotels, 162 approved B&B establishments, and a wide range of additional accommodation facilities, including unapproved B&Bs, hostels, holiday centres, caravan and camping sites, and self-catering facilities.

The survey found that one-half of the premises started up in the previous five years, indicating rapid recent growth in the sector, in line with government objectives for tourism in general. Two-thirds of the respondents reported working more than eight hours per day, with over one-half working more than twelve hours. While clearly this pattern would not be maintained throughout the year, it does indicate a lot of hard work on the part of the women involved. Three-quarters of respondents regarded their B&B business as a full-time job.

Almost all the respondents identified aspects of the business which they did not like, the principal ones being the amount and type of work involved, and the fact that they were tied down to their work all the time and got little chance of a break. At the same time, most respondents also identified aspects of the work which they liked, almost all of which had to do with meeting people. The great majority of respondents thought that doing B&B suited their lifestyle. The small number who expanded on this mentioned such things as being able to work at home (especially where children had to be cared for also) or to be one's own boss, or that they would not be working otherwise.

Only three respondents had given up paid work to start their B&B business: the rest were not gainfully occupied immediately prior to starting the business. Most had been in unskilled employment earlier in their lives. There was strong evidence that many respondents were involved in B&B out of economic necessity: no less than one-half said there was no one else in the household in employment. In addition, six cited the cost of educating their children as a specific reason for being in B&B: almost all of these had no other source of earned income.

The overall picture to emerge from this survey was of an occupation involving long hours of what amounts to a lot of drudgery, doing work which men refuse to do, either because of the nature of the work, or because of the economic returns. While information on income was not obtained, we would suggest that, in most cases, the rate of return is low relative to the number of hours worked and the responsibility involved, and relative to what one would have to pay someone else to do the work in question. Nevertheless, most of the respondents intended to continue with the business, whether because of economic necessity, the zero 'opportunity cost' (lack of alternatives), or the limited expectations of women who mainly came from an unskilled background.

CONCLUSION

The tourism industry in Ireland portrays characteristics which are essentially no different from the situation in most other areas. It is a highly seasonal and unstable economic sector in which part-time and unskilled employment are common features. The fact that these types of employment are mainly taken up by women is primarily a reflection of the generally marginal status of women in the Irish workforce.

Serious questions must be raised concerning the high levels of resources currently being invested in tourism development by both the Irish government and the European Community. The high proportion of poor-quality employment which typifies tourism ensures that the industry holds out little hope of helping Ireland close the income gap with the EC heartland. A strong emphasis on tourism growth therefore serves to confirm Ireland's peripheral status within the Community, relying on the spending in Ireland of wealth generated in highly productive advanced economic activities in the core regions of Europe and other parts of the developed world.

It can be argued that, in the long term, the resources currently being invested in tourism development in Ireland might be better spent in building up an alternative economic base in similar advanced sectors. Of course, if such were to be the case, the types of job which would be created would present limited employment opportunities for Irish women, given existing social structures. However, for the present authors, it seems preferable to challenge these structures, rather than to acquiesce in the kinds of work offered in such quantity by the tourism industry.

NOTE

*   While CERT (1988) provides a very detailed breakdown of the workforce in the Irish hotel and guesthouse sector in terms of gender division, occupations and skill levels, there remain a number of information gaps which made it necessary to make some assumptions in order to facilitate the analysis which follows. Further elucidation of these assumptions is available from the authors on request.

REFERENCES

Atkinson, J., 1985, Flexibility: planning for an uncertain future, *Manpower Policy and Practice*, **1**: 26–9.

Bagguley, P., 1990, Gender and labour flexibility in hotel and catering, *Service Industries Journal*, **10**(4): 737–47.

Blackwell, J., 1989, *Women in the labour force*, Employment Equality Agency, Dublin.

Bord Fáilte, 1991, *1990 Annual Report*, Bord Fáilte, Dublin.

Breathnach, P., 1993, Women's employment and peripheral industrialisation: the case of Ireland's branch plant economy, *Geoforum*, **24**(1): 19–29.

Callender, R., 1990, Women and work: the appearance and reality of change, *Labour Market Review*, **1**: 18–36.

Central Statistics Office, 1989, *Census of population of Ireland 1986: summary population report*, The Stationery Office, Dublin.

Central Statistics Office, 1991a, *Census of population of Ireland 1991: preliminary report*, The Stationery Office, Dublin.

Central Statistics Office, 1991b, *National income and expenditure 1990*, The Stationery Office, Dublin.

Constitution of Ireland, nd, The Stationery Office, Dublin.

Council for Education, Recruitment and Training (CERT), 1987, *Scope of the tourism industry in Ireland*, CERT, Dublin.

Council for Education, Recruitment and Training (CERT), 1988, *Manpower survey of the Irish hotel and catering industry*, CERT, Dublin.

Council for Education, Recruitment and Training (CERT), 1991, *A profile of employment in the tourism industry: non food and accommodation*, CERT, Dublin.

Deegan, J., Dineen, D., 1991, Irish tourism policy: employment, economic development and environmental interdependencies. Paper presented to the 14th Annual Economic Policy Conference of the Dublin Economics Workshop, Kenmare.

Dineen, D., 1989, *Changing employment patterns in Ireland: recent trends and future prospects*, The Irish National Pensions Board, Limerick.

Dunne, J., 1992, World recession leads to empty rooms, *Irish Times*, 1 August.

Gertler, M., 1988, The limits to flexibility: comments on the post-Fordist vision of production and its geography, *Transactions of the Institute of British Geographers*, **13**: 419–32.

Gillmor, D., 1985, Recent changes in the employment of women in the Republic of Ireland, *Irish Geographer*, **18**: 69–73.

Henry, M., 1992, The impacts of tourism: a literature review, MA Qualifying Thesis, Department of Geography, St Patrick's College, Maynooth.

Hicks, L., 1990, Excluded women: how can this happen in the hotel world?, *Services Industry Journal*, **10**(2): 348–63.

Maher, B., 1992, Heritage attractions: effective marketing through research, in Bord Fáilte, *Heritage and tourism*, Bord Fáilte, Dublin, pp. 5.1–5.13.

Ó Cinnéide, M., Walsh, J., 1991, Tourism and regional development in Ireland, *Geographical Viewpoint*, **19**: 47–68.

O'Dowd, L., 1987, Church, state and women: the aftermath of partition, in Curtin, C., Jackson, P., O'Connor, B. (eds), *Gender in Irish society*, Galway University Press, Galway, pp. 3–36.

Price Waterhouse, 1987, *Improving the performance of Irish tourism*, Price Waterhouse, Dublin.

Quinn, B., 1989, Imagery in tourism promotion: A case study of the promotion of Ireland as a tourist destination in continental Europe, MA Thesis, Department of Geography, St Patrick's College, Maynooth.

Schoenberger, E., 1988, From Fordism to flexible accumulation: technology, competitive strategies, and international location, *Environment and Planning D*, **6**: 345–62.

Scott, D., Godley, G.C., 1992, An analysis of adult play groups: social versus serious participation in Contract Bridge, *Leisure Sciences*, **14**(1), quoted in the *Newsletter* of the Association of American Geographers, **27**(7): 4.

Services, Industrial, Professional and Technical Union (SIPTU), 1991, *The SIPTU better hotel guide*, SIPTU, Dublin.

Tansey Webster and Associates, 1991, *Tourism and the economy*, The Irish Tourist Industry Confederation, Dublin.

4
Gender dimensions of tourism in Greece: employment, sub-cultures and restructuring

Lila Leontidou

INTRODUCTION

In the context of the Greek tourism industry gender dimensions have received scant attention. Data availability is poor. The literature distinguishing any gender aspects of tourism, especially from a socio-cultural perspective, is minimal.[1] Women are silent in tourism surveys.[2] If we exclude a couple of anecdotal references, gender dimensions have not been discussed in the literature on tourism as an industry or as a consumption sector, on tourism and economic or regional development, on tourism and the labour market. The following exposition therefore relies on the few specialist works, on passing references in works with a different focus, on the few statistical surveys, and on the personal experience of the author.

Tourist arrivals in Greece are currently doubling every five years (Leontidou, 1991, p. 86). The number of annual foreign visitors are as many as the population of Greece – 8,053,052 (1987) and 10,264,156 (1991) respectively. Other Europeans form the bulk of tourist arrivals (90 per cent in 1987), having overtaken Americans in the early 1970s. Among gender dimensions of tourism development examined, types of labour commitment and cultural tensions in sun and beach resorts have been those most stressed in Greece. The former pertain to informal female work, where tourism creates an invisible 'formal market', especially in the very countries where tourist development is rapid and massive. Cultural aspects have to do with tensions emerging in tourist localities, especially between local and foreign women.

However, tourism 'resources' are heterogeneous, and have several gender implications. Gender divisions are changing. For example, conference tourism, which concentrates in cities, especially Paris and London (Law, 1985; Tuppen, 1985; Williams and Shaw, 1991b, p. 20), used to be male-dominated; this is gradually changing. The bulk of tourism, with extreme coastal concentration, has a strong and apparently growing female element. Sunshine beach holidays, urban/cultural tourism, business/conference tourism, and rural tourism (Williams and Shaw, 1991a, pp. 18–20) are all to be found in Greece. The country also presents a typical case study of ways in which tourism, as an industry, redistributes income between North and South in Europe (Commission of the European Communities, 1985). The predominant tourism types for holidays, especially beach and Alpine tourism, tend to divert visitors from industrial to underdeveloped areas and between city and countryside, and promote the economic development of the latter. This underlines core/periphery, North/South, rich/poor binary distinctions, but also the important role of tourism in a spatial depolarisation process.

However, this is where the international/regional comparison must stop. Studies at the regional level indicate that depolarisation is often far from the case. In fact, there are interactions between national and regional development, such as national investment schemes, international currency fluctuations, etc., affecting the regions (Williams and Shaw, 1991a, p. 4). In addition, social depolarisation is another matter, since the dividing line between natives and tourists is a class line, and there are sharp class and gender divisions within the labour force employed in tourism.

At the local level, the redistributive impact of tourism is often reversed or viewed in a completely different light. This is hidden by the insistence of research on tourist arrivals and uneven socio-economic development of regions of destination of tourists, their transformation through the tourist inflow, their economic and social restructuring, and their protection. This is very important, no doubt; but uneven regional, economic and social development is also evident in the differential access to leisure of residents of various regions, inequalities between regions of origin of tourists and the tensions created in poor localities serving the tourist inflow. These different aspects and binary distinctions will be seen in the following, with special attention given to the gender dimension.

LEISURE: PLACES, PREFERENCES, ACCESS AND CULTURAL TENSIONS

Vacation is a kind of flight from everyday routines, a means to realising dreams, and requires a population working hard to create an ideal environment. Inequality and tension are inherent in such a relationship. As for the definition of female work and leisure and the concepts of work, employment, activity, unemployment, idleness and inactivity, difficult problems are raised in every social formation and historical period. The limits between work and leisure are clearer for women during the tourist season, and this often creates a tension between groups of women – working versus idle women, locals versus foreigners – in tourist resorts. Traditionally, Greece has lived with the divisions of traveller/host, tourist/servant, movement/stasis, male/female. In other words, gender distinctions in the past had men as travellers and women as hostesses. This is no longer the case. As women increasingly travel in groups without men, the disturbance of local societies and relationships between women are restructured in a completely different manner.

Access to tourism and leisure

There has been a spectacular growth of international tourists as incomes rise along with leisure time, from 25 million in 1950 to 69 million in 1960, 160 million in 1970 and 280 million in 1982

(Williams and Shaw, 1991a, p. 13). Tourism consumption con-tributes to national income, especially in Mediterranean Europe. In 1986, 47.4 million tourists visited Spain, 20 million visited Italy, 6.7 million visited Greece, and 5.4 million visited Portugal (plus 7.5 million excursionists). Today 100 million annual tour-ists arrive in the Mediterranean and the forecasts are that they will have doubled by the year 2000. One of the major destina-tions may be Greece, which 36 per cent of the Europeans con-sidered attractive for future holidays (Commission of the European Communities, 1987, p. 77). This is mainly because mass tourist attractions, which by far outnumber other types of attractions, are sea and sun, as well as skiing conditions. Over half of tourists from the EC take their main holidays at the seaside. Greece, with its 15,021 km of coastline, of which 3,000 are sandy beaches, and with its 337 inhabited islands, is a major destination. It is a pity that no information on tourist differentia-tion by age and sex is available, but there seems to be a tendency among visitors from the Mediterranean to travel in couples or families or in mixed company, while northerners are more likely to travel as couples and, increasingly, in groups of women or mixed groups. Among domestic tourists there is a prepon-derance of women with children, as discussed below.

Seaside tourism is highly seasonal, and this is amplified by the increasing involvement of tour operators in the industry. Sea-sonality by nation, but not yet by region, has been well docu-mented (Williams and Shaw, 1993). In the Mediterranean, 35 per cent of tourists arrive in two summer months, while countries with skiing seasons have double peaks. The lowest degree of seasonal peaking is found in the Netherlands, Germany and the United Kingdom (24–27 per cent). Spain has a low index, 29 per cent, despite its attraction of mass tourism (Williams and Shaw, 1991a, pp. 22–3). In Greece, seasonality is always acute and appears to be increasing, despite efforts to spread activity more evenly by the encouragement of other types of tourism. In 1981, 61.6 per cent of arrivals and 66.7 per cent of overnight stays by foreigners were concentrated between June and September. By 1987 this had grown to 65 per cent of arrivals and 68.5 per cent of overnight stays (ESYE, 1990, pp. 21, 137).

Accessibility to tourism is a function of income levels and free time at the disposal of populations. Tourism is characterised by a positive income elasticity of demand: demand rises are proportionately greater than increases in income levels. High-income countries and regions generate the bulk of international tourists. EC residents are foremost in international tourist activity, representing 180 million tourists a year (Williams and Shaw, 1993), with the USA closely following. It has been estimated that EC households spend an average of seven per cent of their budgets on holidays (Commission of the European Communities, 1985).

However, it was found that 44 per cent of EC residents did not take a holiday at all in 1985 (Commission of the European Communities, 1987). Of these, older people, those with large families and those living in rural areas were the groups most likely to fall into this category. National variations are also significant. Mediterranean countries do not usually generate large numbers of tourists. The OECD (1988, p. 82), analysed receipts and expenditure on international tourism (see also Williams and Shaw, 1991a, p. 33), and revealed the highest positive balance to be realised by Spain and Italy, while (West) Germany had the greatest negative balance. In Portugal, only 44 per cent of the population surveyed in 1985 had any paid holidays at all, and half of them were of very short duration (Lewis and Williams, 1991, p. 112; Williams and Shaw, 1993).

Within the EC regional disparities are due mostly to poverty: in Portugal, Ireland and Greece, 67, 61 and 55 per cent respectively of non-holidaying respondents in 1985 could not afford to take a holiday (20–50 per cent in other EC countries) (Williams and Shaw, 1993). Economic constraints, as well as the problem of leave of absence, affected manual workers. Gender dimensions have not been included in such surveys, but they would probably favour women, as in the case of Greek domestic tourism: as children are given priority in family holidays, they are often escorted by mothers, while fathers remain behind to work during the summer.

Cultural preferences and segmentation

Different places in the Greek islands are particularly attractive for certain nationalities. It has been demonstrated in Greece that tourists have tended to be drawn to particular locations by nationality during the early 1980s (Leontidou, 1991, pp. 92–3): tourists originating in the UK have concentrated in Corfu, those from Western Germany in Crete, those from the Netherlands in Rhodes and Crete, Yugoslavians in Pieria, Austrians and all Scandinavians in Rhodes.[3] This concentration is largely due to decisions by tour operators, besides accommodation available, that is, decisions taken abroad.[4] In fact, tour operators dominate Greek tourism, and the level of dependence of certain localities on particular countries creates high risk at periods of crisis.

On the other hand, cases can be discerned where the destinations of tourists vary according to cultural orientations of the holidaying groups: in international (but not domestic) tourism, southerners tend to be drawn to cities, northerners to the countryside and the beaches. It is interesting to note in this connection the positive cultural orientation to urbanism of Mediterranean people (Leontidou, 1990, pp. 257–9), which tends to concentrate their demand in cities and cultural tourism, although Athens does not attract many visitors any more.[5] By contrast, the far more numerous northern Europeans tend to concentrate at seaside and mountain locations for beach and alpine tourism. This can reflect their negative attitude to urban congestion and need to escape to nature and the countryside. In 1982, of the overnight stays of Italian and Spanish tourists in Greece, 26 per cent and 73 per cent respectively were spent in Athens. The figures for French and Belgian tourists were 20 per cent and 13 per cent respectively, while the proportion of tourists from all other European countries was much lower at 3.5–8.5 per cent (Leontidou, 1991, pp. 92–4).

Another North/South division can be discerned in the spending habits and preferences in mass tourism. A broad segmentation of the market between two groups of tourists appears to be developing, a factor that Greek authorities are particularly sensitive to. One group, originating in the industrialised regions of the European core, will be much more demanding of tourist services than another group, drawn from the South, agricultural and poor regions. This segmentation of the market is discussed with respect to the economic benefit to localities of destination, and policy is formulated in order to attract richer tourists. However, it can also be seen in another light: the expansion of affluent but also mass tourism, in the end, undermines exploration and the unexpected as one of the joys and advantages of travelling. Especially in Mediterranean countries, independent holiday-takers are increasingly excluded from certain localities of mass tourism and foreign ownership. It is increasingly difficult for domestic tourists to arrange their own holidays independently from commercial networks, or spontaneously, as they behave in several areas of social life (Leontidou, 1990).

Their reluctance to rely on travel agents should not be negatively evaluated as a 'lack of professionalism and institutionalism in the organisation of the industry' (Lewis and Williams, 1991, p. 112). After all, the right to spontaneity and last-moment choices, the right to wander and discover, should at least be allowed (if not encouraged) during days of leisure. But it is not. Such an attitude emanates from female approaches to tourism (Ammer and Leontidou, 1989): exploration, as one of the best aspects of tourism, is precluded both in localities with mass tourism and foreign-owned areas. Through tour operators, moreover, foreigners obtain better bargains in local hotels than domestic tourists. Organised package holidays exclude individual tourists from booking accommodation, which is held long in advance by tour operators. In foreign-owned localities, even some beaches are closed to the public. The host populations of many tourist destinations are becoming increasingly excluded from holidaying in their own country.

Places are unique; attractiveness and location, physical beauty and cultural tradition are scarce resources, and competition for them is unequal and increasingly excludes low-wage populations and spontaneous tourists. The 'free' market and the monopolistic market in the tourism industry thus create regional polarisation on the demand side.

Local cultural tensions and latent conflicts

Besides the provision of jobs and the stability of the balance of payments between North and South as positive results of tourism, the EC has already stressed closer relationships between states, the contact among people reinforcing European integration (Williams and Shaw, 1993). However, things are often not so pleasant in tourist regions. There has been an unresolved controversy about the effects of tourism on local cultures, arts and crafts. The invasion of foreigners in a locality no doubt interferes with indigenous cultural manifestations, and population succession in rural areas can be a blow to cultural tourism.

The reversal of seasons of work and leisure for the host population and some conspicuous consumption by tourists in poor countries can create grievances against extravagance: in Tunisia, tourists spend in one week what a resident may spend in one year (Tsartas, 1989, p. 44). In Greece the difference is not so sharp, but other tensions mount. On the one hand, there is the relatively well researched issue of the disturbance of local society by daring young foreign women and the tension between them and local women, loyal to tradition. On the other hand, there are the women who search for culture, and ancient and sacred places, as opposed to those seeking pleasure and vacation (Ammer and Leontidou, 1989).

As the post-modern condition saturates tourist resorts, several reversals can be observed there, besides that of the seasons of work and leisure. From the point of view of gender relations, there is a stunning reversal of roles in commercialised love. The importance of female prostitution is limited in Greek tourist regions. *Kamakia* who pursue ephemeral relations with tourists in Greece are males, but their role is controversial. While there are examples of male prostitution in other tourist countries (Tsartas, 1989, p. 51), the Greek men sometimes marry their 'victims'.

This is an aspect of tourism in Greece which has been stressed repeatedly by gender studies, and has been surveyed in Kos (Castelberg-Koulma, 1989a), Ios and Serifos (Tsartas, 1989). Domestic female tourists know how to handle these men, while foreigners sometimes complain that they are annoyed.[6] Many foreign female tourists, however, tend to behave in a liberated way, often quite different from their attitudes in their countries of origin, influenced by the atmosphere of holidays. Local women, for their part, are not free to express their sexuality. In Kos, they complained about the disadvantages of tourism, and stressed that their social life was disturbed and men were lost to foreigners (Castelberg-Koulma, 1989a, p. 129). Nudist beaches and ephemeral love affairs are invasions detested by women secluded in traditional villages, where there is a shortage of men anyway, because they sail or migrate (Tsartas, 1989, p. 220; Panayotopoulou, 1990, p. 15). Despite its economic benefits, about 35 per cent of both sexes of the sample in the Cyclades islands (Tsartas, 1989, pp. 119–20) considered tourism to create 'ethical' problems.

WORK AND PROPERTY: INFORMALITY, POLYVALENCE, SEASONALITY

Before discussing gender in the tourist labour force, a short discussion of female work in general is necessary, in order to stress Greek particularities. Tourism comes somewhere between rural and urban work. In rural areas, despite gender divisions of labour, the forms of male and female employment are closer. Time allocation is governed by the needs of each activity rather than some formal work schedule or timetable. In rural societies, the allocation of tasks is quasi-precapitalist, in that the organisation of work time is subdivided into periods of exhausting work (such as harvesting) and periods of non-activity. These are 'natural' rhythms, close to nature (Thompson, 1967), which contrast with urban work, where time of work is regular and measured by the clock.

Workers and employees in tourist localities work in the summer and are idle, or take up other tasks, during the winter. This reversal of seasons is especially evident in countries with a high seasonality of the tourist industry, such as Greece. Tourism here re-establishes the dominance of nature and seasons, but in an inverse manner from the one familiar to Western societies: work and overpopulation during the summer, pause and depopulation during the winter. This reversal of seasons involves labourers very unevenly in work, and places undergo massive population fluctuations. It also disturbs everyday life: women must often dismantle their homes every summer to rent out the rooms, often leaving the family to sleep on the terrace. In tourist localities, the tourist/native distinction is a class distinction: the idle class versus the labourers.

Segmentation in the Greek female labour force

The National Statistical Service of Greece first started to classify workers by sex in 1907, when only eight per cent of the labour force was female.[7] The massive integration of women into the labour market followed the arrival of 1.5 million refugees in Greece from Asia Minor with population exchanges in 1922. There were many women among these refugees, widows and orphans of the war, who were integrated as low-paid but skilled workers in industry, comprising about 26 per cent of the total labour force (Leontidou, 1989a). At the time, whole industry groups, such as textiles and carpets, were established in Greece with female workers whose wages were half or one-third those of men. They were a proletariat in large factories, while men were dominant as petty entrepreneurs; but they were barred from labour unions and unable to organise themselves. Some of them became home workers in the informal sector.

For many Greek women it has been impossible to undertake paid work because of heavy domestic tasks, especially in shanty towns and poor rural localities, and, sometimes, seasonal tasks in tourist regions. This partly explains the low activity ratios in Greece. By 1951, one year before Greek women won the right to vote, their participation in the economically active population had dropped from 26 to 18 per cent but was higher (22 per cent) in towns with over 20,000 inhabitants. This remained stable until 1971, but rose to one-third of the active population by 1981. By 1989, women represented 52.3 per cent of the total population and 37 per cent of the economically active population. A rapid growth of female unemployment in the 1980s, brought it to over double the percentages of male unemployment, especially in cities (Leontidou, 1993). In the total Greek population, only 48 per cent work, compared with 60–71 per cent in the rest of Europe. This is not only due to reduced female activity, but also to the delay of the young in entering the labour market and the early retirement of elderly populations (Tsoucalas, 1986, pp. 227–31). Both of these create demanding tasks for women in the house.

For a very long period since the inter-war years, the Greek female labour force evidenced some class homogeneity along the lines of a continuum: all their groupings, whether in services or factories, worked in the worst-paid jobs as junior clerks, manual labourers in factories or the informal sector, and as servants. Though there were some teachers, writers and artists, it was difficult to speak of class polarisation on any broad scale. Dividing lines were between working and idle women, between integrated and marginal labourers, and much less between higher and lower classes. This is no longer the case: the latter division is now very strong and has come to the forefront. The female labour force is much more polarised and segmented than the male one (Leontidou, 1989a).

At the one extreme, educated women working especially in the tertiary sector in Athens, Piraeus and Salonica increased in number, following the rapid changes in the sex composition of the student population in the 1970s. The massive entrance of girls into higher education affected all universities, especially those specialising in preparing students for employment in the public sector. Liberal professions and entrepreneurial activities are still dominated by men, though no longer monopolised by them; women also occupy higher professions, but especially salaried public employment.[8] Occupational mobility is faster for the female than the male labour force (Shapiro, 1985, pp. 303–16). Greek researchers speak of a 'new female middle-class elite' (Lambiri-Dimaki, 1983, p. 191), and of family strategies to direct women to the public sector, where secure salary, paid leave and holidays facilitate raising a family. Researchers refer to a strategy of investment in 'educational capital' and even speak of 'quasi-dowry', which is more durable and secure than traditional dowry (Eliou, 1985, p. 59).

At the other extreme, there is the usual lower-paid, exploited female labour force, working in factories and services. Besides traditional manual jobs, new de-skilled ones emerge in the service sector with the generalisation of new technology.[9] Besides Greek women, ethnic minorities, such as Filipinas, Albanians and other Eastern Europeans, arrive to work in urban services and rural temporary jobs, in the informal sector as piece-workers at home, or as domestic servants. The discordance between census data at place of residence and place of work is an indication of large numbers of women in seasonal activities and the informal sector. In many industries, female workers at place of residence were found to be over double those in establishments for some industries, while the number of men was almost the same during the 1970s (Kavounidi, 1982). In clothing industries there were 117,00 men and women officially working in factories in 1988, but this amount is estimated to double if piece-workers, mostly female, are added. Leather and fur, printing, toys, various fitments, etc., are also run by such an unprotected, unstable, seasonal or temporary labour force, unable to unionise. Today informal work in manufacturing industry and services absorbs much of Greek feminist research (Vaiou and Stratigaki, 1989). A glaring gap in this is the tourist sector, to which we now turn.

Employment in activities related to tourism

It is difficult to approach employment in tourism, not least because of indirect employment on the one hand, and hidden, undeclared employment on the other. Attempts have been made to quantify the former. The World Tourism Organisation (1984, p. 81) suggested that tourism-related jobs accounted for 15.5 per cent of total employment in the 1970s. An EC report (Commission of the European Communities, 1985) estimated that tourism provided 5 million direct and 10–15 million direct and indirect jobs in Europe, which means a multiplier of 2–3.[10] Direct tourist employment is usually considered that in the accommodation sector, hotels, restaurants, transport (including travel agencies), recreational and cultural services. The industry is far larger, however. Sectors prospering around tourism range from recreation, tourist attractions, shops, local services, to agriculture, wholesaling and manufacturing.[11]

In Greece, direct employment in tourism was estimated at 23,500 persons in 1966 (Spartidis, 1969) and later at 26,100 people in 1970.[12] Employment grew largely during the subsequent period. The labour force in hotels and restaurants, recreational and cultural services and transport increased by 59,680 persons in the period 1961–71, and then again by 88,460 in the period 1971–81 and grew from 6.12 to 10.46 per cent of total employment, with women as a minority (Leontidou, 1991, p. 102). However, these numbers should be used with caution, because of undeclared beds and undeclared employment, especially female. By 1984, employment in hotels alone had risen to 50,000 (OECD, 1988). The 1983–87 five-year development plan estimated total direct employment in tourism would rise to 160,000 people by 1987 at peak period,[13] and to 200,000 if indirect employment was added (Greek Parliament, 1984, p. 61). Among these, 25,000 qualified and 50,000 less-skilled labourers were absorbed in hotels.

The recent availability of data from the 1988 census makes an analysis feasible. Registered employment is only part of the story, but its diachronic development, fluctuations and sectoral structure can lead to certain important conclusions. Tables 4.1–4.3 compare the sectoral structure of employment in activities related to tourism in Greater Athens and the most important tourist region of Greece, the Aegean islands. Greater Athens is the largest agglomeration, concentrating 30.2 per cent of the Greek population in 1991 and 14.3 per cent of foreign tourist overnight stays in 1987, which are in decline, while the Aegean islands, with 4.44 per cent of the Greek population represent a dynamic tourist area concentrating 30 per cent of overnight stays in 1987, of which 88 per cent in the Dodecanese (Rhodes, Kos, etc.).

The major complications on Tables 4.1–4.3 arise from the fact that all sectors presented, except hotels, serve local residents as well as visitors. Their degree of inclusion into the tourist sector is different in different localities: in the islands, the small entrepreneurs in commerce insist that their occupations are tourism-oriented. Their main argument is that the largest part of their profits comes from tourist-season sales, and that they would not have opened up at all if tourism did not exist.[14] In Greater Athens, by contrast, such activities serve mainly residents. It is noteworthy that the overall percentage of employment in sectors related to tourism appears the same in both Athens (Table 4.2) and the Aegean (Table 4.3); just over 27 per cent in both regions. Structural differences, however, are evident.

With respect to seasonality, average annual employment represents a smaller percentage of employment in September where seasonality is more marked: the population from outside migrates toward tourist localities to work, or more family members are involved in paid employment during the peak season. The

Table 4.1 Greece: employment in sectors related to tourism, 1978–88

		By place of work (except columns 5 and 7)									
		1978				1981			1978–88	1988	
		1	2	3	4	5	6	7	8	1	2
Retail commerce	Total	160,599	287,457	295,645	97.23	252,321	301,805	83.60	1.64	184,821	338,132
	% Female			35.19		29.50					
Restaurants, hotels of which:	Total	54,166	135,594	157,845	85.90	108,803	149,618	72.72	3.34	76,737	188,243
	% Female			36.24		26.87					
Hotels	Total	4,177	34,138	50,196	68.01		36,177		1.95	5,581	41,421
	% Female			45.96							
Transport	Total	7,124	118,102	119,668	98.69	229,148	112,942	202.89	-1.48	8,701	101,763
	% Female			10.69		7.18					
Communications	Total	1,539	32,545	32,930	98.83	36,028	33,357	108.01	0.82	1,708	35,331
	% Female			22.49		21.14					
Renting goods and property	Total	628	1,631	1,712	95.27	275	2,703	10.17	18.34	4,898	8,785
	% Female			20.68		32.73					
Recreational and cultural services	Total	4,328	14,371	15,253	94.22	32,705	15,156	215.79	1.79	6,559	17,158
	% Female			30.73		25.88					
Personal services	Total	19,762	28,942	29,342	98.64	31,244	29,369	106.38	0.49	19,978	30,390
	% Female			39.18		50.64					
Total in tourism related employment	Total	652,780				690,524	681,127	106.66	1.53		761,223
% of total employment						19.22					
Total employment	Total					3,543,797					
	% Female					27.07					

Sources: Adapted from ESYE censuses of establishments 1978, 1988 (unpublished), and population census, 1981.

Columns 1. Number of establishments. 2. Average annual employment. 3. Employment in September. 4. Column 2 as a percentage of column 3. 5. Total employment by place of residence. 6. Total employment by place of work. 7. Column 5 as a percentage of column 6. 8. Percentage average annual rate of change.

Table 4.2 Greater Athens: employment in sectors related to tourism, 1978–88

		By place of work (except columns 5 and 7)									
		1978				1981			1978–88	1988	
		1	2	3	4	5	6	7	8	1	2
Retail commerce	Total	50,492	104,026	105,492	98.61	105,837	109,086	97.02	1.60	57,188	121,872
	% Female			38.05		33.44					
Restaurants, hotels of which:	Total	8,983	33,559	34,451	97.41	33,004	35,467	93.05	1.86	12,019	40,353
	% Female			31.64		24.87					
Hotels	Total	678	10,497	10,873	96.54		10,083		-1.33	580	9,178
	% Female			41.71							
Transport	Total	3,701	84,337	85,361	98.80	109,991	77,592	141.76	-2.74	3,998	63,877
	% Female			12.27		11.00					
Communications	Total	185	15,084	15,268	98.79	14,630	14,978	97.68	-0.24	225	14,732
	% Female			27.21		25.71					
Renting goods and property	Total	202	955	975	97.95	163	1,423	11.46	14.21	1,562	3,606
	% Female			21.23		30.67					
Recreational and cultural services	Total	1,757	7,765	8,022	96.80	18,012	8,461	212.89	2.90	2,745	10,336
	% Female			36.69		30.82					
Personal services	Total	8,044	13,350	13,522	98.73	14,659	13,458	108.93	0.27	7,889	13,713
	% Female			47.41		54.18					
Total in tourism related employment	Total		259,076			296,296	261,865	113.15	0.36		277,667
% of total employment						27.82					
Total employment	Total		1,064,942								
	% Female					29.41					

Sources: Adapted from ESYE censuses of establishments 1978, 1988 (unpublished), and population census, 1981.
Columns 1. Number of establishments. 2. Average annual employment. 3. Employment in September. 4. Column 2 as a percentage of

Table 4.3 *Aegean Islands: employment in sectors related to tourism, 1978–88*

By place of work (except columns 5 and 7)

		1978				1981			1978–88	1988	
		1	2	3	4	5	6	7	8	1	2
Retail commerce	Total	8,725	12,875	13,630	94.46	9,883	13,643	72.44	1.95	10,133	15,618
	% Female			34.12		26.85					
Restaurants, hotels	Total	4,396	11,437	14,870	76.91	10,705	13,284	80.59	5.12	7,366	18,837
of which:	% Female			40.36		33.25					
Hotels	%	15.20	41.76								
Transport	Total	302	1,930	2,096	92.08	12,062	2,058	586.23	2.16	585	2,389
	% Female			14.17		5.49					
Communications	Total	173	1,516	1,567	96.75	1,741	1,555	111.94	0.86	179	1,651
	% Female			14.74		19.76					
Renting goods and property	Total	119	153	183	83.61	1,481	249	594.95	17.61	608	775
	% Female			11.48		31.87					
Recreational and cultural services	Total	227	615	781	78.75	1,386	506	274.16	-6.32	196	320
	% Female			17.41		20.13					
Personal services	Total	807	1,033	1,049	98.47	1,320	1,021	129.23	-0.37	720	995
	% Female			27.07		39.47					
Total in tourism related employment	Total		29,559			38,578	32,316	118.67	3.22		40,585
% of total employment						27.57					
Total employment	Total					139,918					
	% Female					20.12					

Sources: Adapted from ESYE censuses of establishments 1978, 1988 (unpublished), and population census, 1981.
Columns 1. Number of establishments. 2. Average annual employment. 3. Employment in September. 4. Column 2 as a percentage of column 3. 5. Total employment by place of residence. 6. Total employment by place of work. 7. Column 5 as a percentage of column 6. 8. Percentage average annual rate of change.

latter culminates in August, which would be a more appropriate month for comparison, but official censuses are carried out in September. Tables 4.1–4.3 do not reveal any acute seasonality, whereas a comparison between August and February would, and official censuses underestimate the informal economy in tourist regions. The highest seasonality is observed in Aegean hotels and restaurants (average annual employment is only 76.9 per cent of employment in September), recreational and cultural services (78.7 per cent) and agencies renting goods and property (83.6 per cent). Seasonality in the same sectors is more acute in the Ionian Islands (where the respective percentages are 68.2, 74.7 and 76.4 per cent), and less so in Crete (88.5, 94.8 and 95.9 per cent respectively). As for Greater Athens, even the hotel sector does not evidence any remarkable seasonality. In more specialised surveys, however, employment in hotels and restaurants has been found to be highly seasonal, unlike that in transport, recreation and cultural services. Seasonality of employment in hotels in 1969–78, as studied on the basis of data from the Hotel Employees' Insurance Fund, was not found to improve over time (Komilis, 1986, pp. 127–35). Fluctuations were almost negligible in larger cities, but important in certain tourist towns and small seaside settlements.

With respect to gender, sectors run by women in Greater Athens to the largest extent are the personal services (47.4 per cent women in establishments and 54.2 per cent at place of residence), a case which is different in the Aegean islands (27.1 and 39.5 per cent respectively). By contrast, restaurants and hotels are more male-dominated in Athens (31.6 per cent and 24.9 per cent women respectively) than in the Aegean (40.4 and 33.2 per cent), or in Greece as a whole. The participation of women is also high in retail commerce, especially in Athens (38 per cent at place of work), where this sector is addressed at residents to a larger extent than at tourists. The comparison of employment data collected at place of residence and place of work offers further conclusions as to the extent of the informal sector and its gender dimensions. As mentioned above, the population census reveals women more involved in the personal services than the census of establishments, which means that they are more involved in the informal economy in this sector, while there is greater male involvement in the case of hotels and restaurants.

This seems to be systematic, and reveals an interesting gender dimension of the hidden economy.

Finally, with respect to growing/declining sectors in 1978–88, an unprecedented growth in agencies renting goods and property should be stressed: employment in this sector has grown by 17.6 per cent annually in the Aegean, and 14.2 per cent in Athens. Restaurants and hotels are rapidly growing in the Aegean (5.1 per cent annually) but less so in Athens (1.9 per cent). In this city the tourist wave is in decline, as amply demonstrated by the negative growth rate of hotel employment (−1.33 per cent, Table 4.2); see also Leontidou (1991, pp. 94–5). Employment in transport also declines in Athens (−2.7 per cent) while growing in the Aegean (probably much more than the rate of 2.1 per cent, if data at place of residence are taken into account). A very interesting contrast involves recreational and cultural services: this sector increases rapidly in Athens (2.9 per cent), apparently for the resident population, while it declines in the Aegean (−6.3 per cent). This virtual collapse is vividly demonstrated by the fact that while there are huge hotels not a single theatre or library exists. 'Window-shop buildings', addressing the needs of tourists, abound in the island of Kos (Castelberg-Koulma, 1989a, p. 118).

Social polyvalence and segmentation

Double job-holding, underestimated in official statistics, or what can be characterised as multiactivity or 'pluriactivity' (Lewis and Williams, 1991) or 'social polyvalence' (Tsoucalas, 1986), is very widespread in Greece. In 1984, 5.1–9.4 per cent of the economically active population used to have a second job, and these rates did not oscillate much in 1983–86 (Kasimati and Allison, 1989, p. 64). A 1988 survey on multiple employment indicated very high rates of second job-holding among rural rather than urban populations; the former have been five times as high as the latter in all of Greece (Kasimati and Allison, 1989, p. 69), and high rates are also evident in the Aegean islands, where 51.6 per cent of women and 52.6 per cent of men working in agriculture hold a second job, usually in seasonal tourist activities (Panayotopoulou, 1990, p. 23). If it is taken into account that interviewees are usually working in secret, the rates must be higher than shown in the tables. In a survey in Ios and Serifos, all interviewees seemed to have at least two jobs and to be hiding this fact (Tsartas, 1989, pp. 158, 186).

Although pluriactivity is stigmatised by the Greek authorities, especially for reasons of tax evasion, and by political parties for the informal work arrangements it implies, it does not necessarily have a negative impact on the level of regional development. Job creation in multiactivity regions often brings about the repopulation of certain rural tourist areas, diffuse urbanisation along the coast and in the islands, as encountered in Mediterranean Europe during the late 1970s and 1980s (Leontidou, 1990, pp. 185–8), or diffuse industrialisation. In fact, while the role of industrial restructuring in the new depolarised regional pattern is often stressed, the role of tourism is definitely underestimated, as has been argued for the 'Third Italy' (King, 1991, pp. 78–80).

Jobs in tourism can be classified as seasonal/all-year, formal/informal, part-time/full-time, family-labour/wage-labour, voluntary/waged labour, manual/non-manual, skilled/unskilled, etc. (Williams and Shaw, 1991a, p. 4). While indirect employment may be highly skilled and well rewarded, direct employment is usually inferior, with seasonal, part-time and unskilled jobs amounting to 98 per cent of employment in tourism.[15] Pluriactivity usually combines with seasonality: agriculture or industry in the spring or winter, services for tourism combined with part-time agriculture in the summer. Social polyvalence, informal work and gender divisions constitute the main elements in household strategies, which aim at increasing income sources of poor households, especially in multiactivity regions. Tourism has been found to broaden the economic base and open up employment prospects in some regions, while elsewhere, 'monoculture' of tourism has been found to dominate regions of destination.[16]

Aversion from traditional activities was found during a survey in the Cyclades islands in Greece, and preference of the young for tourism-related jobs, involving easy profits and less effort: 75 per cent of the young in Ios took jobs related to tourism, and 65 per cent of entrepreneurs were under 35 years old (Tsartas, 1989, p. 185). For the total population, however, 'monoculture' of tourism is not evident on Tables 4.2 and 4.3: tourism-related employment is just over 27 per cent of total employment in both Greater Athens and the Aegean islands. The difference is qualitative and cannot be found in census material.

Female employment in the tourist sector is increasingly segmented, as in the labour market in general, but with much larger numbers in the lower-paid and manual jobs – servants, cleaners, craftspeople (handicraft, repairs), who have no ambition for a career but work out of economic need. There are only few women office employees and specialists (guides, interpreters), while in transport and communications women appear in 'occupations with gender', such as stewardesses, catering and ticket sales people, rather than pilots or managers. An additional axis for segmentation is the preponderance of small-scale family tourism, reproducing informality, and contrasting with organised tourism, where contractual bonds predominate, even where seasonality is acute.

Jobs in the accommodation sector are gendered, and male/female in the Greek language shows this clearly, as in new-technology sectors (Stratigaki, 1989). Bed-makers, cleaners and servants are women, especially in the small-scale informal sector, where such jobs in unrecorded rooms come 'naturally' as an extension of domestic work (Hadjimichalis and Vaiou, 1992, p. 144). In the organised tourist sector, women maintain the 'housewife' role in hotel employment – in Chalkidiki, about one-third are now paid for what used to be regarded as inferior work, such as cleaning, and acquire economic independence (Iakovidou, 1992, p. 472). Female employment in that area is 47.4 per cent of the total, and a strict differentiation by gender is evident: women as above, men as gardeners and drivers, while waiters and the administrative staff are more mixed, with a male majority. The attraction of 'housewives' into tourist employment has been encouraged by the Greek government since the mid-1970s (Centre of Planning and Economic Research (KEPE), 1976, pp. 51–2). In the informal rented rooms sector, on the other hand, a division of labour reappears according to gender: women take care of the guests and rooms (usually parts of family houses), and men collect clients at the port (usually accompanied by sons), negotiate prices, and, where the rooms are declared, contact the authorities (Hadjimichalis and Vaiou, 1992, p. 144; Leontidou, 1989a). In family taverns and restaurants, men manage the business and do the accounting, children set and clean the tables, and women cook and wash dishes.

Legal and illegal exploitation of property

The main difficulty in the above quantifications stems from illegal exploitation of property and informal work, especially during the peak season. The quality of jobs in tourism is controversial, not only because of seasonality, but also because of informalisation and hidden employment in the para-hotel business, *paraxenodocheia*. This stems from the exploitation of small property during the peak season in tourist localities. It is important from every point of view, because it has been calculated that in the Greek islands over the tourist season, for every formal overnight stay there are three informal ones (Panayotopoulou, 1990, p. 30); and it is important from a gender point of view, because these businesses are often run by women (Iakovidou, 1992; Hadjimichalis and Vaiou, 1992, p. 144).

The accommodation sector is polarised to varying degrees in various countries. In Italy the small-scale sector is dominant, with 250,000 different enterprises and family effort in the fragmented tourist industry, so that tourism is actually integrated in most local economies (King, 1991, p. 77). An obvious contrast is Spain, with multinational and foreign capital involvement predominant in the industry. In 1969–78 the average size of hotel and restaurant establishments in Greece grew from 2.21 to only 2.50 employees per establishment and that of recreational and cultural services decreased (Leontidou, 1991, pp. 101–2). By 1988 there were 2.45 employees per restaurant/hotel. Greece promoted small and medium capital in the 1980s, with some negative side-effects as a result.[17] It was more recently realised that this sort of antidote to mass tourism promoted informal and unauthorised development, amateurism and environmental deterioration by the concentration of several small businesses in specific areas (Kalokardou-Krantoneli, 1988, p. 18).

Dualism can be found within the very same region, as a study of Chalkidiki has shown (OAOM, 1977). The accommodation sector in this region was severely polarised between large hotel complexes, built especially during the period of the 'colonels' junta' in Greece (1967–74), and small rooms of the informal sector. Another comparative study of tourism in the Greek islands (Loukissas, 1982) found a more beneficial impact of tourism in larger islands with more diversified economies and limited leakage effects. In small islands, it was found to dominate the economy and to lead to unstable, short-term and dualistic development (Williams and Shaw, 1991a, p. 9).

It is difficult to generalise about gender characteristics of real estate owners, and it seems that the exploitation of property for tourism and recreation is very often undertaken by male entrepreneurs in Greek tourist resorts. But there are some traditional bonds worth stressing, and they all relate to the institution of dowry. This has been a form of family contribution to young couples by the bride's family,[18] which was abolished by the PASOK legislation on family institutional arrangements in 1983, but only formally. For a very long period, land plots or houses were a popular form of investment by rural families, often as dowry to daughters, and savings were channelled to cities, to the point where a peculiar matrilocality developed (Leontidou, 1989b): a large number of real estate owners have been female, because of dowry, reproducing conditions of spatial inertia of women in urban neighbourhoods. An unpublished 1986 survey by EKKE found that 25 per cent of owner-occupiers in Greater Athens had acquired their houses through dowry, parental donation or inheritance, while 41 per cent and 29 per cent respectively had purchased or built their houses on plots, 35 per cent of which had been acquired through parental donation.

Conditions are different for rural land, which has usually been passed through inheritance, where male family members have had priority, except in certain Cyclades islands. In the past, peasants used to let their property as they migrated to cities. As soon as they were established, and as demand for their rural land by domestic and foreign tourists rose, they used to sell it and buy urban property as residence or dowry (Karapostolis, 1983, p. 226). Today, however, tourist areas are starting to form an alternative to urban-oriented investment. Land appreciation because of rising tourist demand forms an important source of income for the host population. Already by the early 1960s there were increasing land transactions along the Greek coast, while the share of plots sold increased personal income from 5.3 per cent in 1958 to 16.8 per cent in 1971–73 (Papandoniou, 1979, p. 166).

As new types of tourism emerge, time-sharing and second homes dominate the market and visitors are succeeded by owner-occupiers in certain tourist resorts, where retired populations buy out land and traditional houses. Local landowners do profit initially from land sales to developers or individuals. They are lured by the high prices offered, choose to sell, and often sub-divide their property for speculative purposes. After this, however, the landowners in such tourist regions are mostly absentees and export local income in the long term (Valenzuela, 1991, p. 52). Prices soar, real estate markets emerge which are inaccessible to domestic buyers, agricultural land changes into residential, and excessive land fragmentation often emerges, with resulting environmental problems. Population invasion/ succession processes also follow.

Alonnisos, Myconos, Paxi, small islands near Paros and Naxos, and other islands in Greece, are cases in point. A survey in the land registry during the mid-1980s indicated interesting differences between tourist- and less tourist-oriented islands (Tsartas, 1989, p. 197). In the former, exemplified by Ios, real estate prices are 4–5 times as high as in Serifos. Several seaside plots have passed to foreigners, and there are three times as many foreign buyers in Ios than in Serifos, as well as many Athenian entrepreneurs opening up bars, taverns and shops. Serifos, by contrast, a less tourist-oriented island, has attracted returning migrants and Athenians for the purchase of a second residence. Another interesting finding is the secrecy of transactions with foreigners, with the use of names of companies located in Greece, or locals as a front. In some peripheral localities where sales to foreigners are prohibited, a new parasitic occupation has emerged, acting in transactions as a 'front' (Tsartas, 1989, p. 198). This illustrates the difficulty of the study of such phenomena and the discovery of any gender dimensions.

Population succession often results in social segregation between outsiders and tourists on the one hand, and inhabitants on the other (as found in Rhodes; Loukissas, 1982). Overcommitment of resources to tourism is balanced out by preservation of natural beauty, which higher-income groups preserve with great care, and the reduction of acute seasonality in some of the areas sold to retired foreigners.

In such areas and mass-tourism localities, population pressures cause shortages of technological and social infrastructure. It is difficult to quantify summer versus winter population in coastal areas, but in some Greek islands the population can rise four-fold or more during the peak summer season (Hadjimichalis and Vaiou, 1992, p. 144), without a corresponding rise in public services. For example, the population of the Cyclades islands in 1981 rose from 88,500 in spring to 205,000 during peak season (Leontidou, 1991, pp. 97–9), or more if seasonal labour migration and tourists sleeping in informal lodgings or even on beaches are counted. Infrastructure becomes overloaded and the public sector suffers from limited number of doctors, pharmacists, municipal and public servants. Such services do not increase in the summer in proportion with the additional population and activity.

In the initial stages, mass tourism may create jobs and an intensification of agriculture. Later, however, negative consequences are felt, by overcommitment of resources to tourism (Williams and Shaw, 1991b, p. 37). As there are critical numbers of tourists which can be integrated into regional structures and localities, the number of tourists in attractive sites may exceed the tourist carrying capacity (de Kadt, 1979) of a region. Congestion and later desertion may follow. The EC has recognised overcrowding, over-exploitation and depletion of resources for tourism in many regions (Williams and Shaw, 1993). With the entrance of large and multinational entrepreneurs, land use conflict also arises. Various economic activities, especially agriculture, industry and tourism, compete for 'optimum' sites on the coast, limited water supplies and often limited labour reserves. Certain activities may be destroyed by tourist development, which are basic in certain regions in the long term for local employment.

WOMEN IN ALTERNATIVE FORMS OF TOURISM: A CONCLUDING NOTE

Although in general most tourist regions occupy leading positions in listings of per capita income (Valenzuela, 1991, p. 54), the host populations sometimes realise that tourist development does not contribute to their well-being. The domination of tour operators in some areas reduces the locally remaining income: in 1983, each tourist paid an average of $625 per trip, and Greece only received 40–50 per cent of this sum (KEPE, 1984; Tsartas, 1989, p. 91). Besides complaints about the limited income remaining in the locality, as in Chalkidiki, the host populations may object to the conflicting land uses tourism implies, or stress other priorities set by the community. Most social mobilisations in the Greek countryside (Delphi, Pylos etc.), were conflicts between groups of residents with contradictory interests. The community was all but unanimous about environmental protection and tourist development: some groups mobilised in favour of alternative activities, such as manufacturing industry, which are contradictory to tourist development, but bring more employment and income to the locality. Usually, however, there is a favourable attitude towards tourism, because of its perceived economic benefits, irrespective of questions of locally remaining income.

Gender dimensions are difficult to discern here, but another form of grass-roots action is significant. Agro-tourist co-operatives have been set up and run by peasant women (*agrotisses*). Their conception came from the General Secretariat for Equality (set up by the PASOK government in 1985), which wished to promote development and interaction between local and foreign women, as well as domestic tourists. Loans to renovate houses were approved to peasant women and they were later taught how to manage an enterprise (Castelberg-Koulma, 1989b, pp. 132–3). The first co-operatives emerged in Ampelakia (Thessaly), Petra (Lesvos), Pyrgi (Chios), Arahova (next to Delphi), Ag. Germanos (Prespes lakes) and Marona (north-east). Others followed, combining hostels and restaurants with handicraft enterprises. Peasant women with economic independence were becoming so emancipated as to storm the *kafeneia*, the male-dominated coffee shops of Greek villages, and sometimes exclude men from them (Castelberg-Koulma, 1989b, pp. 136–7). Besides tourists, now also local women are entitled to leisure and social interaction, which they combine with work in the co-operatives.

This is an optimistic point on which to conclude a study of the gender dimensions of Greek tourism, instead of the usual deploring of womens' cultural inertia and their informal labour commitment and exploitation (Ammer and Leontidou, 1989). This chapter has stressed acute class boundaries created by tourism in certain areas, work/leisure conflicts and segmentation in the female labour force. Classes of tourists, foreign and domestic, and classes of the host population, complicate the issue, but the basic division between people at work and people at leisure cannot be overcome. Even in Athens, beautiful sites like the Acropolis, Plaka, Greek and Roman Agoras, but also squares, hills, Piraeus ports and the coastal walks, are taken by tourists from spring to autumn, and almost no Greek is spoken there, while the natives used a congested, traffic jammed, unfriendly, often hostile, city, with precariously built streets and offices. Dividing lines between natives and tourists are more acute in the Third World, providing a context for gender divisions. As more people have access to cheap tourism, however, tensions are eased and polarisation is limited to specific localities. The sound of foreign languages in public urban spaces is welcome and pleasant; it feels like welcoming the summer, again.

NOTES

1   The most useful collection, *The Greece of women*, was written as an alternative tourist guide by women, first in German (Ammer and Leontidou, 1989) and subsequently in Greek. Content analysis – places included and omitted, landscapes and built forms mentioned – is useful for a cultural geography of female tourism in Greece.

2   In a recent survey in the Greek islands, women have been negative towards interviews, some asking for the presence of their husband, and 'while in our sample there were over 70 women in each island, in Ios only 16 answered and in Serifos only 18' (Tsartas, 1989, p. 149).

3   For the distinction of foreign and domestic tourism in the Aegean islands in 1977–87, see also Panayotopoulou (1990, pp. 61–2). In general, foreign tourism has increased, but the main destination remained the Prefecture of the Dodecanese, with Samos maintaining second place and Cyclades third.

4   In the formal tourist sector, at the other extreme, capital in both travelling and the accommodation sector concentrates in a few large

firms. In western Germany, almost 66 per cent of the tours are sold by two operators, and in the United Kingdom three groups (the Thomson group, Thomas Cook and Lunn Poly) dominate the package holiday market (Williams and Shaw, 1993). These have access to capital resources, such as Thomas Cook and its (former) parent Midland Bank (Williams and Shaw, 1991a, p. 10). There are several examples of large multinational enterprises in tourism (Williams and Shaw, 1991b, pp. 23–8): Holiday Inns, Avis car rental, Centre Park Holiday Centres, Inter-Continental, Hiltons International, tour companies such as Thomson, Tjaereborg, etc. Travellers and workers in tourism are thus influenced by decisions taken away from the local region, often at international focal points, which influence the availability of certain types of accommodation, marketing and other issues.

5   The role of Athens as a national and international centre of cultural tourism and recreation is constrained. Tourism continues to grow in the rest of Greece, but is declining in Athens. Reasons are mainly environmental, as well as the outlet of charter flights, which leave the option to many visitors to bypass Athens, especially in the summer. Greek islands are gaining momentum through tour operators' policy and direct charter flights (Leontidou, 1991). Land use factors are also important in tourism decline. The concentration of hotels in the polluted Athens centre discourages tourists who seek a pleasant environment. Some central Athens hotels have closed down or changed their use. Grande Bretagne and Astir are the most recent and conspicuous examples, while a Sheraton hotel is among current projects on the seafront.

6   But in a milder way than in other countries, such as Morocco (Castelberg-Koulma, 1989a, pp. 120–3). This author analyses a documentary film about men in tourist localities, shot in 1983 but never shown on the Greek TV.

7   By 1920 their ratio had almost doubled, especially in cities with an economic role (Athens, Piraeus, Kalamata, Hermoupolis, Volos, Patra), mainly because of wars, which drew the male labour force away and created a vacuum filled by women. Female participation in the labour market has changed in the course of history. Women have developed from idle urban dwellers in the 19th century to a proletariat in the early 20th, and today the female labour force evidences a sharp segmentation in every economic sector, including tourism (Leontidou, 1989a).

8   It was found in 1983 that the number of women in higher and secure categories of scientists and white-collar workers, approached or surpassed the number of men in younger generations, while in older

generations men outnumbered women in those jobs. The same was also found for the educational level of the labour force: in 1983, educated women outnumbered men in younger generations (Tsoucalas, 1986, pp. 245–6).

9   Computer-related occupations are gendered, as reflected in the Greek language: male for the programmer, female for the 'girl' on the keyboard (Vaiou and Stratigaki, 1989).

10   Multiplier effects of tourism involve the amount of income and employment generated in an area by an additional unit of tourist spending. Regional multipliers are usually calculated with respect to income, but sometimes, rarely, in terms of employment. A concise relevant discussion, with references to research in the United Kingdom, concludes that income multipliers range between 1.24–1.47 (Archer, 1982; see also Williams and Shaw, 1991b, p. 38). Another estimate on the basis of international data, has found direct income from tourism in the EC to account for four per cent of GDP in 1979 and ten per cent when multiplier effects are considered (Commission of the European Communities, 1985). This means a multiplier of 2.5. The methods are different, but the divergence is also real. Multipliers demonstrate considerable variance among nations, but especially among regions, because of the wide range of varying types of tourism and different degrees of economic polarisation.

11   For example, Italy came to lead the world in the manufacturing of products like power boats, beach apparatus and ski equipment, through tourism and leisure activities of Italians and foreigners (King, 1991, p. 74).

12   Estimates by the Ministry of Coordination (1971). More analytically, in 1966 there were 16,600 people employed in accommodation (15,900 in hotels, 54 per cent of whom in seasonal employment, and 700 in auxiliary places of accommodation), 3,450 in transport, 1,450 in the personal services (personnel and travel agencies, tourist guides) and 2,000 in shops. In 1970 there were 14,000 in hotels (65 per cent in seasonal employment), 500 in auxiliary accommodation, 2,500 in boats, 6,600 in restaurants, entertainment and recreation (Tsartas, 1989, p. 88; Leontidou, 1991, p. 102).

13   The ratio of tourist overnight stays to the number of the persons employed in the whole country rises to 4.88 during peak season and remains at 2.40 for the rest of the year (Komilis, 1986, p. 128), but is sharply differentiated by area (ibid, p. 135).

14   In the total sample of the 1988 survey in tourist and less tourist localities, 36 per cent of commercial entrepreneurs declared no relation with tourism and 47.4 per cent declared a close relation (Tsartas, 1989, pp. 157–8).

15   This is the percentage of semi- or unskilled jobs in tourism in Spain (Williams and Shaw, 1991b, p. 35).

16   Some activities decline and are replaced by new ones. As summarised in a recent study (Williams and Shaw, 1991a, p. 8), farming areas have been abandoned in the Basque region, the young have been attracted away from traditional activities in Southern Spain and in Alpine communities.

17   There is a substantive difference between 1982 legislation, which would permit tourist investment in 'viable' regions, and later policy (Kalokardou-Krantoneli, 1988, p. 16). The need for small-scale developments and locally run hotels was stressed in the 1988–92 five-year plan of economic and social development, and family, cooperative or local authority enterprises in the accommodation sector were encouraged.

18   The opposite form of wedding system, *agarliki*, a sort of compensation to the couple by the groom's family, did not survive.

REFERENCES

Ammer, S., Leontidou, E. (eds), 1989, *Griechenland der Frauen*, Frauenoffensive, Munich.

Archer, B.H., 1982, The value of multipliers and their policy implications, *Tourism Management*, 3: 236–41.

Castelberg-Koulma, M., 1989a, Frauen und Tourismus, in Ammer, S., Leontidou, E. (eds), 1989, *Griechenland der Frauen*, Frauenoffensive, Munich, pp. 118–31.

Castelberg-Koulma, M., 1989b, Tourismusgenossenschaften der Landfrauen – eine Alternative?, in Ammer, S., Leontidou, E. (eds), 1989, *Griechenland der Frauen*, Frauenoffensive, Munich, pp. 132–7.

Centre of Planning and Economic Research (KEPE), 1976, *Programme for development 1976–80: tourism*, KEPE, Athens (in Greek).

Centre of Planning and Economic Research (KEPE), 1984, Data from the study of KEPE for the five-year programme, *Economy and Tourism*, January–April: 23–5, 60 (in Greek).

Commission of the European Communites (CEC), 1985, *Tourism and the European Community*, CEC European File 11/85, Brussels.

Commission of the European Communities (CEC), 1987, *Europeans and their holidays*, CEC VII/165/87–EN, Brussels.

de Kadt, E., 1979, *Tourism: passport to development?*, Oxford University Press, London.

Eliou, M., 1985, La formation inutile des femmes grecques, in *A la recherche du temps des femmes: communication, education, rhythme de vie*, Tierce-ACCT, Paris.

Greek Parliament, 1984, *The five-year plan of socio-economic development 1983–1987*, National Publishers, Athens (in Greek).

Hadjimichalis, C., Vaiou, D., 1992, Intermediate regions and forms of social reproduction: three Greek case studies, in Garofoli, G. (ed.), *Endogenous development and Southern Europe*, Avebury, Aldershot, pp. 131–48.

Iakovidou, O., 1992, Impact of tourist development on the peasant society of Chalkidiki: findings of a survey, in Agricultural University of Athens, *Greek agriculture in the 1990s: economic and social prospects*, Ministry of Agriculture, Athens, pp. 469–74 (in Greek).

Kalokardou-Krantoneli, R., 1988, Tourism: policy and implementation, *Synchroma Themata*, **36**: 26–39 (in Greek).

Karapostolis, V., 1983, *Consumption behaviour in Greek society 1960–1975*, EKKE, Athens (in Greek).

Kasimati, K., Allison, E., 1989, *Survey for the social characteristics of employment: the morphology of the second job*, EKKE, Athens (in Greek).

Kavounidi, J., 1982, Capitalist development and women's employment in manufacturing in Greece, *Synchroma Themata*, **14**: 57–63 (in Greek).

King, R., 1991, Italy: multi-faceted tourism, in Williams, A.M., Shaw, G. (eds), *Tourism and economic development: Western European experiences*, Belhaven, London, 2nd edition, pp. 61–83.

Komilis, P., 1986, *Spatial analysis of tourism*, KEPE, Athens, (in Greek).

Lambiri-Dimaki, I., 1983, *Social stratification in Greece 1962–82*, Sakkoulas, Athens.

Law, C.M., 1985, *The British conference and exhibition business*, University of Salford, Manchester.

Leontidou, L., 1989a, Frauenarbeit in den Stadten, in Ammer, S., Leontidou, E. (eds), *Griechenland der Frauen*, Frauenoffensive, Munich, pp. 97–109.

Leontidou, L., 1989b, Athen der Frauen: matrilocale Wohnfolge-Aneignung des Stadtraums, in Ammer, S., Leontidou, E. (eds), *Griechenland der Frauen*, Frauenoffensive, Munich, pp. 147–56.

Leontidou, L., 1990, *The Mediterranean city in transition: social change and urban development*, Cambridge University Press, London.

Leontidou, L., 1991, Greece: prospects and contradictions of tourism in the 1980s, in Williams, A.M., Shaw, G. (eds), *Tourism and economic development: Western European experiences*, Belhaven, London, 2nd edition, pp. 84–106.

Leontidou, L., 1993, Postmodernism and the city: Mediterranean versions, *Urban Studies*, **30**.

Lewis, J., Williams, A., 1991, Portugal: market segmentation and regional specialisation, in Williams, A.M., Shaw, G. (eds), *Tourism and economic development: Western European experiences*, Belhaven, London, 2nd edition, pp. 107–29.

Loukissas, Ph.J., 1982, Tourism's regional development impacts: a comparative analysis of the Greek islands, *Annals of Tourism Research*, **9**: 523–41.

Ministry of Coordination, 1971, *Study on employment in hotel and other tourist enterprises*, Ministry of Coordination, Athens (in Greek).

National and Statistical Service of Greece (ESYE), 1990, *Tourist statistics: years 1986 and 1987*, ESYE, Athens.

OAOM, 1977, *Chalkidiki: regional plan*, Ministry of Coordination, Athens (in Greek).

OECD, 1988, *Tourism policy and international tourism in OECD countries*, OECD, Paris.

Panayotopoulou, R., 1990, *Problems and prospects of the island regions: quality of life*, University of the Aegean, Athens (in Greek).

Papandoniou, G., 1979, *Allocation of income and accumulation of capital*, Papazisis, Athens (in Greek).

Shapiro, R., 1985, Echange matrimonial et travail feminin, in Piault, C. (ed.), *Familles et biens en Grèce et á Chypre*, L'Harmattan, Paris, pp. 300–20.

Spartidis, A., 1969, *Research on the magnitude and the characteristics of employment in tourist enterprises*, EOT, Athens (in Greek).

Stratigaki, M., 1989, Technological evolution and 'gendered' skills, *Synchroma Themata*, **40**: 31–8 (in Greek).

Thompson, E.P., 1967, Time, work-discipline, and industrial capitalism, *Past and Present*, **38**: 56–97.

Tsartas, P., 1989, *Social and economic impact of tourist development in the Cyclades Prefecture, and especially the islands of Ios and Serifos during 1950–1980*, EKKE, Athens (in Greek).

Tsoucalas, C., 1986, *State, society, work in postwar Greece*, Themelio, Athens (in Greek).

Tuppen, J., 1985, *Urban tourism in France*, University of Salford, Manchester.

Vaiou, D., Stratigaki, M., 1989, Women's work: between two worlds, *Synchroma Themata*, **40**: 15–23 (in Greek).

Valenzuela, M., 1991, Spain: the phenomenon of mass tourism, in Williams, A.M., Shaw, G. (eds), *Tourism and economic development: Western European experiences*, Belhaven, London, 2nd edition, pp. 40–60.

Williams, A.M., Shaw, G., 1991a, Western European tourism in perspective, in Williams, A.M., Shaw, G. (eds), *Tourism and economic development: Western European experiences*, Belhaven, London, 2nd edition, pp. 13–39.

Williams, A.M., Shaw, G., 1991b, Tourism policies in a changing economic environment, in Williams, A.M., Shaw, G. (eds), *Tourism and economic development: Western European experiences*, Belhaven, London, 2nd edition, pp. 263–72.

Williams, A.M., Shaw, G., 1993, Tourism: opportunities, challenges and contradictions in the EC, in Blacksell, M., Williams, A.M. (eds), *The European challenge: geography and development in the European Community*, Belhaven, London.

World Tourism Organisation (WTO), 1984, *Economic review of world tourism*, WTO, Madrid.

5
Tourism, gender and development in the Caribbean

Janet Henshall Momsen

INTRODUCTION

Tourism has long been seen as a panacea for the economic problems of the small islands of the Caribbean (Tripartite Report, 1966; Bryden, 1973; de Kadt, 1979; and West Indian Commission, 1992). In 1987 the Caribbean Tourism Research and Development Centre went so far as to state that

> The tourism sector offers the best, indeed in many cases, the only hope for successfully addressing the major socio-economic problems of the Caribbean while at the same time providing a strong motivation for stability and security in the region. (CTRC, 1987, p. 1)

Unfortunately, this focus on economic and political considerations has meant that insufficient attention has been paid to the socio-cultural impacts of an industry which is embedded in the realities of spatial and cultural differences.

Tourism seeks consciously and specifically to capitalise on differences between places and when these include differences in levels of economic development then tourism becomes imbued with all the elements of domination, exploitation and manipulation characteristic of colonialism. Indeed, as Antrobus

(1990, p. 1) states, 'tourism is a powerful mechanism for the incorporation of poor countries into an essentially exploitative global economic system'. For the small nations of the Caribbean, economic dependence on tourists, who come mainly from North America, can be interpreted as selling themselves into a new slavery incorporating racial, class and gender dimensions.

Gender issues in tourism are of critical importance in this industry which has depended on 'presumptions of masculinity and femininity' (Enloe, 1989, p. 28). The regional 'tourist gaze' includes clear sexual imagery with woman portrayed as both the strong mother and the quintessential exotic temptress to be experienced by man, the adventurer. Yet in practice these roles are being reversed with lonely women tourists seeking sexual excitement with West Indian 'beach boys'. Such paradoxical elements of image and reality in terms of gender roles and relations will be explored in this chapter.

The first part of the chapter looks at the growth of the tourist industry in the Caribbean and the spatial dimensions of its importance. The second part outlines the economic roles of men and women in the industry and how these have changed over time. Finally, I consider differences in cultural attitudes to gender in tourism source and recipient areas and the problems these cause.

THE DEVELOPMENT OF THE CARIBBEAN TOURIST INDUSTRY

Only in the last three decades has the Caribbean ceased being a winter resort area for the rich and begun to develop mass tourism (Tripartite Report, 1966). Cuba and the Bahamas, being closest to the United States, were the first to develop tourism. Although time series data for visitors to the Caribbean are not always strictly comparable or reliable, it would appear that the total number of tourists rose from 45,000 in 1919 to 131,400 in 1929 and reached 430,000 in 1938 when 37 per cent went to Cuba and 13 per cent to Nassau (Anglo-American Caribbean Commission, 1945). However, the main growth of tourism is a post-war phenomenon with the region receiving 1.5 million visitors in 1959 and 2.5 million in 1965. Between 1970 and 1991 Caribbean tourist arrivals (excluding cruise passengers) increased from 4.24 million to 11.65 million, an increase of 175 per cent compared to 180 per cent growth for international tourism in the world as a whole (CTO, 1992, p. 9). Since 1985 the annual rate of growth of tourist arrivals in the Caribbean has been seven per cent which is faster than the world average of 5.8 per cent for the same period (CTO, 1992, p. 7), despite reductions in Caribbean tourist numbers in 1981 and 1991 (CTO, 1992, p. 9).

Both the number and distribution of tourists depend on the level of affluence in the tourist-supplying countries and the relative accessibility, attractiveness and political stability of the recipient countries. The vagaries of fashion and fluctuations in the comparative advantage of resorts add to the fickle nature of the industry. The Cuban revolution brought tourism in that island to an abrupt halt and the industry is only just beginning to recover, increasing from 94,000 arrivals in 1980 to 424,000 in 1991 (CTRC, 1982; CTO, 1992, p. 10). After 1959 Puerto Rico replaced Cuba as the Caribbean territory receiving the most visitors. Further growth has been related to distance from major United States population centres, cultural links, accessibility to airports and convenience of airline connections. Thus growth came first to the northern tier of islands, especially Puerto Rico and the United States Virgin Islands, followed by the Bahamas and Jamaica. Pollard (1976) distinguishes between the northern islands dominated by American visitors, an eastern group with more European and Canadian visitors, and a southern group with more Latin American visitors, based on a complex of travel costs and political and cultural links.

These differences are reinforced by the physical environment of the islands. The low-lying coral islands offer both good construction and operational weather conditions for airports. The white coral sands and shallow reefs are ideal for recreational development. Unfortunately, increasing exploitation of these resources is leading to beach depletion, damage to fringing reefs and contamination of coastal waters in some areas (Archer, 1985). At the same time a growing awareness of the dangers of skin cancer is decreasing the attractiveness of sunbathing on tropical beaches while new public awareness of the environment is creating a demand for ecotourism in the less developed, rugged, volcanic islands such as Dominica.

The seasonal variation in visitor arrivals noted in 1966 (Tripartite Report, 1966, p. 20) has become less marked. There are now two annual peaks: December to April and July to August with the lowest month, September, having about 60 per cent of the number of visitors recorded in the most popular month (CTO, 1992, p. 13). Puerto Rico, the Dominican Republic and the Bahamas attract the most visitors with the fastest growth since 1987 being in the Dutch West Indies, the Dominican Republic and Cuba (CTO, 1992, p. 10).

The Barbados-based Caribbean Tourism Research and Development Centre estimated that while visitor expenditure in the region in 1982 was US$4 billion, it had risen to US$9.2 billion in 1991. The share of the Caribbean Common Market (CARICOM) countries of the Commonwealth Caribbean increased from one-quarter to one-third. The contribution of tourism to Gross Domestic Product (Table 5.1) is most marked in the smaller and least diversified regional economies, varying as the prices for export staples fluctuate, but in most territories it has shown a gradual increase in the 1980s (CTO, 1992, pp. 164–5). In the archetypal sugar plantation islands of Barbados and Antigua earnings from tourism surpassed those from the traditional export crop of sugar as early as 1966 in Antigua and 1969 in Barbados. Today, visitor expenditure is greater than the value of merchandise exports throughout the Lesser Antilles, except in St Vincent and in Trinidad and Tobago (CTO, 1992, p. 163). As a percentage of Gross Domestic Product in 1990 it ranged from 96 per cent in the British Virgin Islands to four per cent in Puerto Rico and two per cent in Trinidad and Tobago (CTO, 1992, p. 165). The foreign exchange earned through tourism pays for a large proportion (estimated at 40 per cent) of the region's total annual imports from the United States and Canada and more than offsets the ostensible payments deficit which North America has on its travel account with the Caribbean (CTRC, 1987, p. 18). Unfortunately, much of the economic benefit from tourism is lost to the islands, although the extent of this loss depends on the level of local participation in the industry, the tourist multiplier and the leakage of earnings.

The proportion of locally produced food consumed by tourists varies with the ownership of hotels and restaurants, the type of tourist and the ability of the islands' producers to respond to

Table 5.1 Visitor expenditure in selected Caribbean islands as a percentage of GDP, 1970-90

Island	1971	1980	1985	1990
Antigua & Barbuda	50	32	76	88
Bahamas	77	46	54	47
Barbados	20	25	28	33
Jamaica	6	11	22	21
St Lucia	40	28	48	51

Sources: World Bank (1975, p. 1); CTRC (1982, p. 98); CTO (1992, pp. 164-5).

tourist demand. Since women farmers are more likely to be producing crops for local consumption than are men (Henshall, 1981) there is a gendered effect on agriculture. In 1973 66 per cent of the food used in hotels in Barbados was imported (Gooding, 1971, p. 91) but this had fallen to about one-third according to a field survey I carried out in 1990. In St Lucia in 1971 some 70 per cent, by value, of the food consumed by tourists was imported but the proportion was much lower in the smaller locally owned establishments than in the large foreign-owned hotels (Momsen, 1972). In 1983 a survey of only the largest hotels in St Lucia found that the proportion of imported food had fallen to only 58 per cent (CTRC, 1984). In most of the islands there has been a growing interest in offering local dishes to tourists as the industry matures and tourists become more sophisticated. Linkages between agriculture and tourism have improved considerably and public awareness of their importance is such that the Barbados Hotel Association now advertises on television the amount of money it spends on locally produced food purchases.

Ownership of tourist accommodation has changed from being almost 90 per cent foreign owned in 1975 to 66 per cent local ownership ten years later (CTRC, 1987, p. 15). Ownership affects employment as locally owned hotels are less likely to lay off staff during quiet periods (Momsen, 1986). However, some of the change of ownership may be more apparent than real in that several foreign hotel owners took out local citizenship during this period. The total number of persons employed in accommodation establishments in the Caribbean in 1991 is estimated to be 162,000, compared to 82,000 in 1983 (CWIC, 1984, p. 9), and total employment generated by tourism is thought to be three times greater than this (CTO, 1992, pp. 91–2). Ten years ago almost half the working population of the Bahamas and a quarter in Antigua were employed by the tourist industry. In Barbados the figure was 14 per cent, a considerable rise from two per cent in 1970 (Gill, 1984, p. 28) and 10 per cent in 1975 (Marshall, 1978, p. 5), while in St Lucia it was 18.2 per cent and in St Kitts-Nevis 13.1 per cent (Boxill, 1982). Most of these workers in tourism are young, semi-skilled and increasingly likely to be female (CTRC, 1987, p. 21).

GENDER AND TOURISM-RELATED EMPLOYMENT

The image of Caribbean women in the tourist industry is ambivalent. As Dagenais (1993, p. 83) points out

> Popular representations of the region portray them as sexual objects and publicity props; the tourist industry presents them as sensual mulattoes with endless free time to enjoy the beaches and, of course, the (male) visitors.

This is but one side of the mother/whore dichotomy which characterises much of the literature on the Caribbean family. The local (male) view sees women's economic role in the Caribbean tourist industry as being based on their caring, mothering role as interpreted through service to tourists as chambermaids, receptionists and landladies (McKay, 1993).

Parish tax returns in Barbados for the late 19th century show that one of the few ways for women to achieve economic success in their own right was to run a guesthouse or tavern. The 1891 Census of Montserrat recorded only one hotel keeper, a woman. This is still seen as an acceptable form of employment. In Negril, in western Jamaica, West Indian men will provide capital for women of the family to establish guesthouses offering accommodation for tourists, as this is seen as an extension of their domestic role. The powerful mother image of the Caribbean woman is sometimes quite blatantly utilised in advertisements for these guesthouses in order to attract the tourist. However, McKay (1993) shows that women are resisting this job stereotyping because running a guesthouse is hard work, time-consuming and restrictive of spatial mobility. In addition, women complain of male relatives' attempts to control the running of the guesthouse and to claim part of the profits. They also complain of troublesome male guests.

Another extension of the caring image of women is for them to offer food, clothing and other hand-made items for sale to tourists. In Negril women often preferred working as vendors in the market to running guesthouses (McKay, 1993). In Barbados, women beach vendors were older than their male counterparts, and were in the job because it offered flexibility of time, which was convenient for family responsibilities, yet could provide a reasonable income. Women tended to have less capital and to depend on selling home-produced food, produce or clothes, while men sold imported jewellery or souvenirs (Momsen, 1993b). The services offered by these vendors also differed by gender. Women would braid hair while male vendors offered to anoint the tourist with aloe to prevent sunburn or to provide drugs and sex.

Work may also increase disproportionately for women if the tourist market creates a commercial demand for craft items formerly produced for domestic use, as happened among the Kuna on the Caribbean coast of Panama (Swain, 1989) and in Nevis (Olwig, 1987). In such situations, the former balance between male and female contributions to the household may change. But the demand for traditional craft work varies, with the intricate needlework of the Kuna being more in demand than the crude pots of the Nevisians. The introduction of tourist demand may also change the nature of the craftwork and involve a new group of workers. Attempts to teach the women potters of Nevis to use a wheel and to make items specifically aimed at tourists led to younger women becoming involved and items being more standardised (Olwig, 1987). In other cases, if a tourist market does not develop, craft work will decline, as occurred in Margarita Island where freeport status failed to sustain or encourage craft work, with men and women shoemakers continuing to cater only for local demand and just a few traditional potters and hammock-makers selling to tourists (Monk and Alexander, 1986).

The main form of employment for women in the tourist industry is as maids in hotels. This can quite clearly be seen as an extension of their domestic role, and thus is classified as un-skilled and paid accordingly. When tourism began to develop in the Caribbean in the early 1970s it was thought that it would compete with agriculture for labour. This competition would be exacerbated by a seasonal conjunction of labour demand with the sugar and cotton harvest coinciding with the peak of the tourist year. However, most of the workers in tourism have never worked in agriculture. They are younger and better edu-cated than most agricultural workers. Wages in the two indus-tries do not differ significantly at the bottom of the scale but the possibilities of vertical mobility are thought to be greater in tourism. Working as a hotel maid, although menial, is at least out of the hot sun.

Most management positions were until recently held by for-eigners and there was in reality little chance of promotion for an unskilled maid (Louis, 1983). However, the development of training institutions for the tourist industry in several islands has enabled better educated women to move into positions as receptionists and housekeepers. Yet men are still more likely to have been given training. In a survey of hotel workers in Bar-bados in 1986 it was found that 21 per cent of the men but only nine per cent of the women had attended hotel school (Levy and Lerch, 1991, p. 74). These figures can be compared to those ob-tained from a 1970 survey of hotel workers in Barbados where it was found that women workers had a higher level of schooling than men. However, men workers had both confidence in their ability and wished for further training while more women ex-pressed confidence in their ability to be trained than wished for training. This was possibly due to domestic reasons which made it difficult for them to attend a training course (Doxey and Asso-ciates, 1971, p. 51). Not surprisingly, in 1986, 14 per cent of men but only two per cent of women held management positions, yet there was no significant gender difference in upward mobility in employment (Levy and Lerch, 1991, p. 78).

In the 1970 survey some of the older women workers com-plained that preference was given to younger women from the hotel school (Doxey and Associates, 1971, p. 51). This preference for younger women seems to be supported by a comparison of the two Barbados surveys: in 1970 74.3 per cent of the male workers were below the age of thirty while only 47.1 per cent of the women were (Doxey and Associates, 1971, p. 47), while in the 1986 survey the mean age of male hotel employees was 37 compared to 35 for women (Levy and Lerch, 1991, p. 72). In general, women came to the tourism industry from clerical, sales or other non-tourism service jobs, while men were more likely to have started in manufacturing. A common pattern for women was to have moved from domestic service in a private household to work as a maid in a hotel because hotels provided higher pay, regular hours, more company and less maternalistic work relations (Levy and Lerch, 1991, p. 78). In the 1970 survey only 34.4 per cent of the male hotel workers as compared to 60.4 per cent of the women had been in their current job for more than three years (Doxey and Associates, 1971, p. 48). But by 1986 men averaged eight years in the same job as compared to only five years for women (Levy and Lerch, 1991, p. 74) and men felt more secure and satisfied with their job, were more likely to be unionised and earned a third more than the women hotel workers interviewed (Levy and Lerch, 1991, p. 74). In his work on St Lucia, Louis (1983) found that there was a very rapid turnover among maids because of arguments with employers, fellow employees and guests. While there was a constant flow of maids between the main hotels, men who left hotel work tended to use their contacts to set up small tourism-related businesses.

Louis (1983) noticed an increasing feminisation of the work force in St Lucia, and Doxey noted that some smaller facilities in Barbados used females exclusively. It was also noted that some hoteliers felt that women were more easily trained and more amenable than men (Doxey and Associates, 1971, p. 43). However, the rigid yet often changing shiftwork times and the hours of work caused many problems for women with family responsibilities.

Tourist work and family life

Around 40 per cent of Afro-Caribbean families are female-headed. Levy and Lerch (1991, p. 80) found that while men were likely to come from nuclear families, most women hotel workers lived in female-headed and single-parent households while in 1970 more women workers than men were married (Doxey and

Associates, 1971, p. 47), probably reflecting the difference in the mean age of women workers in the two surveys. Women tended to have fewer dependants in both the 1970 and 1986 surveys, perhaps because of their stage in the life cycle (Doxey and Associates, 1971, p. 48 and Levy and Lerch, 1991, p. 80), but were more worried about combining employment and childcare. Both men and women hotel workers often have secondary jobs. If they are part-time farmers they will use their contacts to sell produce to the hotel. They may also act as a conduit for friends who have farm produce to sell. Thus even the biggest hotels build up a network of local suppliers of fresh produce (Momsen, 1986).

SOCIO-CULTURAL ROLES IN TOURISM

Some West Indians feel that tourism has a corrosive effect on the values and cultures of the host society. The idea of the islands being turned into playgrounds for wealthy North Americans repels many people. This is most strongly felt in the more recently independent countries, some of which are at a critical stage in their cultural metamorphosis from colonial dependency to independent nation.

Most visitors to the Caribbean come from the industrialised North and are relatively wealthy, white urbanites over 35 years of age while the Caribbean peoples are predominantly black, poor, rural and young. Even with goodwill on both sides the meeting of these two groups is bound to cause friction, exacerbated by historical inequalities. The visitors provide a positive reference group leading to feelings of relative deprivation among the local population. It has also been suggested (Sethna, 1979, pp. 54–5) that this demonstration effect, diffused by the cultural imperialism spread by tourists, may destroy the Caribbean character and lifestyle. Surprisingly, surveys show that West Indians recognise the benefits of tourism and accept the need for planning aspects of its development in order to prevent problems (Doxey and Associates, 1971, p. 64). Overall, all the male workers interviewed in 1970 but only 73.3 per cent of the women thought that tourism had a generally good effect on life in Barbados (Doxey and Associates, 1971, p. 54) but only 57.2 per cent of the male workers and 46.1 per cent of the women workers thought it had a positive effect on their own lives (Doxey and Associates, 1971, p. 52). In the survey of residents 23.6 per cent thought their lives had been affected positively and only 6.1 per cent negatively, and the rest felt unaffected (Doxey and Associates, 1971, p. 64). On the whole, Barbadians see the effect of tourism on the environment as positive (Doxey and Associates, 1971, p. 67; Momsen, 1993a).

Clearly, there are gender differences in the impact of tourism. In Havana in the 1930s prostitution was a major occupation of women. The 1959 revolution ended this exploitation but economic restructuring has recently led to women again being forced to become prostitutes in Cuba as in many of the other islands. Antrobus (1990, p. 8) even notes an increasing trafficking from some islands such as the Dominican Republic to others with implications for the vulnerability of these women in relation to police and immigration officials as well as local prostitutes. However, female prostitution is generally directed towards local customers rather than tourists. On the other hand, male prostitutes, known as 'beach boys', are a direct response to tourist demand. This has long been seen as a major problem in Barbados. Some hotel managements complained that even groups of guests were

> sometimes approached by beach boys who were not always polite or willing to take refusals happily. However, a few managements blamed the encouragement given to beach boys by some of their guests – and it was probably for this reason that some hotels and apartments claimed that they preferred either couples or even refused reservations for single girls. (Doxey and Associates, 1971, pp. 42–3)

Thus the growth of feminism in the North which gives women both the economic and social ability to travel alone is being exploited by Caribbean tourism. As Antrobus (1990, p. 9) notes, this is not a change in behaviour for West Indian men but is much resented by West Indian women. For visiting women it offers the possibility of a 'holiday romance' or the threat of sexual harassment. In the case of male prostitution, the male drive for sexual power is matched by the female's quest for sexual adventure, although the West Indian male often hopes to use his tourist conquest as a ticket to North America. For the female prostitute whose aim is an income to support her children, her vulnerability makes her an easy prey to the unscrupulous male, whether local pimp or clients, local and visitor.

The tourist image portrayed in the source countries is still one of scantily clad, young women in exotic surroundings appealing to the fantasies of middle-aged businessmen who are feeling threatened by the empowerment of women in the North. Tourism encourages an essentialist view of difference: beach boys of white women and tourist males of black women. But gender relations in host and source countries may differ. West Indian men often have many sexual partners and, in the era of AIDS, interaction with tourists contributes to the rapid spread of the disease and to even more unstable relationships for West Indian women.

However, the undermining of moral values extends beyond those of sexual morality. The whole ethic of hedonism and materialism runs counter to the traditional values of hospitality and concern for others and to the need for discipline and hard work which is essential to national development. The perception of psychological inferiority noted by Sethna (1979, pp. 56–9) is reinforced by tourism and needs to be considered further.

CONCLUSIONS

Tourism affects men and women differently. Increased incomes generated by tourism can lead to a redistribution of authority within the family and resulting tensions in gender relations which the commodification of sex further undermines.

Despite such problems, community attitudes to tourism are quite positive as current rising unemployment and inflationary pressures make economic benefits outweigh social problems in public perceptions (University of Newcastle, 1990). This leads to a rapid public response to events which are seen as discouraging to fickle tourists. The United States government advice to tourists not to travel to Barbados, issued in May 1992 as a result of increasing violence on the island, was seen as a devastating blow to the island's tourist industry, even though it was lifted in October 1992. National economic problems resulting in unemployment and poverty lead to crime based on resentment of rich tourists, which frightens them away, thus reinforcing the downward cycle of poverty. The society becomes polarised between those who benefit from the employment opportunities created by tourism and those who fall outside the 'formal' economy. Gender is an important factor in assessing the socio-cultural impact of tourism on Caribbean peoples and societies. Development affects men and women differently through their specific gender roles and, because tourism is an export industry based on interaction between peoples, it also affects gender relations.

REFERENCES

Anglo-American Caribbean Commission, 1945, *Caribbean tourist trade. A regional approach*, Washington D.C.
Antrobus, P., 1990, Gender issues in tourism. Paper presented at CTRC conference: Tourism and socio-cultural change in the Caribbean, June 25–28, Barbados.
Archer, E., 1985, Emerging environmental problems in a tourist zone: the case of Barbados, *Caribbean Geography*, 2(1): 45–55.
Boxill, B., 1982, *Employment generated by tourism in the Caribbean*, CTRC, Barbados.
Bryden, J.M., 1973, *Tourism and development: a case study of the commonwealth Caribbean*, Cambridge University Press, London.
CTO (Caribbean Tourism Organisation), 1992, *Caribbean tourism statistical report*, CTO, Barbados.
CTRC (Caribbean Tourism Research and Development Centre), 1982, *Caribbean tourism statistical report, 1981*, CTRC, Barbados.
CTRC (Caribbean Tourism Research and Development Centre), 1984, *A study of linkages between tourism and local agriculture in Grenada, St Vincent, St Lucia and the Bahamas*, CTRC, Barbados.
CTRC (Caribbean Tourism Research and Development Centre), 1987, *The contribution of tourism to economic growth and development in the Caribbean*, CTRC, Barbados.
CWIC (*Caribbean and West Indies Chronicle*), April/May 1984, 99 (1579).
Dagenais, H., 1993, Women in Guadeloupe: the paradoxes of reality. In Momsen, J.H. (ed.), *Women and change in the Caribbean: a pan-Caribbean perspective*, James Currey, London; Ian Randle, Jamaica; Indiana University Press, Bloomington, Indiana, pp. 83–108.
de Kadt, E., 1979, *Tourism: passport to development?* Oxford University Press, Oxford and New York.

Doxey, G.V. and Associates, 1971, *The tourist industry in Barbados: a socio-economic assessment*, Dusco Graphics, Kitchener, Canada.

Enloe, C. 1989, *Bananas, beaches and bases – making feminist sense of international politics*, Pandora, London.

Gill, M., 1984, Women, work and development in Barbados 1964–1970, in Gill, M., Massiah, J. (eds), *Women, work and development*, Institute for Social and Economic Research, University of the West Indies, Barbados, pp. 1–30.

Gooding, E.G.B., 1971, Food production in Barbados with particular reference to tourism, in Doxey, G.V. and Associates, *The tourist industry in Barbados: a socio-economic assessment*, Dusco Graphics, Kitchener, Canada, pp. 73–116.

Henshall (Momsen), J.D., 1981, Women and small-scale farming in the Caribbean, in Horst, O.H. (ed.), *Papers in Latin American geography in honor of Lucia C. Harrison*. Special publication no. 1, Conference of Latin Americanist Geographers, Muncie, Indiana, pp. 44–56.

Levy, D.L., Lerch, P.B., 1991, Tourism as a factor in development; implications for gender and work in Barbados, *Gender and Society*, 5(1): 67–81.

Louis, M., 1983, Tourism in St Lucia. Unpublished PhD dissertation, Rutgers University, New Jersey.

McKay, L. 1993, Gender and tourism in Negril, Jamaica, in Momsen, J. (ed.), *Women and change in the Caribbean: a pan-Caribbean perspective*, James Currey, London; Ian Randle, Jamaica: Indiana University Press, Bloomington, Indiana.

Marshall, D., 1978, *Tourism and employment in Barbados*. Occasional paper no. 6, Institute of Economic and Social Research, University of the West Indies, Barbados.

Momsen, J.D., 1972, *Report on vegetable production and the tourist industry in St Lucia*, Department of Geography, University of Calgary, Canada.

Momsen, J.H., 1986, *Linkages between tourism and agriculture: problems for the smaller Caribbean economies*. Seminar paper no. 45, Department of Geography, University of Newcastle upon Tyne, Newcastle upon Tyne.

Momsen, J.H., 1993a, Gender and environmental degradation in the Caribbean, in Drakakis-Smith, D. (ed.), *Island studies*, Routledge, London.

Momsen, J.H., 1993b, Women and the life course in the Caribbean, in Katz, C., Monk, J. (eds), *Full circles*, Routledge, London.

Monk, J., Alexander, C.S., 1986, Free port fallout: gender, employment and migration on Margarita Island, Venezuela, *Annals of Tourism Research*, **13**: 393–416.

Olwig, K.F., 1987, Tourism and pottery in Nevis. Paper read at the annual conference of the Society for Caribbean Studies, Hoddesdon, Hertfordshire.

Pollard, H.J., 1976, Geographical variations within the tourist trade of the Caribbean, *Journal of Tropical Geography* **43**: 49–62.

Sethna, R., 1979, The Caribbean tourism product – an appraisal, in Holder, J.S. (ed.), *Caribbean tourism policies and impacts*, CTRC, Barbados, pp. 51–60.

Swain, M.B., 1989, Gender roles in indigenous tourism: Kuna Mola, Kuna Yala, and cultural survival, in Smith, V.L. (ed.), *Hosts and guests: the anthropology of tourism*, University of Pennsylvania Press, Philadelphia, 2nd edition, pp. 83–104.

Tripartite economic survey of the eastern Caribbean report (*Tripartite Report*), 1966, HMSO, London.

University of Newcastle, 1990, Tourism survey, University of Newcastle upon Tyne, unpublished.

West Indian Commission, 1992, *Time for action: the report of the West Indian Commission*, Christ Church, Barbados.

World Bank, 1975, *Report on the Caribbean regional study Vol. VIA Tourism*, World Bank, Washington D.C.

6
Gender, culture and tourism development in Western Samoa

Peggy Fairbairn-Dunlop

INTRODUCTION

Women's work in developing countries has generally been analysed in terms of economic-growth models, each of which conclude that women have been adversely affected in the change from traditional to modern economic systems. Liberal-Feminist[1] Women and Development theorists such as Boserup (1970) and Rogers (1980) identify the decline of women's traditional roles in production and the importation of Western concepts of women's inferiority as the causes of an erosion of women's status. Increased workloads in subsistence and cash cropping and informal trading and also the diminution of women's traditional rights in land, education and decision-making in the new national institutions and policy-making bodies are used as evidence to underscore women's worsening position. Marxist-Feminist theorists, on the other hand, see women's low status as resulting from the sexual division of labour which emerges as an expression of women's role in reproductive activities and the articulation of these with production outside the home (see Beneria and Sen, 1981; Nash, 1981). They draw attention to women being forced by economic circumstances to work long hours for very low wages, as well as the increasingly more common practice of women working a 'double day'.

These Women and Development models are based on two assumptions. First, that developing nations will unthinkingly adopt development initiatives (such as tourism) in the form in which they are introduced. Secondly, that the emergence of exploitative competitive relationships between gender is an inevitable feature of the development process.

This chapter challenges these assumptions, and in doing so questions the appropriateness of these models to explain women's experiences in all societies. Tourism development in Western Samoa is employed as the vehicle for this analysis.

Admittedly the tourist industry in Western Samoa is not well developed. However, it appears that contrary to the predictions of the Women and Development models, Samoan women have not been marginalised in this industry. In fact, Samoan women have shown considerable initiative and used the opportunities available in the tourism industry to develop their entrepreneurial skills. In a society where there are very few income-generating avenues, tourism has provided opportunities for learning new skills and applying old skills in new fields.

I propose that Samoan women's experience has been different from that of women in other developing nations because the Samoan people continue to live according to the *faaSamoa* (the Samoan ways of doing things). As a result, women's rights and resources have been safeguarded by customary norms.

The impact of traditional ways on development programmes is a whole area of understanding not satisfactorily accounted for in the prevailing Women and Development models which explain women's situation in terms of gender and/or global economic relations. An analysis of women's work must also include an examination of ideologies of gender, which articulate the sexual division of labour.

This case study will show how the maintenance of traditional ways not only influences the development of an enterprise, but also affects women's level of participation. The commitment to cultural ways has both positive and negative effects on the industry in general. First, I establish the social and economic context of the case study and in doing so predict some of the ways in which cultural mores may influence tourism. Next, I describe the industry, and lastly, women's participation in the industry.

WESTERN SAMOA

The country

Western Samoa has a total land area of 1,100 square miles, covering two main islands, Savaii and Upolu, and five other small islands. Samoa's population of 160,000 is mainly of Polynesian descent and over 50 per cent of this population is under 15 years of age. Seventy-two per cent of the population live on Upolu – 21 per cent live in Apia, the commercial and administrative centre of the country. Land and agriculture are the country's major resources. There are no mineral resources and there is little potential for industrial development. Seventy per cent of agricultural production is from the smallholder sector, the predominant farming mode being semi-subsistence production. Eighty per cent of the land is held in customary tenure.

Since gaining independence in 1962 Western Samoa has maintained strong links with New Zealand and, until recently, enjoyed relatively easy access into that country. Returning migrants (on family business, to bring their New Zealand born children 'home' to see the country and meet their relatives) form the bulk of travellers to and from the country. Although not officially counted as 'tourists', these returning migrants add to the 'needs' market which the tourist industry must satisfy (entertainment, souvenirs, travel and tours, for example). The large number of expatriates in the country (on aid projects, conducting research or workshops, for example) also swells the demand for tourism-related services.

The people

Samoans live in villages, their extended families being under the control of the family chiefs (see below). They take pride in the fact that they continue to live according to the *faaSamoa* despite the influx of modern goods and ideas (see for example Mead,

1966; Davidson, 1967; Fairbairn-Dunlop, 1991). As summed up by Farrell and Ward (1962, p. 232):

> Tradition dies hard in Samoa. The many aspects of the Samoan way of life are vigorously and steadfastly protected. Nowhere else in the Pacific is innovation so resolutely resisted, and in few other territories is the cult of custom so deeply revered.

The Samoans' extreme pride stems from the belief that Samoa is the 'cradle of Polynesia' and hence the creator and curator of the true Polynesian material culture and traditions. The feelings of 'rightness' that *faaSamoa* engenders are strengthened by the perception that community survival has been achieved because people observe the *faaSamoa*. In commenting that the *faaSamoa* supplies the basics of life, Meleisea (1987, p. 235) contrasts the standards of living in Samoa today with the 'chaotic plight of many other third world countries' which, by implication, have sacrificed their culture as well as their identity to economic ends.

What is the *faaSamoa*, and how has this influenced the development of the tourist industry?

The *faaSamoa*

The *faaSamoa* is a system of chiefly rule in which every person is expected to know their place and the correct behaviour patterns of their place. 'Correct behaviour' is the dynamic which ensures the smooth running of the chiefly system, the norm being that one gives service and respect to those of higher status and can expect to receive the same from those of lower status.

Status is determined according to the application of a sacred/secular ideological division at three levels of social interaction – family, gender, and within gender. The sacred/secular elements at each level are bound together in a relationship incorporating 'service', 'respect' and 'personal allegiances'.

At the first level there is a distinction between chiefly families (and their rankings) and non-chiefly families. All chiefs are sacred because they represent the ancestral gods of the family, village or district. However, the most revered chiefly lineages are those which can trace their linkages back to the gods of the creation story. Although ascribed, chiefly rankings are not 'set', but can be raised or lowered according to the actions of those holding the title. This factor has three important behavioural implications. First, family members must continuously work to maintain family prestige. Secondly, it places families in a competitive relationship. Thirdly, although an ideological division of labour based on sex is upheld (see below), in practice work is allocated according to what will bring the best returns for the family.

In the *faaSamoa*, prestige is achieved by giving – by sharing rather than accumulating resources. Hence, the system is marked by a continuous exchange of goods and services. Traditional foods (the products of the men) and fine mats and *tapas* (hand-made cloth made from beating the bark of a mulberry tree and used in ceremonial exchanges today) (the products of the women) are essential items in the formal exchanges associated with rites of passage and other important social occasions. These sharing exchanges not only nurture the bonds between the givers and the receivers, but hold the obligation to reciprocate when needed. The status of the chiefly title, then, is demonstrated by the amount of support that title can call upon in times of need.

In practical terms, the chief, who is elected by family members

> . . . serves as a kind of family patriarch who must promote family unity and prestige, administer all family lands, settle disputes amongst kinsmen, promote religious participation, and represent the family as its political spokesman in the village council. (Holmes, 1984, p. 22)

Family members (secular) 'serve' their chief by contributing their labour and resources to enable the chief to fulfil these duties. In serving the family in this way members consolidate their own social identity as well as their individual security, both of which are located in a family's ability to act independently. Further, all family members, regardless of sex, share the resources and prestige associated with their title. For example, both males and females are eligible for election to the chiefly positions, for participating in family decision-making, and for using the family lands.

While family rank is the prime ordering principle, a second division separates women (as the holders and transmitters of *mana*, supernatural power to foretell the future, heal or control natural events), from men, who hold the secular power. The bond between the two domains is symbolised in the sacred covenant (*feagaiga*), whereby brothers are responsible for the welfare of their sisters. The division of labour is based on this sacred/secular distinction:

> Political authority, defence and warfare, and the production of food was the sphere of men. Moral authority, ceremony and hospitality and the production of exchange valuables was the sphere of the ladies. (Schoeffel, 1977, p. 5)

Ceremony and hospitality play a central role in village and family alliance-building strategy. They are the means by which a village demonstrates its prosperity, the dignity of its chiefs and the honour of its families. In traditional times girls learnt how to provide 'correct hospitality' in the *aualuma*, the village grouping of the 'daughters of the village' (this group included widows and other women not presently living in a marriage relationship and was autonomous in action). The *aualuma* stayed together in the large guest house of the village under the tutelage of the *sao tamaitai* (leader of the women) where they learnt tasks such as how to prepare *kava* (roots and stem of the *Piper methysticum* plant, used to make ceremonial drink) and how to make the fine mats used in ceremonial exchanges.

The third division of status separates daughters (virginal, sacred – the most privileged group in the village) from wives (not virginal, secular – the lowest ranking adult status group). Wives perform the utilitarian household duties, and are expected to serve their husbands' sisters and family, just as he does.

Of these three classifying principles (family, sex and unmarried/married status) family needs always have precedence. For example, although agriculture is the work of males, females do agricultural work if it is necessary (when not enough males are available for the work, or there arises an urgent need for agricultural produce). However, it is more likely that a 'wife' will help than a 'sister', and that a wife of an untitled male assist, rather than the wife of a chief. An interchange of tasks results from the fact that 'work' is shared according to the labour available and what will bring the best returns for the family. For example, if a woman runs a business/secures a waged job, it is unlikely that she will be expected to do the household tasks as well. Instead, these jobs will be done by another member of the family (grandmother, aunt, husband). Hence, women do not automatically work a 'double day'.

Influence of the *faaSamoa*

This brief overview highlights three factors which are of particular importance in the following discussion. First, because the prime motivating factor is to promote the family good, little antagonism is displayed towards women pursuing their own entrepreneurial activities, because this is perceived to be in the 'family interest'. Secondly, most Samoan women have the basic skills and positive attitudes needed to undertake development enterprises because they have equal access with males to the family resources. For example, Samoan women enjoy equal educational opportunity[2] and are accustomed to participating in decision-making (Fairbairn-Dunlop, 1991). Thirdly, 'acting correctly' is the guiding force in the *faaSamoa*. Social interactions are characterised by a personalised, face-to-face relationship incorporating the giving and receiving of respect. Although 'village hospitality' is still the responsibility of women, today these tasks are done by the village Women's Committees, a corporate group made up of village wives and daughters. In many villages the Women's Committees have widened their role to become the major implementers of successful development programmes and income-generating activities. This will be described below.

THE TOURIST INDUSTRY

Like other similar Pacific nation states, Samoa's economic development is constrained by factors such as its small population and workforce, limited land area and resources, isolation from major trade routes, restricted range of marketable products and limited number of markets and suppliers. Given these circumstances, it has been argued that tourism, a 'service' rather than a 'production' industry, could play an important role in national development. To this end, successive Development Plans have featured ambitious schemes for the industry and devised government incentives, such as duty exemptions, loans and tax holidays, to speed its growth. The Pacific Area Tour Association (PATA), was formed in 1965 to provide professional expertise to the fledgling industry.

The tourist industry has focused on Samoa's 'unique', 'untouched' and 'unchanging' beauty in its advertising campaigns. In the 1970s Samoa was featured as 'the best kept secret', a slogan reflecting not only Samoa's lack of promotion as a tourist mecca, but its small numbers of tourists compared with Fiji, Tahiti or New Caledonia, for example. In the mid-1980s, tourist promotions portrayed a 'family' image for Samoa, linking this to the country's natural unbounded beauty. Under the caption 'I call it home, you call it paradise' air hostesses and stewards were pictured in everyday family situations mingling with laughing children on seemingly endless white sand beaches or participating in dignified *kava* ceremonies. The theme for the 1990s, 'Samoa: the Cradle of Polynesia', builds on Samoa's historical significance and unchanged landscapes.

Beginnings

Tourism 'officially' began with the printing of the first tourist advertisement in the *Samoa Times* (10 August 1967). This read:

> In Samoa, stay at Aggie's Hotel.
> Leisurely comfort combined with gracious
> and typically Samoan hospitality and cuisine.
> No visa for up to 3-day visits.
> 78 rooms now available for tourists and guests
> or Pago Pago holiday makers.
> Handy to Apia yet quiet and secluded.

By way of contrast, today there are 16 hotels/boarding houses in Samoa, with a capacity of 432 rooms and 892 guest spaces (Tourism Council of the South Pacific, 1992). Each of the hotels is a locally run family business with the exception of the Tusitala, renamed the Kitano Tusitala following its take-over by the Japanese Kitano Holdings. Current figures show the number of tourist arrivals during the period 1984–90 grew by 2.8 per cent per annum, with approximately 48,000 arrivals in 1990. As stated earlier, these figures do not include returning migrants, or people arriving on aid projects, research or workshops, for example. Gross foreign exchange earnings from tourism amounted to WS $47.1 million in 1990, contributing 17.4 per cent to foreign exchange earnings.

The industry has developed according to the *faaSamoa* values. For example, it is characterised by home-based traditional hospitality (family and village), in contrast to the mass 'Club Med' model which has become the mode in other Pacific countries such as New Caledonia and Fiji. Further, hotel floorshows feature village groups performing traditional songs and dances, the men dancers as prominent as the women, rather than the South Seas image of sarong-clad dusky maidens wiggling their way through frenzied hulas. Probably the most telling example of the *faaSamoa* attitudes which mould the industry are the indignant responses aroused by the advertisement for the national carrier, Polynesian Airlines, depicting scantily clad women. According to the Marketing Manager for the airline:

> We had a bit of trouble with that ad . . . we had to withdraw it . . . the ladies, and not only the ladies, didn't like the clothes Ursula was wearing . . . They said 'Samoan women don't go around in public like that . . . she should be more dignified'. (Moore, 1992)

So the advertisement was replaced with a far more dignified, acceptable picture of Samoan life (depicting men!).

In line with the family image promoted in the brochures, the tourist is offered small, scattered, 'intimate' family accommodation (Figure 6.1). The majority of today's hotels began the same way as the legendary Aggie Grey's: from a small spare-room in a family house – used by the family when there were no guests.

An estimated 720–30 were employed in the tourist sector in 1990 (excluding those employed by airlines and the transport sector), and according to unofficial estimates, 80 per cent of these were women. However, as has been well documented by Rogers (1980) and others, selective statistical enumeration practices, such as those represented by these data, do not satisfactorily account for activities in the informal sector.

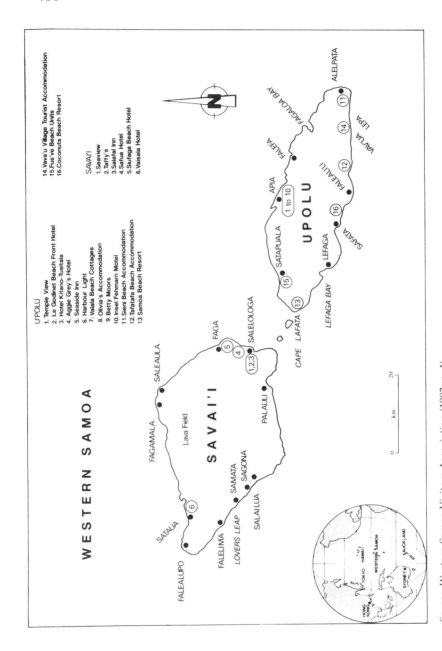

Source: Western Samoa Visitors Association (1992, p. 4).

Figure 6.1 *Location of tourist accommodation, Western Samoa, 1992*

Factors influencing the growth of tourism

A growth from 78 rooms to 432 over a 25-year period does not represent a thriving growth from the point of view of capital development. This is supported by comments from those in the tourism business which suggest that tourism has never really 'taken off' in terms of credibility/respectability:

> (Government) still treats tourism as a low-priority enterprise . . . we're like amateurs in a professional game. (Margraff, 1992)

The slow growth of the industry has been attributed to a number of factors. Attention has been drawn to the inefficiency of national support services, ranging from the provision of basic physical infrastructure such as roads and ports to telecommunications. Others comment that government's cautious attitudes regarding infrastructural development are understandable, given that heavy investment in an enterprise subject to fluctuations in external economies and rising energy costs presents inevitable risks (Meleisea and Meleisea, 1981, p. 46). The lack of available finance for capital investment has been raised as another factor influencing the industry. In many cases, the organised capital market in Samoa is narrowly based and generally poorly developed, while the lending practices of established institutions, including development banks and commercial banks, tend to be highly inflexible (Fairbairn, 1992, p. 220).

The major factor affecting the industry, however, is the widespread fear that tourism will undermine the *faaSamoa*. The tourist industry conjures up attitudes of suspicion, apprehension, dislike and disgust:

> . . . tempting tourist dollars might subvert the real function of Samoan ceremonies, and cruise-day hawkers with begging children [are] a hazard to Samoan dignity. (Alailima, 1988, p. 289)
>
> Tourists bring too many bad ways . . . our children will copy them . . . Tourism is an overseas way of making money . . . do we really want lots of people walking around our villages? (Anonymous interviewees, 1992)

These negative attitudes, incidentally, are not lost on tourists:

> They [Samoans] make no effort to cater to a tourist market . . . in fact, it's almost like the Samoans are saying 'You [tourists] are very lucky to be coming to our country!'. (Anonymous interviewee, 1992)

It is believed that tourism not only demeans the cultural ways (the *faaSamoa* ideology is a 'lived' one, not a 'display'), but also directly challenges these because each of the skills involved in the industry is contrary to customary behavioural norms. For example, in the *faaSamoa* hospitality is freely given, representing the reinforcement of personal bonds between the two parties. The idea of 'paid' respect and service is anathema. Further, whereas *faaSamoa* communication interactions are marked by an eye to seniority and correct dialogue (for example, people communicate with people of similar status; they do not voluntarily pass information on because that is presuming that the other person does not have that knowledge), tourism requires interaction with people of differing status and the need for Samoans to take the initiative in passing on information.

Practical constraints arising from the *faaSamoa*, such as village autonomy, the communal nature of land holdings and consensus decision-making, also hinder the smooth development of tourist initiatives. For example, despite the institution of a national government on the gaining of self government in 1962, the village councils of chiefs are still responsible for village law and order and any development initiatives the villages undertake. This fiercely guarded village autonomy negates the 'efficiency' of national policies the government may hope to introduce, while time-consuming consensus decision-making blunts 'progress'.

The fact that 80 per cent of the land is held in customary tenure necessitates that tourist ventures be village/family ventures. Enthusiastic negotiations for tourist ventures have foundered on questions of land ownership.

WOMEN AND TOURISM

As stated previously, women form an estimated 80 per cent of the formal tourist sector workforce. Women are not confined to the secretarial and sales fields in these enterprises, but hold management positions. For example, Gina Moore, the Deputy General Manager and Commercial Manager for the national carrier, Polynesian Airlines, was previously Airport Manager. At the Western Samoa Visitors' Bureau (an incorporated statutory authority), the Product Development Manager, Flo Saaga, is second in command to the General Manager.

A large proportion of women are also engaged in the informal tourism sector (handicraft production, tours, family guesthouses, informal selling, vegetable production). Taxi driving is the only tourism-related enterprise where men outnumber women.

When asked their opinion of why women predominated, the following were typical responses made by both men and women:

> Women are good at hospitality, at looking after people. That's their job . . . and they like doing this.

> Women do it because there's little money in tourism . . . it's not a full time job . . . it doesn't bring in regular money so it's good for women to do as a part-time job in between doing their home jobs.

> In the *faaSamoa* we don't do things for money. If we grow, he'll just give it away . . . I have to go and sell. Same with tourism.

These statements support those of the prevailing Women and Development literature – that women are 'suited' to hospitality tasks, that women are part-time workers in a low-status industry, and that safeguarding male status is important (it is acceptable for women to act against customary norms by taking money for hospitality).

I propose that the major difference of the Samoan example is that Samoan women's participation has not remained at the subsistence level. Women have built new and lucrative enterprises out of the initial small-scale activity by skilfully identifying a market and responding to opportunities. This has been possible because the endurance of customary values has ensured that women have not been denied an education; are used to taking the initiative and being responsible for their decisions; and are willing to work hard at any task which may benefit the family. In addition to these personal skills, the *faaSamoa* has provided women with a loyal family support network which has enabled women to take risks as they explore new business directions. Women have utilised the family system-operating norms to the advantage of the business itself, and to the advantage of family members.

The following three case studies demonstrate this point. Although I have deliberately chosen one large business (Aggie's) and one middle-scale operation (Moelagi Jackson), the development path I describe is one commonly followed by the hundreds of women who run small businesses in Samoa. The third example featuring a Women's Committee, is again typical of the Samoan focus on 'group development' rather than individual development.

Case 1: 'Aggie's' — the home away from home

'Aggie's' undisputably holds pride of place as the most well-known hotel in the South Pacific. To tourists it is a Pacific landmark, to economic experts it is proof that an indigenous business enterprise can 'take off'. To the Samoan government 'Aggie's' is a major source of foreign exchange; and on the local scene 'no-one laughed at her [Aggie] at Chamber of Commerce meetings any more; in fact, she was unanimously selected to represent the business community at a formal dinner on the royal yacht when the Queen of England came to visit' (Alailima, 1988, p. 295).

Aggie reportedly went into the hospitality business when her husband's business went bankrupt in the depression. She progressed from selling baskets of fruit and vegetables to New Zealand administrators' wives, to handicrafts, then hospitality, because she was determined that her younger children would enjoy the same education as had her older children (Alailima, 1988, p. 203). Today, the modest two-roomed guesthouse Aggie began in the 1930s is an internationally recognised multi-million complex, incorporating a 154-room hotel, gift shop, tours, and an extensive farm developed specifically to meet the hotel's food needs (Figure 6.2).

Each new development has represented a reaction to changing conditions: the stationing of thousands of GIs in Samoa in the 1940s; the growth of air travel (the introduction of three-day package TEAL flights, Pan Am flights from Hawaii to American Samoa, and the development of Polynesian Airlines, the national carrier); the shooting of a movie in Samoa featuring box-office stars Gary Cooper and Roberta Haines (*Return to Paradise* based on a James Michener story).

What is notable is that it was a woman who capitalised on the business potential that these changing conditions offered.

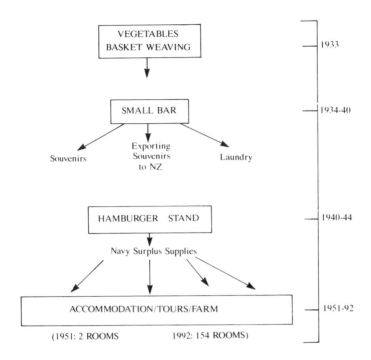

Figure 6.2   The growth of Aggie Grey's hotel

Further, male businessmen and friends advised and assisted her as she developed her business (see Alailima, 1988). It was not until the mid-1950s that Aggie sought financial assistance from 'outside her cookie jar' (Alailima, 1988, p. 274). On being advised that the Bank of New Zealand would only give a loan if the hotel were incorporated, Aggie formed 'Aggie Grey Hotel Ltd.,' and the bank gave her a loan of £25,000. Aggie used this money to build the first six modern rooms for her hotel.

'Aggie's' is run like a chiefly system with Aggie at the head' was once a common saying around Apia. The relationship between the Grey family and their staff has been described as 'personal rather than directive', with the result that workers feel they have a personal stake in the business.

> Aggie . . . (looked at her staff) not as employees but as members of her own extended families. Many of them were really her kin . . . Though

> Aggie held no title, they thought of her as the chief of this large house-
> hold. She assigned jobs, gave instruction, inspected progress, and
> scolded malingerers. She made very clear what she expected and was by
> no means easy to please. (Alailima, 1988, p. 294)

In return for this, Aggie:

> . . . provided more than wages. She acted like a parent, designing their
> clothes, sticking flowers over their ears, and dabbing her 'daughters'
> with perfume . . . she advised them about sex . . when they were sick
> she nursed them; when they were in trouble she stuck by them; and
> when they had a *faalavelave* (family obligations) she was generous. (Al-
> ailima, 1988, p. 294)

Aggie utilised family links or forged business links based on
personal loyalty. She always purchased handicrafts and other
goods from certain villages and buyers, thus guaranteeing these
people a market. In return, they brought their best goods to
stock her shop. She created work for those urgently in need of
cash and in many cases gave higher prices than a piece of handicraft warranted. Today Aggie's employs over 250 people: 'We
could run the Hotel with fewer, but you don't fire "family" '
(Grey, 1992).

As in a family, staff members are adept at most of the jobs
needed to keep the hotel running smoothly: the girls who clean the
rooms by day become the dancers at the floorshow in the evening,
while the pool attendants and gardeners provide the music.

As fitting its prominent 'chiefly' status, the Grey family give
generously to national and local fund-raising efforts. These gifts
reinforce the relationships between the enterprise and the
people: as in traditional times, true wealth is displayed in giving.

Not only is the hotel run on 'family lines', its success is largely
due to the family image it promotes. In earlier days Aggie was
the major draw-card, as GIs who had been posted to Samoa in
the 1940s came to introduce their family to the lady who had
made them a 'home away from home'. It became the tradition
for a member of the Grey family to perform the *taualuga* (last
dance, the most important) at the weekly *fiafias* (traditional con-
cert). In the early days Aggie was the *taualuga*. Then her grand-
daughters were given this prized honour. More recently, her
daughter-in-law Marina Grey has taken this role. Today, members of the Grey family are highly visible around the complex
and very approachable.

The chiefly concept of working for the good of the family is again exemplified in the second case study. However, in this instance, the business has expanded to include educational and income-generating opportunities for the local village women.

Case 2: Moelagi Jackson and village development

Moelagi Jackson has a chiefly title, *Vaasili*. She assumed complete charge of the Safua Hotel (Savaii island) when her husband died in 1987. The set of nine *fales* (Samoan houses) which make up the hotel, is built on customary land, within her family village. It can accommodate approximately 40 people and has a restaurant, gift shop and library facilities.

The development of the Safua Hotel (Figure 6.3) progressed from hospitality to include tours of historical sites, and to village tours where tourists see women making *tapa* and other traditional hand-crafted goods. Next, Moelagi turned her attention to helping women produce 'modern' articles for the tourist market. She was instrumental in starting a Women's Advisory Committee for the district and gaining local and international donor agency interest in sponsoring educational workshops for the women's groups. In 1991–92 three day dying workshops were held, and these were subsequently followed up with business skills courses. Moelagi's new venture is eco-tourism, and she is currently working with a national conservation group to explore the possibilities of this concept.

The development of the Safua Hotel complex, and its supporting services, has featured a deliberate educational input at each step, each centred around the demands of the hotel. The small nature of the business probably facilitates its ability to respond to changes.

Case 3: Producing handicrafts for home use/tourist sale? The Women's Committee solution

The endurance of traditional ways presents women with a dilemma very similar to the agricultural food sufficiency/cash cropping debate: should women produce the goods needed for daily household use and the prestige fine mats and *tapa* which

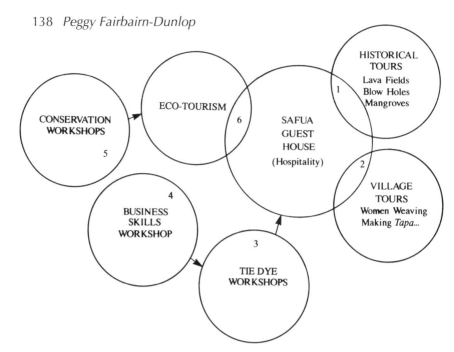

Figure 6.3   *Tourism, education and village development*

play a crucial role in ceremonial and more formal exchanges, or should they produce the goods tourists like to buy?

Numerous workshops have been sponsored by government and aid agencies to encourage women to produce quality hand-icraft goods for the tourist market. Each have failed. The Women's Committee members have found that producing handicrafts for the tourist market is both risky and uneconomical. For example, the National Council of Women (NCW) recorded how long it took to produce a piece of *tapa*, and then the price the *tapa* could be sold for. They found that the price tourists were willing to pay did not even cover labour time costs. Nor did tourists appreciate the cultural value of the *tapa*. It was suggested that the large pieces of *tapa* would have better sales appeal if they were cut into small pieces such as would cover a piano top, coffee table, or be framed. In the ladies' opinion, however, if they cut up the larger pieces these would be unusable in traditional exchanges, and there was still no guarantee that the tourists would buy the smaller sections.

As a result of this experience, the NCW impressed on women the need to be aware of, and clearly differentiate between, the two separate 'markets' – goods for traditional purposes and household use (cultural maintenance) and goods for the tourist market (income-generating activities).

About that time, tie dyed *pareus* (a length of flowered cloth wound around the body as a sarong), imported from Tahiti and the Cook Islands, became extremely popular through Samoa. Numerous Women's Committees ran tie dying workshops, in which the women used natural materials, such as bread fruit leaves and coconut midribs, to copy the designs of the imported products.

Realising the visual beauty of the *tapa* geometric patterns, a few women began using their *tapa* boards to print materials and sweaters. These products were an instant success. The brightly dyed *tapa*-designed materials were made into traditional dresses, modern styles, bags and table-cloths. By combining the new technology and the old, the women are producing goods which are particularly Samoan. These are in high demand locally, regionally (women are selling these goods in Fiji) and with the international tourist market. Today, women's stalls selling brightly printed tie dyed goods line the pavements of Apia.

By carefully identifying and separating the demands of the two markets, women have made sure that traditional goods are still available for home and ceremonial use. It is notable that the goods women customarily produce are still the validating core of exchanges – these have not been replaced by commodity goods. Hence, women's goods are still highly valued in society.

CONCLUSION

These three examples are a few of many which could have been employed to illustrate how Samoan women have used the opportunities presented in the tourism industry to develop their entrepreneurial skills. In a society where there are few income-generating avenues, the tourism enterprise has enabled women to learn new skills and apply old skills in new fields. I propose that Samoan women have been able to capitalise on the opportunities the industry offers because their rights have been safeguarded by customary norms. Further, again in line with customary norms, women's efforts have not been confined to improving only their own welfare, but to giving other women within their family/ villages the opportunity to progress and learn new skills also.

The Samoan case draws attention to the inappropriateness of the prevailing Women and Development theories to explain women's situation in all societies. Instead, an analysis of women's experiences must also include an examination of ideologies of gender which articulate the sexual division of labour. It could be argued that the effects of tourism have been limited, in Samoa, because of the small-scale nature of the industry. The industry could be at a turning point. As noted earlier, the Tusitala hotel has been taken over by a Japanese investment firm which is upgrading it completely so that it will provide the atmosphere and service Japanese tourists are accustomed to. These moves could hold changes for the industry, and women's work in the industry.

NOTES

1 I am using the Bandarage (1984) classification. She identifies three approaches in the 'Women in development' literature which can be differentiated on conceptual and methodological grounds. The dominant approaches which she labels Liberal-feminist and Marxist-feminist are predominantly economic models. The Liberal-feminist paradigm underlies most interventionist strategies. A third model incorporates an understanding of the significance of cultural and symbolic aspects of gender and points to the need for a multi-dimensional interventionist strategy.

2 For example, in 1986 the percentage distribution of persons attending school by gender was

5–9 years	80% female	79% male
10–14	89	99
15–19	84	79

(Government of Western Samoa, 1986, Table 4.16, p. 28.)

REFERENCES

Alailima, F., 1988, *Aggie Grey: a Samoan saga*, Mutual Publishing Company, Hawaii.
Bandarage, A., 1984, Women in Development: Liberalism, Marxism and Marxist-Feminism, *Development and Change*, **15**: 495–515.

Beneria, L., Sen, G., 1981, Accumulation, reproduction and women's role in economic development: Boserup revisited, *Signs*, **7**(2): 279–300.

Boserup, E., 1970, *Women's role in economic development*, George Allen and Unwin, London.

Davidson, J.W., 1967, *Samoa mo Samoa*, Oxford University Press, Melbourne.

Farrell, B.H., Ward, R.G., 1962, The village and its agriculture, in Fox, J.W., Cumberland, K.W. (eds), *Western Samoa: land life and agriculture in tropical Polynesia*, Whitcombe and Tombs Ltd., Christchurch, New Zealand.

Fairbairn, T.I.J., 1992, *Private sector development in the South Pacific: options for donor assistance*, University of New South Wales, Centre for Pacific Studies, Pacific Studies Monograph, no. 3, Sydney.

Fairbairn-Dunlop, P., 1991, E au le inailau a tamaitai: women, education and development, Western Samoa, Unpublished PhD thesis, Macquarie University.

Government of Western Samoa, 1986, *Census report*, Statistics Department, Apia, Western Samoa.

Grey, M., 1992, Personal communication, Co-Manager, Aggie's Hotel.

Holmes, L.D., 1984, *Samoan village*, Holt, Rinehart and Winston, New York.

Margraff, V., 1992, Personal communication, Director of Tourism, Western Samoa.

Mead, M., 1966, *Coming of age in Samoa*, Penguin, New York.

Meleisea, M., 1987, *The making of modern Samoa*, Institute of Pacific Studies, University of the South Pacific, Suva, Fiji.

Meleisea, M., Meleisea, P.S., 1981, 'The best kept secret': tourism in Western Samoa, in Institute of Pacific Studies, *Pacific tourism: as islanders see it*, University of the South Pacific, Suva, Fiji.

Moore, G., 1992, Personal communication, Managing Director, Polynesian Airlines.

Nash, J., 1981, Ethnographic aspects of the world capitalist system, *Annual Review of Anthropology*, **10**: 94–119.

Rogers, B., 1980, *The domestication of women*, Tavistock, London.

Schoeffel, P., 1977, The origins and development of women's associations in Western Samoa 1930–1977, *Journal of Pacific Studies*, **3**: 1–21.

Tourism Council of the South Pacific, 1992, *Pre-feasibility study of tourism training facilities and institutional frameworks in the South Pacific*, Tourism Council, Suva, Fiji.

Faafetai lava also to the following people who had time to talk: Taofi Atoa, Moelagi Jackson, Sosi Annandale, Jim Dunlop.

7
Gender and economic interests in tourism prostitution: the nature, development and implications of sex tourism in South-east Asia

C. Michael Hall

INTRODUCTION

Sex tourism is one of the most emotive and sensationalised issues in the study of tourism. Although it is prevalent in Western capitalist nations, sex tourism has generally come to be associated with 'Western' (including Japanese), usually male, visits to the Third World. Otherwise known as tourism prostitution, sex tourism can be defined as tourism for which the main purpose or motivation is to consummate commercial sexual relations (Graburn, 1983; Hall, 1991a). Sex tourism has become substantial fare for Western media over the past decade, a factor which has fed into often sensationalist reports of tourism prostitution in Thailand or the Philippines. However, much of the recent attention given by commercial media to sex tourism has not arisen because of any new-found concern for the disempowering nature of tourism prostitution, rather it has emerged because of the spread of AIDS. Therefore, current concern with sex tourism does not reflect a discovery of relationship between gender issues and tourism development, but is instead often regarded as a health concern (Ford and Koetsawang, 1991).

Sex tourism is a major component of international travel to South-east Asia and has been given both overt and covert encouragement by government as a source of foreign exchange. For example, the Philippine Women's Research Collective (1985, p. 8) reported that sex tourism is the third largest source of foreign exchange for the Philippines. Although exact figures are impossible to obtain, one estimate suggests that 70–80 per cent of male tourists travelling from Japan, the United States, Australia, and Western Europe to Asia do so solely for purposes of sexual entertainment (Gay, 1985, p. 34). While Gay's estimate is almost certainly on the high side, especially given contemporary concerns over AIDS, it is likely that 'sexual entertainment' is a major motivating factor for many male travellers to the region.

This chapter will present an account of the various dimensions of sex tourism in South-east Asia. The chapter is divided into several sections. First, there is a discussion of the methodological difficulties encountered in the study of sex tourism. This is followed by an overview of the development of sex tourism. Thirdly, this chapter will note the various dimensions in the growth of sex tourism in two South-east Asian countries: South Korea, and Thailand. Finally, the chapter will acknowledge that sex tourism can only be understood within a framework which addresses the varieties of structural inequality that occur within the South-east Asian region.

STUDYING SEX TOURISM

The study of sex tourism is difficult because of a number of factors:

(i) the seeming blindness of many tourism researchers to actually acknowledge that a link exists between sex and the tourism industry, particularly in respect of sex as a motivating factor for travel and the sexual relationships between hosts and guests;

(ii) the extreme difficulties to be had in conducting research on tourism prostitution, which is typically an illegal informal activity, often with substantial crime connections, and which may place both researcher and subject at risk from brothel owners, criminal gangs and syndicates, and police and politicians who wish to keep the subject hidden and away from public examination;

(iii) the lack of common methodological and philosophical frameworks with which to explain the complex web of gender, productive, reproductive and social relations which surround sex tourism.

BLINDED BY THE LIGHT

With few exceptions, there is an apparent blind spot or natural reticence among academics to acknowledge the relationship between tourism and sex (Cohen, 1982; Crick, 1989; Hall, 1991b). Nevertheless, if an effective analysis of the proposition that 'tourism is prostitution' is as true of metropolitan tourist resorts of the first world as it is of the third world (Graburn, 1983, p. 441), then such studies are necessary. For example, despite claims by Mathieson and Wall (1982, p. 149) that there is little evidence to confirm or deny a positive link between prostitution and tourism, there has been a long history of this relationship (Turner and Ash, 1975). Just as Miami has become synonymous with vice, the combination of sun, sea, sand and sex has become associated with tourism resorts in general (Hall, 1991b). Tourist promotion often focuses on the more licentious attributes of the tourist and highlights the erotic dimensions of a tourist destination:

> Tourism promotion in magazines and newspapers promises would-be vacationers more than sun, sea, and sand; they are also offered the fourth 's' – sex. Resorts are advertized under the labels of 'hedonism', 'ecstacism', and 'edenism' . . . One of the most successful advertizing campaigns actually failed to mention the location of the resort: 'the selling of the holiday experience itself and not the destination was the important factor. (Baillie, 1980, pp. 19–20)

Most observers who have examined the motivations of tourists have overlooked the very explicit messages purveyed in tourist advertisements. Despite the self-confessed selling of hedonism by the tourist industry, it is interesting to note that several studies of tourist brochures and images have failed to identify the pervasive use of erotic images in promoting travel destinations (Buck, 1977; Dilley, 1986). Furthermore, the 'red light' districts of many cities are tourist attractions which draw the sensation-seeking tourist as participant or observer.

CONDUCTING RESEARCH

There is a substantial lack of systematic research on sex tourism. This is because of the often informal and illegal nature of tourism prostitution, and the general unwillingness of police, government authorities, and politicians to acknowledge its existence. Given the circumstances surrounding sex tourism it is therefore extremely difficult to measure the scale of sex tourism at any given location and obtain interviews with prostitutes and other sex industry workers and their customers (Wihtol, 1982). Furthermore, Burley and Symanski (1981, p. 239) suggest that widespread disdain for prostitutes inhibits researchers and hinders the reliability of informants' accounts.

The analysis of sex tourism is also complicated by the several forms which tourism prostitution takes (Hall, 1991a):

(i) casual prostitutes, who move in and out of the pursuit according to financial need. This may be regarded as incompletely commercialised and the nature of the relationship between partners is ambiguous (Cohen, 1982);

(ii) prostitutes ('callgirls', 'callboys') who operate through intermediaries and who visit tourists in their accommodation;

(iii) sex workers who operate out of clubs and brothels, which are often regarded by authorites as a mechanism for the containment of prostitution (Symanski, 1981);

(iv) bonded prostitutes working in brothels who have often been sold in order to pay debts or reduce loans. Bonded prostitution is a form of slavery in which the body of the prostitute is treated solely as a commodity to be bought and sold without the prostitute's consent.

In addition, it should be noted that prostitution is often 'spatially, economically and socially differentiated between locals and tourists, a point that is often forgotten by many researchers who tend to blame all prostitution on tourism' (Hall, 1991a, p. 65).

FINDING COMMON GROUND

A major problem in studying sex tourism, as with any analysis of gender issues, are the considerable divergences in approaches towards feminist and gender studies. Most theoretical developments in the study of women and gender have emerged from the studies of women in the First World, not from Third World studies (Brydon and Chant, 1989). Indeed, Barrett (1986, p. 8) has described that a feminist theoretical framework remains 'fragmentary and contradictory'. Nevertheless, research into the nature of sexual politics and the interrelated structures of gender relations may shed some insights on sex tourism.

Sexual politics examines the links between sexuality and power. Gender and sexuality are socially constructed at both the personal level of individual consciousness and interpersonal relationships and the social structural level of social institutions. The control of sexuality through, for example, such mechanisms as formalised tourism prostitution, is a key component of domination. Sex tourism serves to establish certain erotic images of Asian women in Western society which are then perpetuated within the social institutional structures of the destination. For example, Davidson (1985, p. 18) reported a Frankfurt advertisement which stated, 'Asian women are without desire for emancipation, but full of warm sensuality and the softness of velvet'. More recently, South-east Asian airlines such as Thai Airlines, Singapore Airlines and Cathay Pacific have portrayed 'submissive' Asian women in their promotional material, with Singapore Airlines running a campaign of 'Singapore Girl – you're a great way to fly'. The control of sexuality harnesses erotic power for the needs of larger, hierarchical systems by controlling the body and hence the population (Foucault, 1981). Therefore, there is a need to examine the processes by which power as domination occurs on the social structural level –

namely, the institutional structures of racism, sexism, and social class privilege – and annexes the basic power of the erotic on the personal level (Collins, 1990).

Connell (1987) identified three interrelated structures of gender relations: first, the division of labour; second, power, particularly as connected to masculinity; and third, 'cathexis' – 'the construction of emotionally charged social relations with objects [that is, other people] in the real world' (p. 112). The three structures contribute to the institutionalisation of a 'gender order' which described the historically constructed pattern of power relations between men and women at the societal level. From this perspective, which relies heavily on notions of structuration, gender relations are stable to the extent that groups constituted in the network of gender relations have interests in the conditions for cyclical rather than divergent practice (Connell, 1987, p. 141; Crompton and Sanderson, 1990, p. 19).

Gendered perspectives on sex tourism which place significant emphasis on the exercise of power in gender relations will have substantially different insights on the conditions which allow sex tourism to prosper. For example, the economic justification provided for sex tourism in Fiji in the early 1970s by Naibavu and Schutz (1974, p. 6) argued that prostitution as a fully localised industry provided income for unskilled female workers for most of whom no other employment would be available. It required no foreign capital investment, but attracted significant foreign exchange with minimal leakage. By contrast, a gendered perspective (ISIS, 1984, p. 4) views the acceptance of the inevitability of prostitution as being vested in the assumption that access to sexual relations is a male right, and that viewing prostitution as woman's choice reduces all women to the lowest and most contemptible status within male-dominated society.

> Prostitution is both an indiction of an unjust social order and an institution that economically exploits women. But when economic power is defined as the causal variable, the sex dimensions of power usually remain unidentified and unchallenged. (Barry, 1984, p. 9)

Any oversimplified utilitarian justification for prostitution may obscure the gender and class interests associated with tourism prostitution. According to Thanh-Dam (1983, p. 536), prostitution is differentiated in response to the processes of 'capitalist development and conditioning labour relations, demand and supply'. In contrast, feminist researchers such as Hawkesworth (1984) and Rogers (1989) argue that prostitution is a direct result of the patriarchal structure of society. The reality for many of the women involved in the sex tourism industry lies somewhere in between. The roots of disempowerment are found not only in economic status and within the sphere of production but also in reproduction and social and cultural structures. As Connell and other writers on gender issues have indicated, the explanation for the exploitation of women through tourism prostitution lies in the interweaving of class relations and gender relations. The present chapter therefore draws upon empirical evidence and attempts to synthesise the interpretations and arguments used by authors working from different theoretical perspectives in arriving at an understanding of sex tourism in South-east Asia.

THE DEVELOPMENT OF SEX TOURISM IN SOUTH-EAST ASIA

The economic and social problems of Asian women tend to be viewed by Western feminists as stemming from the patriarchal nature of local cultures (Hall, 1991a). Yet there is not an undifferentiated Asian model of women and gender relations, although the state as a structure is dominated by patriarchal interests (Agarwal, 1988). Each region within South-east Asia needs to be examined in terms of its own particular set of gender, class and social relations. However, certain generalisations about the role and position of women within South-east Asia and the development of sex tourism can be made.

The growth of the newly industrialised economies within South-east Asia through the relocation of multinational export-processing manufacturing forms to the region has led to the highest rates of female employment in the Third World. In each country of South-east Asia women constitute at least 26 per cent of the labour force, and 36–45 per cent in the Philippines, Laos, Burma and South Korea (Seager and Olson, 1986). The transfer of export-processing plants to South-east Asia from Japan, North America and Europe has led to a demand for young, unmarried, relatively educated women who are assumed to have the manual dexterity and docility needed for the tedious, repetitive and monotonous work. The new international division of labour has perpetuated existing gender disparities in wages, except in situations where labour market shortages have significantly improved the status of women in the workforce (Phongpaichit, 1988). Despite the high rates of female labour force participation,

> women's 'status' in Southeast Asia is not necessarily 'better' than in regions where their involvement in remunerated work is lower, since many of the activities engaging women are those which reinforce patriarchal power structures, such as prostitution and sexual services in Thailand and the Philippines. (Brydon and Chant, 1989, p. 43)

Ong's (1985, p. 2) argument that the new trade in the labour and bodies of Asian women is more rooted in corporate objectives of profit-maximisation than in the persistence of indigenous values, is only partially correct. The new international division of labour and the spread of consumerism to the Third World has had substantial impacts on gender, racial, and social relations in Southeast Asia, but rather than supplant indigenous values, it has built on them. Indeed, as noted above, it was the indigenous set of gender relations which helped to provide a female labour force for various multinational enterprises and which has assisted in the development of sex tourism. In spite of high rates of remunerated employment among women in east Asia, religious and cultural ideals emphasise that their primary responsibility is to home and family (Brydon and Chant, 1989). Women who have fled rural poverty, only to be forced into prostitution by urban unemployment, are victims of a double standard (Claire and Cottingham, 1982). Brydon and Chant (1989, p. 44) point to the fact that economic development has had an equally important role to play in reinforcing women's secondary status. When women move into the labour force their work is often of a highly exploitative nature, whether in a multinational-owned factory or brothel.

Sex tourism may be conceptualised as a series of linkages between a legally marginalised form of commoditisation (sexual services) within a national industry (entertainment), dependent upon, but performing a dynamic function within, an international industry (travel) (Thanh-Dam, 1983, p. 544). The post-war development of the new international division of labour has meant radical restructuring of the economies of South-east Asia through their closer integration within the global economy. The influx of rural women to urban centres in order to support village families has encouraged the marginalisation of female participation in the labour market (Hall, 1991a). In both the light manufacturing industries of the electronics revolution and in the sex industries, women have been integrated into the global economy. Indeed, Ong (1985) argued that women who have lost jobs in the industrialised sector have been forced to seek work in hotels and brothels. However, the new international division of labour should be seen as only one stage in the development of sex tourism in east Asia.

In east Asia the institutionalisation of international sex tourism commenced with the prostitution associated with American and Japanese colonialism and militarism and has now become transformed through the internationalisation of the regional economy (Hall, 1991a). Prostitution is illegal in most South-east Asian countries, but laws regarding tourism prostitution are poorly enforced by authorities in the region's patriarchal societies (Sentfleben, 1986).

Prostitution in South-east Asia clearly existed before the arrival of tourists. One of the ironies of the current Japanese involvement in sex tourism is that the Japanese used to export their own prostitutes *Kara-Yuki San* to their colonies. *Kara-Yuki San* were bonded Japanese women who were sent abroad to serve as prostitutes in ports frequented by Japanese merchants and soldiers (Hawkesworth, 1984; Matsui, 1987a). However, since the 1920s when the Japanese government issued the Overseas Prostitution Prohibition Order, and with the prohibition of legal prostitution in Japan in 1958, women from the former colonies 'are now imported into Japan as prostitutes' (Graburn, 1983, p. 440). In addition, the nature of sex tourism varies from country to country according to different gender, cultural and social factors. For instance, in a report on child prostitution Rogers (1989) states that in Thailand child prostitution is 90 per cent female, in Sri Lanka 90 per cent male, and in the Philippines, young boys account for 60 per cent of child prostitutes.

The evolution of sex tourism in South-east Asia has generally gone through four distinct stages (Hall, 1991a). The first stage is that of indigenous prostitution, in which women are already subject to concubinage and bonded prostitution within a patriarchal society which regards such sexual relations as acceptable and normal. The second stage is that of economic colonialism and militarisation in which prostitution is a formalised mechanism of dominance and a means of meeting the sexual needs of occupation forces. For example, the American presence in Taiwan from the Korean War through to the end of the Vietnam War provided a major stimulus for tourism prostitution centred on Shuang Cheng Street in Taipei. Similarly, until the closure of the bases, the 12,000 registered and 8,000 unregistered hostesses in Olongapo City provided the major source of sexual entertainment for the United States military personnel based at Subic Naval Base and Clark Air Force Base in the Philippines (Claire and Cottingham, 1982, p. 209). In this stage both the indigenous and occupier's set of gender relations are used as a justification by government and occupying forces for economic or military enforced prostitution, thereby encouraging the dependency of host regions on the selling of sexual services as a means of income generation. The commoditisation of sexual relations is marked in the third stage by the gradual substitution of overseas military forces by international tourists. For example, Australian criminal elements made substantial investments in the sex industry in Angeles City near Clark Air Force Base in the Philippines prior to it being closed, in order to offer sexual services to Australian tourists as well as American servicemen. Bacon (1987, p. 21) reported that 'Australians now have a financial interest in more than 60 per cent of the 500 bars and 7,000 prostitutes around the base'. At this third stage, sex tourism now becomes a formal mechanism by which authoritarian governments can further national economic goals.

The fourth, and current, stage for most of the nations of Southeast Asia is that of newly industrialised nation status. Despite the increased material standard of living for many areas, tourism prostitution is still widespread. The series of stages in the development of sex tourism have established and reinforced a network of gender conditions which may take many years to dismantle, particularly given their continued maintenance by patriarchal elite structures. The following overview of sex tourism in South Korea and Thailand indicates the four stages of development of sex tourism.

SOUTH KOREA: *KISAENG* TOURISM

The term *kisaeng* originally referred to females who served a similar social function as the *geisha* in Japan. The word is now, however, synonymous with Japanese-oriented tourism prostitution in Korea. 'No less than 100,000' tourist service girls were estimated to be operating in South Korea in 1978 (Korea Church Women United, 1983, p. 2), although this figure excluded the large number of unregistered sex workers. Gay (1985) estimated that some 260,000 prostitutes were operating in South Korea, the majority of whom originated from economically marginal rural areas. *Kisaeng* girls were required to obtain identification cards from authorities in order to enter hotels. While at the government 'orientation programme' for sex workers, which was a prerequisite for issuance of the card, women were told that their carnal conversations with foreign tourists did not prostitute either themselves or the nation, but expressed their heroic patriotism (Gay, 1985, p. 34). The orientation programme was regarded as similar to that given by the Japanese to the 100,000 Korean women who were forced to serve in the 'women's volunteer corps' as prostitutes to the Japanese troops during World War II (Yoyori, 1977; Matsui, 1987b). Indeed, the relationship between sex tourism and the use of 'comfort women' by the Japanese armed forces during World War II is now expressly made by Korean women's groups. The South Korean Church Women's Alliance adopted the 'comfort women' issue, not so much as a major cause in its own right, but rather in the hope that it could be a vehicle to generate feelings against Japanese sex tours (Hicks, 1993, p. 34). According to Korea Church Women United (1983, p. 27):

> The only difference we can find . . . is the circumstances under which they are conducted – the one during the Japanese invasion days was in a war effort; the other, currently in a sovereign state.

Kisaeng sex tourism is dependent on the Japanese. Following the severing of Japanese diplomatic ties with Taiwan in 1973 there was a massive increase in Japanese tourism, predominantly male, to South Korea (Kikue, 1979). (Conversely there has been a reduction in Japanese sex tourism to Taiwan.) *Kisaeng* sex tourism has taken three major forms:

(i) the establishment of *kisaeng* houses (brothels) in the major urban areas geared towards tourists;

(ii) *kisaeng* act as companions to Japanese businessmen and travel with them during their visit to Korea. This role is regarded as an integral component of the conduct of Japanese business overseas and may be likened to a contemporary equivalent of the 'comfort women' role that Korean women were forced to take during World War II;

(iii) *kisaeng* has been exported to Japan, with at least one report of 'musical talent' being sent to 50 Japanese *kisaeng* houses operating in Osaka (Korea Church Women United, 1983, p. 46).

The authoritarian nature of successive South Korean governments has played a major role in the commoditising of women through *kisaeng* tourism. Existing sets of gender relations, reinforced through periods of colonisation by the Japanese, have been consciously maintained by government policies which have exploited women's bodies for national economic gain. The 1988 Seoul Olympics saw South Korea put on a modern façade for the world but despite the promotion of cultural and natural attractions by the government, *kisaeng* tourism is still a major factor in attracting Japanese male tourists to the country. Korean women's groups have attempted to draw attention to Japanese sex tourism in recent years, most successfully by highlighting the 'comfort women' issue. However, the Korean government appears at pains not to damage its economic relationship with Japan and provides little support for the women's movement. The continued maintenance of the authoritarian, patriarchal institutional structure by the present Korean elite can only continue to perpetuate the existing set of gender relations which allows *kisaeng* tourism to exist.

> The tidal wave to modernize this land has brought along in its wake the spurring on of tourism – a form of 'prostitution tourism' which is condoned and encouraged, for the sake of foreign exchange, by the powerful in our country. This depersonalization of the sex act and through it the dehumanization of Korean women, takes sex from being a soul-body relationship to one of a 'subject-object' relationship, in which the Subject is the man who buys and the Object is the woman who is sold. This deliberate action of earning foreign exchange by selling the flesh and souls of our women for sexual exploitation, is not only stripping the

human dignity from Korean women, but is also an affront to all human-
ity. (Korea Church Women United, 1983, p. 1)

THAILAND: 'LAND OF SMILES' OR 'THE BROTHEL OF ASIA'

Substantial debate has surrounded the indigenous gender relations of Thai society. Several authors have argued that women
have enjoyed relative equality (Davidson, 1985), while others
have noted that women have long been subordinated, with the
patriarchal Buddhist culture maintaining both class divisions
and the exclusion of women from political power (Phongpaichit,
1982; Thanh-Dam, 1983; O'Malley, 1988). Indeed, the importation of elements of Brahminical culture into Thai society has
allowed concubinage and polygamy to be legitimised and has
created a ready-made framework within which sex tourism can
be acceptable to government and local elites.

The promotion of sexual services is an important element in
the marketing of Thailand to tourists. It seems likely that in no
other country has tourist motivation been so explicitly linked
to sex (Cohen, 1988, p. 86). In 1957 there were 20,000 prostitutes, by 1964 400,000, and between 500,000 and a million in
the early 1980s (Phongpaichit, 1982; Taylor, 1984; Gay, 1985;
Hong, 1985). Not all the prostitutes cater to sex tourists.
Indeed, Cohen (1982, p. 409) argued that the women working
with *farangs* (foreigners) are in many ways the 'elite' among the
prostitutes: they earn significantly more than those working
with Thais, enjoy greater independence, and are rarely controlled by pimps or pushed into prostitution against their will.
However, according to Richter (1989, pp. 98–9), Cohen's empa-
thetic and empirical approach describes the lifestyle of only a
tiny minority of female prostitutes. Most have no such protec-
tive ambiguity. Furthermore, many Thai women become
'rented wives' (*mia chao*), somewhat similar to the *kisaeng* of
Korea, who often return to tourist generating regions, particularly Germany, Holland, and Japan, where they may suffer
linguistic and social isolation while often being forced to perform sexual services (Skrobanek, 1983).

The economically marginal rural areas of the north-east and northern provinces of Thailand have been the major source for child and female prostitutes, with many families and villages economically dependent on remittances from the prostitutes (Wereld, 1979; Phongpaichit, 1981, 1982; Cockburn, 1989). The rapid and uneven development of Thailand has been closely viewed as integrating militarisation, tourism, and industrialisation as institutionalised systems of female exploitation (Ong, 1985). Phongpaichit (1982) has argued that the economic condition of northern Thailand stems from the hegemonic power of Britain and the United States which have encouraged export-oriented development on the Central Plain at the expense of the north. The northern provinces are structurally disadvantaged within the Thai economy and in the absence of alternative income sources, a vested interest and dependency upon a continuation of the sex industry is created (O'Malley, 1988, p. 110), providing an assured supply of workers for the sex industry based in the nation's urban and industrial centres.

Until the end of the 1980s the Thai government placed great emphasis on sex tourism as a means to earn foreign exchange, to the extent that ministers often openly advocated tourism prostitution as a means of job creation (Mingmongkol, 1981; Gay, 1985; Barang, 1988). Successive Thai governments therefore continued to perpetuate existing gender relations and exploitation through support of the sex tourism industry. The last five years have seen public statements from the Thai government on the control of sex tourism, but the reasons for this probably lie more within concerns for AIDS and the image of the country overseas than in any intrinsic changes in social attitudes.

In 1989 the Thai Public Health Ministry started campaigning against prostitution and the promotion of Thailand as a sex tour destination. The primary reason for the campaign was the recognition that sexually transmitted diseases such as AIDS could pose major problems for Thailand's rapidly growing tourism industry. A Ministry survey of AIDS indicated that about 3,000 prostitutes in Thailand were carrying the AIDS virus and a World Health Organisation report estimated that the number of infected people in Thailand was between 45,000 and 50,000, compared to an official figure of 14,000 (Corben, 1990, p. 7). In tourist centres such as Chiang Mai, tests have suggested that one of every two prostitutes in the region carries the virus (Robinson, 1989). According to the Thai Deputy Public Health Minister, Suthas Ngernmuen (in Robinson, 1989, p. 11):

> Thailand's profitable tourist industry has been an inhibiting factor in promoting AIDS awareness . . . More than two-thirds of the overseas visitors entering Thailand are single men, and medical officials avoided publicising the appalling AIDS statistics for fear of damaging the country's healthy tourist business . . . But it is long past time for the government to change Thailand's image as a sexual paradise.
> We should promote tourism in more appropriate ways, and campaign more against AIDS.

The Thai government has considered a number of options to curb the spread of AIDS, including operating testing programmes for certain visitors, and distributing condoms in hotels and at the airport. Part of the AIDS programme includes 're-habilitating' and skilling prostitutes, while the Defence Ministry is providing an AIDS education programme for servicemen. The Public Health Ministry has proposed the issuing of health cards to brothel workers which would indicate the holder's personal background and the results of tests conducted for sexually transmitted diseases, including AIDS (Corben, 1990). The issue of three-monthly health cards is only an indirect measure of controlling AIDS and does relatively little to deter the sex tourist. Instead health cards may only further attract visitors to certain brothels or locations and may also allow the possibility of corruption in order to obtain cards which give workers in the sex industry clean bills of health. If the Thai government is to be serious about controlling AIDS a major emphasis has to be given to replacing Thailand's image as a sex tour destination and, more significantly, providing alternative economic and social support mechanisms for those who are forced to use prostitution as a means of employment (Hall, 1993). However, Thailand's tourism authorities are extremely sensitive to reports on the causes and consequences of the rising incidence of AIDS and other sexually transmitted diseases in Thailand (Corben, 1990, p. 9). After a damning examination of the sex trade and the major role it plays in Thailand's tourism industry by the *Far Eastern Economic Review*, the Governor of the Tourism Authority of Thailand (TAT), Dharmnoon Prachuabmoh, attacked the Review and argued that any effective measures adopted by the Thai government to curb the spread of AIDS were acceptable, and that the welfare of the Thais, not the tourist dollar, was top priority (Corben 1990, p. 9).

The AIDS scare has already impacted on some Thai tourist destinations (Hall, 1993). Visitor arrivals by road from Malaysia were estimated to have dropped by over half during 1989 at the southern town of Hat Yai, renowned for its bars and massage parlours (Asia Travel Trade, 1990). Similarly, AIDS has tarnished the image of Pattaya, and this, associated with environmental problems, is believed to have contributed to a sharp decline in the number of visitors to the resort area in the later 1980s.

In order to attract more female tourists and to counteract Thailand's image of sex tourism and AIDS, the chairman of the Tourism Authority of Thailand and a leading anti-AIDS campaigner, Minister Mechai Viravaidya, planned a Women's Visit Thailand year campaign in 1992. According to the Minister:

> We want women to come particularly from countries where some of their men have come here on sex tours . . . We want them to see what their men get up to and how they have exploited uneducated women and children. We want their women to come and see the good Thai women and encourage Thai women to stand up to the brutality and disrespect they have suffered. More action must come from Thai women themselves, otherwise the country will still be seen as the brothel of the world. (Kelly, 1991, p. 44)

The Minister's stance led him to be criticised severely by some members of the tourism industry and accused of a conflict of roles (Hail, 1992). It is readily apparent that some sections of Thailand's tourism industry are still keen to promote sex tourism because of its financial benefits. However, the long-term health implications, through the spread of AIDS and other sexually transmitted diseases, and the social impacts of sex tourism are enormous and represent a potential time-bomb for Thailand's economic and social development. In order to confront the implications of sex tourism for Thai society and economy, the government must overcome official corruption and deep-rooted cultural attitudes towards sex and the role of women. Such a task will not be easy, but unless the government takes firm and decisive action, not only will the broader tourism industry be damaged, particularly that geared towards the family market, but the human base of Thai economic development will be undermined. However, as long as the gap between the city and the rural areas continues to widen, real living standards in the country remain low, and the pre-existing set of gender relations continue to be maintained by successive military regimes, the women of the rural north will continue to furnish Thailand's sex industry with its raw material.

CONCLUSION

Sex tourism is an integral part of the tourism industry of east Asia. It has developed for a number of reasons. The indigenous set of gender relations in many parts of east Asia provided the gender base upon which sex tourism could thrive. However, the post-war militarisation of the region plus the integration of the area in the international economy has provided a further dynamic element in the perpetuation of pre-existing gender and social relations, including institutionalised racism. The significance of economic marginality and racial inequality as a causal factor in prostitution is witnessed in the origins of prostitutes. For example, the majority of tourism prostitutes in Taiwan are not Han Chinese but instead come from the island's aboriginal population which is Polynesian-Malayan in origin and which live in marginal rural areas (Sentfleben, 1986). Similarly, hospitality girls working in the ago-go bars in the tourist nightlife belt of Ermita in the Philippines come mainly from low-income families in economically marginal rural areas (Wihtol, 1982). According to the Philippine Women's Research Collective (1985) many women expend almost a quarter of the total income to support family members in Manila or send remittances back to the home province, a situation which is replicated throughout the region.

The desire for economic development by many of the region's newly independent nation states has led to dependence on tourism as a source of foreign exchange (Center for Solidarity Tourism, 1989; Harrison, 1991; Hall, 1993). Indigenous gender relations have allowed many women to be sold as commodities in order to achieve this goal, whether it be through sex tourism, as cheap labour in multinational manufacturing enterprises, or as migrants. For example, following the campaign against sex tours by Japanese and Filipina women, numbers of Japanese tourists to Manila decreased while the proportion of Filipina women travelling to Japan increased (Matsui, 1987a, p. 32). Economic relations both within the new international division of labour and between the First and Third Worlds has only exacerbated gender inequality. A direct analogy has been drawn between prostitution in the Third World and that in metropolitan resort centres where the women (and men) may be largely drawn from economically and socially disadvantaged sections of the population whose position illuminates forms of 'internal colonialism' commonly found in stratified, industrial societies (Graburn, 1983, p. 442).

The stability of the gender relations which allow the maintenance of sex tourism is a reflection of the interests of the groups which constitute the gender order. The 'insidious tourist first attitude' (Philippine Women's Research Collective, 1985, p. 36) of many governments of eastern Asia has actively promoted the images of subservient women waiting on the needs of the (male) tourist. To change this set of circumstances will therefore require fundamental change both within the host countries and in the international tourism industry.

East Asian sex tourism has further institutionalised the exploitation of women within patriarchal societies although its more overt forms do appear to be on the decline. However, the reasons for this probably relate more to the threat of AIDS to the visitor rather than widespread concern for the sex worker or fundamental changes in gender and economic relations. Indeed, modern mass tourism and its accompanying images only serve to promote unequal gender relations in which women are subordinate to male interests. Tourism will continue to be a mainstay of the region's economies. However, while tourism prostitution may decline, the intrinsic inequality of host-guest relationships in mass tourism can only continue to perpetuate the current set of gender relations. (Mass) tourism is sex tourism.

REFERENCES

Agarwal, B., 1988, Patriarchy and the 'modernising' state: an introduction, in Agarwal, B. (ed.), *Structures of patriarchy: state, community and household in modernising Asia*, Zed Books, London, pp. 1–28.

Asia Travel Trade, 1990, AIDS problem menaces tourism, *Asia Travel Trade*, **22** (November): 56–7.

Bacon, W., 1987, Sex in Manila for profits in Australia, *Times on Sunday*, 19 April: 21, 24.

Baillie, J.G., 1980, Recent international travel trends in Canada, *Canadian Geographer*, **24**(1): 13–21.

Barang, M., 1988, Tourism in Thailand, *South*, December: 72–3.

Barrett, M., 1986, *Women's oppression today: problems in Marxist Feminist analysis*, Verso, London.

Barry, K., 1984, *Female sexual slavery*, New York University Press, New York.

Barry, K., Bunch, C., Castle, S. (eds), 1984, *International feminism: networking against female sexual slavery*, International Women's Tribune Centre, New York.

Brydon, L., Chant, S., 1989, *Women in the Third World: gender issues in rural and urban areas*, Edward Elgar, Aldershot.

Buck, R., 1977, The ubiquitous tourist brochure: explorations in its intended and unintended use, *Annals of Tourism Research*, **4**(4): 192–207.

Burley, N., Symanski, R., 1981, Women without: an evolutionary and cross-cultural perspective on prostitution, in Symanski, R., *The immoral landscape: female prostitution in western societies*, Butterworths, Toronto, pp. 239–73.

Center for Solidarity Tourism, 1989, Impacts of tourism in the Philippines, *Contours*, **4**(2): 29.

Claire, R., Cottingham, J., 1982, Migration and tourism: an overview, in ISIS, *Women in Development: a resource guide for organisation and action*, ISIS Women's International and Communication Service, Geneva, pp. 205–15.

Cockburn, R., 1989, The geography of prostitution, part I: the east, *The Geographical Magazine*, **60**(3): 2–5.

Cohen, E., 1982, Thai girls and farang men: The edge of ambiguity, *Annals of Tourism Research*, **9**, 403–28.

Cohen, E., 1988, Tourism and AIDS in Thailand, *Annals of Tourism Research*, **15**: 467–86.

Collins, P.H., 1990, *Black Feminist thought: knowledge, consciousness, and the politics of empowerment*, Unwin Hyman, Boston.

Connell, R.W., 1987, *Gender and power*, Polity Press, Cambridge.

Corben, R., 1990, Thailand takes another step to curb AIDS, *Asia Travel Trade*, **22**(June): 7–9.

Cottingham, J., 1981, Sex included, *Development Forum*, **9**(5): 16.

Crick, M., 1989, Representations of international tourism in the social sciences: sun, sex, sights, savings, and servility. *Annual Review of Anthropology*, **18**: 307–44.

Crompton, R., Sanderson, K., 1990, *Gendered jobs and social change*, Unwin Hyman, London.

Davidson, D., 1985, Women in Thailand, *Canadian Women's Studies*, **16**(1): 16–19.

Dilley, R.S., 1986, Tourist brochures and tourist images, *Canadian Geographer*, **30**(1): 59–65.

Ford, N., Koetsawang, S., 1991, The socio-cultural context of the transmission of HIV in Thailand, *Social Science of Medicine*, **33**(4): 405–14.

Foucault, M., 1981, *The history of sexuality*, vol. 1, *An introduction*, Penguin, Harmondsworth.

Gay, J., 1985, The patriotic prostitute, *The Progressive*, **49**(3): 34–6.

Graburn, N., 1983, Tourism and prostitution, *Annals of Tourism Research*, **10**: 437–56.

Hail, J., 1992, Thailand: a new approach, *Asia Travel Trade*, **23**(May): 24–31.

Hall, C.M., 1991a, Sex tourism in south-east Asia, in Harrison, D. (ed.), *Tourism and the less developed countries*, Belhaven, London, pp. 64–74.

Hall, C.M., 1991b, *Introduction to tourism in Australia: impacts, planning and development*, Longman Cheshire, South Melbourne.

Hall, C.M., 1993, *Introduction to tourism in the Pacific: development, impacts and markets*, Longman Cheshire, South Melbourne.

Harrison, D., 1991, International tourism and the less developed countries: the background, in Harrison, D. (ed.), *Tourism and the less developed countries*, Belhaven, London, pp. 1–18.

Hawkesworth, M., 1984, Brothels and betrayal: On the functions of prostitution, *International Journal of Women's Studies*, **7**(1): 81–91.

Hicks, G., 1993, Ghosts gathering: comfort women issue haunts Tokyo as pressure mounts, *Far Eastern Economic Review*, 18 February: 32–6.

Hong, E., 1985, *See the third world while it lasts*, Consumers Association of Penang, Penang.

ISIS, 1979, *Tourism and prostitution, International Bulletin*, **13**, ISIS, Geneva.

ISIS, 1984, Prostitution: who pays?, *Women's World*, **3**: 4–5.

Kelly, N., 1991, Counting the cost, *Far Eastern Economic Review*, 18 July: 44.

Kikue, T., 1979, Kisaeng tourism, in ISIS, *Tourism and prostitution, ISIS International Bulletin*, **13**: 23–6.

Korea Church Women United, 1983, *Kisaeng tourism, a nation-wide survey report on conditions in four areas Seoul, Pusan, Cheju, Kyongju,* Research Material Issue No. 3, Korea Church Women United, Seoul.

Mathieson, A., Wall, G., 1982, *Tourism: economic, physical and social impacts,* Longman, London.

Matsui, Y., 1987a, The prostitution areas in Asia: an experience, *Women in a Changing World,* **24**(November): 27–32.

Matsui, Y., 1987b, Japan in the context of the militarisation of Asia, *Women in a Changing World,* **24**(November): 7–8.

Mingmongkol, S., 1981, Official blessings for the 'brothel of Asia', *Southeast Asia Chronicle,* **78**: 24–5.

Naibavu, T., Schutz, B., 1974, Prostitution: problem or profitable industry?, *Pacific Perspective,* **3**(1): 59–68.

O'Malley, J., 1988, Sex tourism and women's status in Thailand, *Loisir et Société,* **11**(1): 99–114.

Ong, A., 1985, Industrialisation and prostitution in southeast Asia, *Southeast Asia Chronicle,* **96**: 2–6.

Philippine Women's Research Collective, 1985, *Filipinas for sale: an alternative Philippine report on women and tourism,* Philippine Women's Research Collective, Quezon City.

Phongpaichit, P., 1981, Bangkok masseuses: holding up the family sky, *Southeast Asia Chronicle,* **78**: 15–23.

Phongpaichit, P., 1982, *From peasant girls to Bangkok masseuses,* International Labour Office, Geneva.

Phongpaichit, P., 1988, Two roads to the factory: industrialisation strategies and women's employment in south-east Asia, in Agarwal, B. (ed.), *Structures of patriarchy: state, community and household in modernising Asia,* Zed Books, London, pp. 151–63.

Richter, L.K., 1989, *The politics of tourism in Asia,* University of Hawaii Press, Hawaii.

Robinson, G., 1989, AIDS fear triggers Thai action, *Asia Travel Trade,* **21**(September): 11.

Rogers, J.R., 1989, Clear links: tourism and child prostitution, *Contours,* **4**(2): 20–2.

Seager, J., Olson, A., 1986, *Women in the world: an international atlas,* Pan, London.

Sentfleben, W., 1986, Tourism, hot spring resorts and sexual entertainment, observations from northern Taiwan – a study in social geography, *Philippine Geographical Journal,* **30**: 21–41.

Skrobanek, S., 1983, The transnational sex-exploitation of Thai women, MA thesis, Institute of Social Studies, The Hague.

Symanski, R., 1981, *The immoral landscape: female prostitution in western societies,* Butterworths, Toronto.

Taylor, D., 1984, Cheap thrills, *New Internationalist*, **142**: 14.

Thanh-Dam, T., 1983, The dynamics of sex-tourism: the cases of Southeast Asia, *Development and Change*, **14**(4): 533–53.

Turner, L., and Ash, J., 1975, *The golden hordes: international tourism and the pleasure periphery*, Constable, London.

Wereld, O., 1979, Sex tourism to Thailand, in ISIS, *Tourism and prostitution, International Bulletin*, **13**: 9–12.

Wihtol, R., 1982, Hospitality girls in the Manila tourist belt, *Philippine Journal of Industrial Relations*, **4**(1–2): 18–42.

Yoyori, M., 1977, Sexual slavery in Korea, *Frontiers, A Journal of Women's Studies*, **2**(1): 76.

8
The masculinisation of Stirling's heritage

Tim Edensor and Uma Kothari

INTRODUCTION

In Britain, tourism and the heritage industry occupy an increasingly central role in local and national strategies of capital accumulation. The dislocation of national and local economies as a result of the ability of ever-more mobile capital to restructure and relocate on a global terrain has resulted in the frantic search for economic alternatives to replace the many industrial casualties. Faced with the obliteration of vast swathes of manufacturing industry, entrepreneurs and administrators have sought salvation in the production and marketing of a commodity based on the rather less finite resource of 'heritage'.

Towns, cities and regions attempt to concoct an attractive and unique image, advertising their heritage in competition with other places. As space and leisure-time increasingly become colonised by consumption-related activities, strategies to create 'consumer-friendly' local environments frequently depend upon the marketing of heritage. Furthermore, a particular prestigious place-image can encourage businesses to site production within, and link their product with, a particular locality. Besides this economic competition between places within the national context, the growth of a world-wide tourist market encourages nations to vie on a global scale, rivalling each other in the touristic qualities they can offer. In this global market, Britain has specialised in marketing a specifically 'unique' heritage.

Despite the deluge of literature dealing with heritage tourism in the past decade, few writers have focused on the way in which heritage production, interpretation and consumption are gendered. In this chapter we want to examine the processes by which heritage is constructed through a study of three sites in Stirling, Scotland. We argue that these processes articulate masculinised notions of place and identity, and male dominated versions of the past which privilege white, male, heterosexual experience and activity. In examining Bannockburn Heritage Centre, the Wallace Monument and the Museum of the Argyll and Sutherland Highlanders at Stirling Castle we will highlight the ways in which these specific sites reflect particular and partial histories and myths, male-defined landscapes and gendered national identities.

MATERIAL AND SYMBOLIC CONSTRUCTIONS OF HERITAGE

In order to look at how power and control over the space and time of a place influence the construction of heritage, we need to discuss particular material and representational practices and processes.

Places and their heritage offer an ontological and epistemological security in everyday life, expressing and being constituted by particular collective and individual identities. Through the advertising of place-images and the propagation of symbolic metaphors that construct 'imagined communities' (Anderson, 1991) and 'imagined geographies' (Said, 1990), representational practices continually reinforce, (re)configure and (re)present local identities. But the construction of place is also concretely recognisable in material culture. Material practices include the investment of capital in the heritage industry and tourist infrastructure (hotels, tourist information, heritage centres, etc.), the designation of areas perceived as 'worthy' of preservation and changing employment patterns; indeed, all those practices which concern the changing economic relations within a locality and link it to wider economic networks.

It is important not to privilege material, representative or imaginative practices over one another.[1] In fact, these processes combine to (re)construct places 'in our memories and affections through repeated encounters and complex associations' (Heidegger, as cited in Harvey, 1993, p. 17), invoking memories and appealing to collectivities. Utilising the emblematic features and sites of localities that operate as 'condensation symbols'[2] signifying the character of a place, such constructions are anchored in the landscape as it were, embodied and legitimated as material evidence of local heritage.

HEGEMONIC CONSTRUCTION OF HERITAGE

The shaping of heritage is a powerful process by which memory and myth, feelings and emotions, and narratives and practices are structured and broadcast. In focusing on material and symbolic practices and processes, it is essential to account for the way in which the construction of heritage articulates the ideological interests embedded in various power relations: class, gender, race and sexuality. Partial representations of national and local identities are transmitted to visitors and attempts are made to delineate a hegemonic and unified sense of the local.

Heritage as a marker of identity, is formulated out of concepts of space and time. Histories and myths, landscapes and place and a search for 'nationhood' are the 'raw material', out of which heritage has been assembled. These constructions are inevitably expressive of particular and partial class, gendered, sexual and racial identities. So we need to ask whose myths, whose histories, whose landscapes and sites, whose nationality, whose identity and whose heritage are being constructed, presented and consumed?

It is evident that constructions of historical and spatial identities will mean that

> in creating our own centres, and our own locals . . . our centres displace others into the peripheries of our making. (Probyn, 1990, p. 176)

However, individuals and groups have differing levels of access to and control over the construction of their own and others' identity. Particular experiences, practices and histories are dominant, are taken as 'true' and have greater power to colonise and exclude the experience of others. Thus we must challenge the notion that there is a single shared sense of place, a coherent local identity, a totalising common history.

The (re)interpretation, (re)construction and (re)presentation of heritage is a process which embodies different power relations. The problem with most explorations of the diversity of spatial practices, which is how we conceive of those activities which construct heritage, is that there has been an overwhelming focus on, and prioritisation of, capital and class relations to the exclusion of other (interacting and interrelating) relations of power and control.

For instance, Harvey focuses almost exclusively on the way in which *capital* shapes spatial practices and continuously transforms previously oppressive customs. He writes,

> Differences that preceded the capitalist order – of gender, race, language, ethnicity, religion and pre-capitalist social class – have been absorbed, transformed and reconstructed by a social system in which the accumulation of capital is assured through the domination of nature and control over wage labour. (Harvey, 1993, p. 21)

Harvey's focus on class and his privileging of the workings of capital mean that racism and homophobia are marginal to our understanding of spatial control, and the power of male-dominated social systems to sustain and normalise power through the control of space is shunted into a siding. As Massey rightly argues, 'there is a lot more determining how we experience space than what "capital" gets up to' (Massey, 1993, p. 60).

What we want to examine and demonstrate in this chapter is the way in which the construction, presentation and consumption of heritage is formed out of the configuration of gendered material, gendered representational and gendered imaginative practices.

Exclusive and inclusive notions of heritage

The collapse of established industries and the subsequent marketing of localities for tourists have contributed to the renewed awareness of a sense of place that characterises the contemporary search for identity. The construction of heritage in these situations where local economic stability seems threatened can exacerbate *conservative* notions of place. Robins argues that such policies often

> represent protective strategies of response to global forces, centred around the conservation, rather than reinterpretation, of identities. The driving imperative is to salvage centred, bounded and coherent identities – placed identities for placeless times. (Robins, 1991, p. 41)

Such constructions often include some people and exclude others within a locality. Thus, while an attractive place-image is fashioned to appeal to visitors, it can also circumscribe the boundary of a place, incorporating only particular residents enclosed in the demarcated space. The local symbolic value of a particular site can then suggest that those who do not identify with the popular myths and histories of the site are not *bona fide* locals. Indeed, they may even be perceived as an 'enemy within'.

At local and national levels, the more recursive notions of place provide a bulwark against the perceived chaos of economic and social change. These conservative forms of identification have been mobilised around the perceived threats of immigration, the influx of 'foreign' culture, different sexualities and radical politics, to question the belonging of black and ethnic groups, lesbians and gays and any form of political opposition. Indeed, these groups may construct very different heritages and feel positioned within different spatial entities. These conservative versions of place and heritage have also been profoundly masculinised. At most major heritage sites there is a focus on particular, valorised masculine spheres of activity (war and militarism, statesmanship, exploration, scientific invention, public life). These preoccupations render invisible women's historical contribution to, and participation in, the nation and locality.

A plurality of heritages?

Although the heritage industry tends to cater to those who seek to anchor themselves to an archaic sense of place when confronted with the ever-shifting terrain of contemporary life, in some ways these conservative narratives, identities and practices are being decentred. Furthermore, there has recently been a proliferation of alternative sites and heritages. Industrial, domestic and political realms have been opened up to the gaze of tourists.

Recent writings[3] have alerted us to the fact that there are many imagined pasts. Oral and subaltern histories have emerged as different and multiple identities[4] struggle to claim and broadcast a heritage. The defensive withdrawal into a conservative, white, male, heterosexual sense of place outlined above, contrasts with the extension of social links outwith the local and national domains. Identities then, are increasingly likely to be constructed through association on grounds of gender, race, sexuality, interest group or political concern. At the local level, as Massey argues,

> If it is now recognised that people have multiple identities, then the same points can be made in relation to places. (Massey, 1993, p. 65)

National and local myths are continually reinterpreted, lose their symbolic power or are reinvigorated. Moreover, at heritage sites meaning cannot be closed and the potential for polyphonous interpretation lurks, whether through the symbolic appropriation by organised groups or through competing historical research which questions official narratives.

While it is true that these trends outlined above appear to provide a greater scope for the multiple interpretation of heritage and the deconstruction of traditional exclusionary and conservative notions, in fact, at most major heritage sites interpretation remains overwhelmingly dominated by white, masculinised stories concerning the actions of 'great men'. Competing accounts continue to be consigned to a historical and spatial ghetto and the powerful constraints placed on interpretation, the directing of the tourist gaze and commercialisation constrain visitor practices and interpretation at such sites. As Samuel and Thompson state, 'The powerful have a breathtaking ability to stamp their own meanings on the past' (Samuel and Thompson, 1990, p. 18).

Before we examine the specific ways in which the heritage attractions we study are constructed, we will place them in their geographical context by briefly discussing tourism in Scotland and Stirling insofar as it relates to our inquiry.

TOURISM IN SCOTLAND

As in other areas of Britain, the tourist industry in Scotland has increased in economic importance. In 1990, more than nine million tourists spent approximately £1.4 billion, some five per cent of Scottish GDP (Scottish Tourist Board, 1990). Most of these tourists are attracted by a particular Scottish heritage and the scenery of the Highlands.

Scottishness has been a marketable commodity since the construction of a romantic aesthetic in the late eighteenth century.[5] During this period, representations of the Highlands became infused with romantic notions of the sublime. The 'discovery' of the 'Ossian' epic provided a basis for metropolitan flights of fancy about 'noble savages' and the authentic virtue of Highland life was praised. With the development of scenic tourism these conceits flourished. Following the invention and marketing of clan tartans, the kilt,[6] and the patronage of Highland garb by royalty, these ideas were sustained.

Developing alongside this tartan fetishism and utilising the symbolic material it produced, was the Scottish military tradition. This was predicated upon a notion of the natural Scottish soldier, a descendant from the warriors of the clan system. The archetypal male Scot was

> . . . the expression of an essence: in a romantic realisation of the neo-classical placing of the barbarian, the Highland zone produces warfare from its own dark interior. There is a striking correspondence between that irrationalism and the rational exploitation of the region as a source of military manpower: for the picturesque tourist, as for the army. (Womack, 1989, p. 38)

The irony of this tradition, created as it was by the imperial imperative to recruit soldiers and an overworked metropolitan imagination, is that it has been incorporated into constructions of popular Scottish identity, influencing notions of heritage and nationalism. This reappropriation sustains the continued transmission of a military-inscribed history: the national popularity

Figure 8.1   *The Stirling tourism logo*

of imposing castles, the Edinburgh tattoo, military museums and battlefields.

STIRLING

The Stirling area is popularly described as the 'Battlefield of Scotland', and by local historian Tom Lannon as the 'Seed-box of Scottish Nationalism' (Lannon, 1983, p. 56). As the location of the major Scottish victories over the English at the battles of Stirling Bridge in 1297 and Bannockburn in 1314, it has long been a place of pilgrimage for nationalistic Scots. Tourism in

Stirling has focused on these sites as well as on the spectacular castle.

The three sites on which we concentrate are often referred to as the 'Stirling Triangle' and reinforce the area's symbolic national(ist) stature. As elsewhere, with the decline of traditional industries, particularly mining in the case of Stirling, the heritage industry has grown in economic importance. These attractions are being marketed with a renewed vigour. And as Lannon remarks, '. . . to revive the history of Stirling . . . is to revive the history of Scotland' (Lannon, 1983, p. 54).

The local and regional councils have been extremely active in promoting tourism in the area as the main plank in their strategy to reinvigorate the local economy. Although the castle annually attracts over 250,000 visitors, Bannockburn nearly 70,000 and the Wallace Monument, before its renovation, attracted around 40,000 (Scottish Tourist Board, 1991) the authorities aim to increase vastly the number of visitors to Stirling. Plans to develop heritage sites and improve tourist infrastructure have met with a considerable degree of success in acquiring funding. Several projects requiring a large financial commitment are part-funded by the European Community. Besides improving the physical infrastructure and the quality and quantity of retail outlets in the Old Town, encouraging a street theatre project and instituting a 'Tartan' Festival, major projects include renovation of the castle and the restoration and re-presentation of the Wallace Monument.

THE CONSTRUCTION OF HERITAGE IN STIRLING

An examination of the historical and geographical materials out of which heritage is wrought highlights its gendered construction. In the case of Stirling, these resources comprise the trenchant national myths that surround the area as well as scholarly historical accounts; a famous place-image and its apparent 'natural' reflection in material features in the local landscape; and nationalist and romantic notions of the meaning of 'Scotland' and 'Scottishness'.

History and myth

Historical narratives exist as folk tales and myths, and as 'official' academic accounts. As with all other narratives, these forms are selective and partial. Formal historical research and study, and the production and transmission of myths are highly gendered activities, for men and women are differentially involved in the construction, dissemination and consumption of all types of historical account.

In order to express the primordial pedigree, mystique and endurance of heritage, tourist boards, locals and nationalists utilise the narrative powers of myth for commercial, political and affective reasons. It is a feature of myths that they are multi-interpretable and are continually adapted through time. Yet at any historical moment, there is usually a dominant version constructed and claimed by the powerful. The heritage industry exerts a powerful influence over the reproduction of myths in present times.

In Stirling, the legends of Bruce and Wallace have been central to the town's image. As examples of mythical national heroes, they are typically 'creatures of excess' who 'perform legendary feats of strength', 'effect miraculous escapes' and through their travails maintain a sense of honour, fairness and equanimity (Samuel and Thompson, 1990, p. 3). These qualities are highly valued and are presented as being exclusively male attributes. This is characteristic of the form of national myths which excludes women from its narratives. As Kay writes,

> . . . women do not ordinarily appear as protagonists in national epics but only in novels and children's fairy tales. Women, if they appear at all in national epics, typically do so as camp followers, titillating distractions, rewards for male heroism or answers to male loneliness. (Kay, 1991, p. 442)

In many cases then, myths are exemplary vernacular narratives that are used to sustain, legitimise and broadcast partial national and local identities. It is worth asking which myths are transmitted and consumed and by whom.

'Official' versions of history have long been a male preserve of expertise. Until the recent rise of social and subaltern history, historical accounts have typically concentrated on the character, actions and influence of great male figures. As we shall see, at all the sites we examine at Stirling, heritage interpretation depends on the rather antiquated version of history which concentrates on the lives of great men and their actions. Particular events, usually military or political, are held up as especially momentous and the stories of women are invisible. Boulding makes the general observation that,

> When we start probing back through history, we find huge blank spaces relieved here and there by fragmentary images of kings, pyramids, temples, battlefields . . . (Boulding, 1992, p. 3)

The history of Scotland and Stirling has concentrated on the man-made icons of castle and monument and the sites of military exploits, stages upon which the great male figures have strode. It is true that the exception to this masculinist history is the romantic figure of Mary, Queen of Scots, yet the emphasis habitually falls on the tragic aspects of her life. Boulding considers the restricted roles consigned to women in grand historical narratives, including queen, tragic figure and great beauty (Boulding, 1992, p. 5), all integral to accounts of Mary.

On the male-inscribed sites of Bannockburn, the Wallace Monument and the castle, the historical obsession with militarism lends itself to an uncritical portrayal of warfare, with its insistent focus on heroism, soldierly virtues and tactics. There is an unwillingness to pose wider questions about the social cost of war, why there has been a continuous historical recourse to war, and the failure to seek alternative strategies that might bypass the use of military engagement.[7]

In the historical accounts we examine there is a highly circumscribed gendering of historical roles which neglects most aspects of the past lives of men and women: as Kay states,

> Casting women only as helpmeets or bit-players in a Euro-American male drama does not do justice to the people who made the past that we study: it simply indicates that (historians) interpret the past in terms of mythic-type-scenes that validate their own ideologies. (Kay, 1991, p. 435)

Place, space and landscape

As already mentioned, the salience of the local and a 'sense of place' has been theorised as increasingly important as a source of refuge from the contingencies of time-space compression

(Harvey, 1989), globalisation (King, 1991; Featherstone, 1990) and restructuring. This renewed focus on the local has been generated by the work of academics and politicians and the increasing mobility of capital. However, it has also changed local everyday practices which respond to these dislocating forces.

These spatial practices involve a range of activities which articulate gender-specific constructions of heritage. For example, the control of capital, land use and administration are controlled by mainly male personnel following particular bureaucratic and commercial goals. However, it is representations of space and place that most concern the heritage industry: those practices which designate, map, interpret and advertise tourist attractions by reworking symbolic material.

In Stirling, the spectacular monuments commemorating the past continue to evoke a particular public sentiment. We have discussed the way in which the 'Stirling Triangle' acts as a concatenation of Scottishness. So dominant are these features on the landscape that they act as constant visual reminders of the heritage of Stirling and of Scotland. Tom Lannon describes the sites as 'installed, like bits of organic furniture in a spiritual home' (Lannon, 1983, p. 54). Even on the most popular streets in the centre of Stirling there is no escape from the presence of Wallace and Bruce. A profusion of Victorian statuary of the two heroes inscribes their presence on the town. Furthermore, the ubiquitous logo of the council features an image of Bruce on horseback (see figure 8.1, p. 171).

The everyday activities of local people occur within and traverse these specifically male local places and tourists are directed to gaze upon these masculinised features. It is this very overt material existence that tends to reinforce a particular reality in which these sites and symbols embody the identity and heritage of Stirling. These material forms serve to celebrate sites of male activity and make aesthetic statements that glorify particular male historical figures. But the public realm contains no heritage sites that celebrate women or are historical locations of female activity. How do women feel in these public spaces, so taken over by masculinised images and male identities? These are most definitely male spaces and male places.

Tourist attractions are distinctive sites where locals and visitors engage in particular spatial practices. As special symbolic sites it might be suggested that they offer an opportunity for visitors to engage in more imaginative practices. In this way they can escape the networks of disciplinary space in which circumscribed activities established by commercial and bureaucratic powers occur. Thus, such spaces may be more amenable to the 'tactics' envisioned by de Certeau, where individuals 'reappropriate the space organised by socio-cultural production' (de Certeau, 1984, p. xiii). These improvisational 'tactics', weave narratives together as they move through space, utilising personal formative memories and myths. For de Certeau, 'to practice space is thus to repeat the joyful and silent experience of childhood' (de Certeau, 1984, p. 110). We would like to question though, whether particular sites and their interpretation only stimulate the replaying of especial memories and stories. As we will argue, at the sites that we examine, heritage interpretation that appeals to and stimulates the fantastical and childish imaginations of visitors, thereby provoking particular spatial practices, appears to be restricted to boyish daydreams.

Although there has been a growing body of work which has examined the way in which landscape can be read as a text,[8] there has been a dearth of analysis on the way in which such readings are gendered. Rose considers that in constructing the natural as female, as either maternal/fecund or wild, it is subject to the penetrating gaze of the male, who is seducer and scientist, coloniser and conqueror.[9] As part of this fantasy, romantic notions of wild areas like the Highlands are thoroughly gendered and Scotland has frequently been represented as a woman. The personification of Scotland as pure and natural, and conversely, as a homeland raped by brutal English colonialism echoes our points about the gendering of landscape. However, the imagined geographies suggested by the monuments, the castle and the battlefields inspire a male-inscribed text. For the tourist, the local landscape, (re)presented and (re)packaged, serves as a theatre in which only particular historical scenes are imagined.

Nationalism

Literature on nations and nationalism rarely addresses the question of women's and men's differential participation in the national project. This is usually mirrored in the way in which myths and symbolic sites that pervade notions of nationhood are constructed and interpreted.

We have cited the national myths whereby heroic male figures are invoked by Scottish nationalists to serve as rhetorical symbols and fantastic exemplary characters. This raises the question as to the role and image of women within the national(ist) project. According to Yuval-Davies and Anthias, women's involvement in national processes occurs in specific areas: as biological reproducers of nationals; in the transmission and reproduction of national ideology and culture; as symbols of nationhood; and as participants in national struggles (Yuval-Davies and Anthias, 1989, p. 7). However, women are generally portrayed as those who must be protected and defended while men are represented as the protectors and defenders.

The contemporary production of the heritage of Scotland certainly fails to include women among the participants for national liberation. The focus is exclusively on heroic male warriors like Bruce and Wallace. The Scottish National Party organises a large annual rally at Bannockburn and its leaders continue to employ the myths of the battle to invoke patriotism and inspire those who struggle for national independence. Most national histories and myths are peculiarly obsessed with military conflict. Indeed, as Enloe has observed, nationalism has 'typically sprung from masculinized memory, masculinized humiliation and masculinized hope' (Enloe, 1989, p. 44). Since states usually emerge out of wars and battles and since men fight in these battles, women tend to be invisible in the history of the nation.

With these gender-specific national roles in mind, we can ask whether male and female aims and desires for national projects are similar. Anthias and Yuval-Davies argue that men and women are equally committed to the national project, but they may contribute in different ways (Yuval-Davies and Anthias, 1989, p. 9). However, Walby maintains that this is not always the case. She asserts that women may support a *different* national project from that of men, but that in the struggle to define what is constituted as *the* national project, women are typically heard less than men (Walby, 1992, p. 90).

Walby describes how the relations between gender and nationalism are mediated by militarism (Walby, 1992, p. 92). A national history which glorifies an overwhelmingly military heritage is gendered by the different relationship that men and women have to war. Walby suggests that women's political activity frequently exists in a different spatial context from that of men.[10]

The heritage sites we examine exist as public spaces in which masculinised nationalist rituals and fantasies are played out. We describe the way in which these sites are presented, interpreted and consumed, and argue that these reflect and influence the reification of the Scottish subject as male.

BANNOCKBURN

Bannockburn Heritage Centre and the battlefield site are located two miles from the centre of Stirling. Bannockburn has retained its significance as a symbol of Scottish independence and the story of the battle continues to be transmitted orally, often via poetry. The citation of the Declaration of Arbroath and historical and semi-fictional volumes evoking the event remain popular. The triumph of Bruce and his outnumbered men is the most momentous victory in Scottish military history and many nationalist-minded visitors make a 'pilgrimage'[11] to Bannockburn on a regular basis.

This battlefield site has been progressively saturated with symbolic forms. A large rotunda contains an enormous flagpole with a battle-axe atop and a memorial cairn. Just beyond the rotunda is an imposing statue of Robert the Bruce mounted on his horse, surveying the scene of his triumph. In the Heritage Centre, there is a retail area, a popular audio-visual programme and an exhibition outlining Scottish history from the date of Bruce's victory to the Union of the Crowns.

It becomes apparent after spending any time at the battle site that the majority of the pilgrim-tourists are male or families 'led' by fathers or grandfathers. These latter exercise their patriarchal and patriotic duty by guiding the junior family members to the cairn or statue to pay tribute to the exemplary figure of Bruce. While there we heard the leaders of family expeditions say:

'Aye, an' we're still battlin' on yet, son.'

'Does it no' make ye proud to be Scottish, eh?'

'There's a wonderful man . . . makes ye feel proud.'

'No' much has changed. We could do wi' him now.'

The transference of the significance of the Bannockburn myth is apparently taken up by male family members.

The symbols of axe and statue elevate weaponry and its use, and the tourist gaze is instructed to follow direction pointers which indicate where particularly significant stages of the battle occurred within the wider panorama. Here, in this theatrical vista, contrary to Rose's discussion of a feminised landscape, the landscape is clearly male inscribed.

It has been mentioned by several commentators that a post-modern, playful imagination is characteristic of contemporary tourist practices (Urry, 1990). We would suggest that here, the resources that stimulate imagination and fantasy are exclusively male. The gaze is directed to features that sustain militaristic fantasies, backed up by tele-visual and literary material that conjure up the adventure of war. How can women interpret, consume or imagine heritage at such sites? Is male imagination stimulated and female imagination cauterised? Does the posses-sion or absence of gendered knowledge based on the replaying of male childhood games and roles exclude women from engag-ing in these fantasies?

The presentation of heritage at Bannockburn is very much centred around the heroic person of Bruce and his chivalric and courageous qualities. The popular audio-visual show empha-sises that the story of Bannockburn is the tale of the qualities of Bruce and his noble comrades-in-arms, and portrays the visceral excitement of battle. That this incites the passions of patriotic Scots is borne out in the visitors' book where effusions of nationalist pride predominate along the lines of 'blood-stirring' and 'time we did it again'.

The battle is dealt with in terms of strategy and military man-oeuvres and as is usually the case, the stories of the bereaved and defeated are neglected as are those of the non-chivalric participants and camp-followers. At Bannockburn, a historical and nationalist narrative is offered in which the exploits of great men are the key to understanding the past and serve as exemp-lars worthy of emulation.

WALLACE MONUMENT

The Wallace Monument is undergoing the final stages of an expensive refurbishment. Designed to express a romantic, rather than political, nationalism in late Victorian times, this gothic memorial is sited on the Abbey Craig Rock overlooking the site of the Battle of Stirling Bridge.

When work is complete, visitors will enter the lower part of the building and confront an English knight guarding a reconstructed battle tent. Inside, Wallace is there to greet them. There follows an interactive dramatised dialogue between the simulacrum of Wallace and five other male historical figures projected onto a screen. Wallace commences the playlet with the following political statement:

> Men must have their power. They seek to influence, to strengthen their position, to be seen as something else in other men's eyes. But no one man can, nor should, hold himself higher than his fellow. For that diminishes us all. For then we all fail. And our society, our humanity is nothing.

Shortly after, Wallace refers to the murder of his wife and children by the English and then comes the inevitable statement, 'English Edward had raped our young nation'. This clearly epitomises the metaphoric engendering of the nation as victim and female. While this short drama is skilfully constructed and imaginatively presented, it selects a highly conservative and masculinised set of characters and events.

Outside the tent there is a combination of words, images and music to convey how Wallace defeated the larger English army in battle. As the pamphlet advertising the attraction puts it, '. . . you are swept into the heat of battle'. Furthermore, the tourist gaze is directed towards the famous authentic symbol of Wallace's heroism, his 'mighty two-handed broadsword'. An attempt is evidently made here to immerse the visitor in the excitement and strategy of the battlefield.

An extraordinary and revealing insight into the 'Great Man' version of national history is found on the floor above. Here we enter the 'Hall of Heroes', a chamber which accommodates the busts of sixteen 'notable Scotsmen'. As the accompanying script admits, the Hall of Heroes 'is typically Victorian, reflecting their romantic notions of heroes, their obsession with the individual and their zeal for memorials and monuments'. Furthermore, it agrees that, 'the exclusion of any heroines from the Hall of Heroes also explains a good deal about Victorian attitudes and values'. It goes on to encourage us to think about what heroes and heroines we would include in a contemporary list, although no suggestions are offered.

The choice of heroes typically reflects an archaic notion of a great man.[12] 'Posterity' and 'eminence' are embodied by men who pursued scientific invention, martial skills, literature, exploration and missionary work. These figures are still regarded as irrefutably 'great' Scots. The Hall of Heroes fortifies the assumption that history has been shaped by men.

A diorama on the third floor points out particular historical events that occurred and these can then be further visualised from the viewing platform at the top of the monument, thus inscribing a network of military happenings across the landscape surrounding Stirling.

THE REGIMENTAL MUSEUM OF THE ARGYLL AND SUTHERLAND HIGHLANDERS IN STIRLING CASTLE

To show how a dominant view of Scottish heritage has been constructed out of militarism, imperial role and Highland romanticism, we examine the presentation of the history of the famous Scottish regiment, the Argyll and Sutherland Highlanders. The regiment has played a prominent role in the many British imperial wars up to the Falklands. Its members have collected a total of sixteen Victoria Crosses – the official stamp of valorous activity. Thus there is a lineage that can be traced through the battles of Balaclava, Lucknow, the Boer War and the Korean War to the present.

In the museum, we are again surrounded by Scottish military glory. Much celebrated is the 'Thin Red Line' which stood its ground against insuperable odds at the Battle of Balaclava. The museum is utterly saturated with a particular militaristic, aesthetic fetishism which enshrines particular objects. There are well-used weapons including swords, bayonets and firearms in profusion. Also, there is a revealing glut of the iconic trophies, medals and testimonials that so preoccupy military signifying practices. This sterile form of symbolism obfuscates the horror of battle and ennobles soldierly virtues. There is nowhere any history about why such battles occurred, the imperialist contingencies that compelled soldiers to die in their thousands, or even details of the consequences of defeat. There is only glory and testimonials to bravery. Even in the presentation of World War I, we are offered a generally humorous and stoical account of life in the trenches from a taped reconstruction of an officer's diary that neglects much of the horror. This is compounded by an account of how three members of the regiment killed seventeen of a party of Germans and put the rest to flight. The text advances the opinion that this episode

> . . . makes one almost believe that the old romance supposed to attach to war is not yet dead, but still lingers on in places, despite the deadly influence of trench warfare.

The aesthetic fetishism presented is not merely a redundant display. This ideological construction successfully merged imperial loyalty with Scottish patriotism, and utilised romantic Celtic mythology to claim Highland military legend as the regiment's legitimate ancestor. Here, the Scottish role of military participation in imperial adventure is normalised. This is most profoundly incorporated in one of the museum's showpieces, a florid centrepiece to commemorate the Highlanders' action in the Boer War. This large and ostentatious item of silverware incorporates the allegorical figures of 'Diarmid of the Wild Boar', Ossian the Celtic bard and 'Cruachan', an embodiment of the Campbell war-cry. Also featured are members of the British royal family, soldiers from various eras, and a feminine 'Victory'.

One has to wonder what the huge number of visitors, men and women, make of the museum. The interpretation of war here is undoubtedly the most masculinised presentation of heritage at the three sites we have studied. The Argyll and Sutherland Highlanders have been a fixture of Stirling life for centuries and the military values perpetrated by the museum are echoed at the other sites we have examined. We can see the persistence of normative notions of Stirling's heritage that concentrate on highly partial, gendered and battle-soaked histories.

THE DECENTRING OF MASCULINE HERITAGE?

In this chapter we have shown the ways in which the heritage industry has been constructed out of, and has drawn from, masculinised versions of history, a masculinised sense of place and masculinised national identities. In looking at the production, interpretation and consumption of heritage at three sites in Stirling, we have examined the specific ways in which this male bias is articulated. We argue that our examples highlight particular persistent masculinised themes that run throughout the heritage industry, such as militarism and the glorification of 'Great Men'.

It is clear that the construction of heritage is a complicated and problematic process, involving the weaving together of different narratives. These include discourses which attempt to construct collective national, historical and local identities by drawing almost exclusively upon male experience and male activity. The construction of heritage thus (re)creates and reinforces male spaces and male places, re-enchants an imaginary masculinist past and (re)confirms the national subject as male.

The issues we want to raise concern not only the way in which heritage is constructed but also how it restricts visitors in their power to interpret, practise and imagine nationalism, place and history. Indeed, can particular heritage sites only appeal to certain people? Or, are individuals' spatial practices and imaginations expressed differently and at different sites?

In this study, we have focused on the way in which the production of heritage foregrounds male characters and activities, provoking further questions. How do women interpret the old Scottish military myths as they are presented at the Museum of the Argyll and Sutherland Highlanders? What childhood memories or fantasies can women invoke at Bannockburn? How do women feel about their very obvious exclusion as participants in the history of Scotland when they visit the Hall of Heroes?

We have pointed out that during a period of rapid change, heritage can provide a sense of security but it does this by reinforcing archaic and reactionary notions of locality, history and nation. The creation of a conservative sense of place is not, however, the only course. The question we need to ask is how can we decentre this male, conservative, hegemonic interpretation of heritage? Following Doreen Massey we ask, how can we create a 'progressive sense of place' (Massey, 1993, p. 66)?

A place does not have to have a coherent essential identity. A single, shared sense of locality constructed out of an inward-looking history can only reflect and reinforce a partial subjectivity. Massey suggests that we should imagine places not as bounded areas but as 'articulated moments in networks of social relations and understandings' and furthermore that,

> if places can be conceptualised in terms of the social interactions which they tie together, then it is also the case that these interactions themselves are not static. They are processes. (Massey, 1993, p. 66)

In order to avoid the construction of a hegemonic, reified and static sense of place, we need to recognise that localities are replete with 'internal differences and conflicts' (Massey, 1993, p. 67) that necessarily reflect power struggles. This recognition helps to decentre static conceptions of place that propagate and utilise a conservative heritage.

By recognising that places exist, and have always existed, within a matrix of different spatial and temporal social relations, we emphasise that there is a plurality of heritages that express different identities and operate within different networks. Although the tourism and heritage industry continues to privilege white male heterosexual knowledge and experience, these dominant versions are becoming decentred. There are now spaces being created within which women, black people, lesbians and gays can construct and define their diverse alternative heritages and articulate their different spatial and temporal realities.

NOTES

1   For a discussion of the usefulness of Lefebvre's framework for an analysis of spatial practices from which we derive these different practices, see Harvey (1993).

2   The term is Cohen's. He asserts that such symbols are mnemonic triggers that engender affective and cognitive responses and act as a form of shorthand for more complicated narratives (Cohen, 1985).

3   See Hobsbawm and Ranger (1983); Samuel and Thompson (1990).

4   See Barrett and Philips (1993).

5   Among accounts of the invention of Scottishness, the most interesting are by Donnachie and Whatley (1992); McCrone (1992); Womack (1989).

6   For a contentious account of the origin of the kilt, see Trevor-Roper (1987).

7   For an account of the interpretation of war, see Uzzell (1989).

8   See for instance, Cosgrove and Daniels (1988); Short (1991).

9   See Rose (1992), for a detailed account of the gendering of the landscape.

10   For example, the feminist, peace and green movements are distinguished by their concern with the local and global.

11   See the *Annals of Tourism Research* special issue on the links between pilgrimage and tourism, January–March, 1992.

12   The heroes are Robert the Bruce; George Buchanan; John Knox; Allan Ramsay; Robert Burns; Robert Tannahill; Adam Smith; James Watt; Walter Scott; William Murdoch; David Brewster; Thomas Carlyle; Hugh Miller; Dr Chalmers; David Livingstone; and W.E. Gladstone.

REFERENCES

Anderson, B., 1991, *Imagined communities: reflections on the origins and spread of nationalism*, Verso, London.
Barrett, M., Philips, A. (eds), 1993, *Destabilising theory*, Polity Press, London.
Boulding, E., 1992, *The underside of history* vol. 1, Sage, London.
Cohen, A.K., 1985, *The symbolic construction of community*, Tavistock, London.
Cosgrove, D., Daniels, S. (eds), 1988, *The iconography of landscape*, Cambridge University Press, Cambridge.
de Certeau, M., 1984, *The practices of everyday life*, California University Press, Berkeley.
Donnachie, I., Whatley, C. (eds), 1992, *The manufacture of Scottish history*, Polygon, Edinburgh.
Enloe, C., 1989, *Bananas, beaches and bases: making feminist sense of international politics*, Pandora, London.

Featherstone, M. (ed.), 1990, Global culture, *Theory, Culture and Society*, 7(2–3), special issue.

Harvey, D., 1989, *The condition of postmodernity*, Blackwell, Oxford.

Harvey, D., 1993, From space to place and back again: reflections on the condition of postmodernity, in Bird, J. *et al.* (eds), *Mapping the futures: local cultures, global change*, Routledge, London, pp. 3–29.

Hobsbawm, E., Ranger, T., 1983, *The invention of tradition*, Cambridge University Press, Cambridge.

Kay, J., 1991, Landscapes of women and men: rethinking the regional historical geography of the United States and Canada, *Journal of Historical Geography*, 17(4): 435–52.

King, A. (ed.), 1991, *Culture, globalisation and the world system*, Macmillan, New York.

Lannon, T., 1983, *The making of modern Stirling*, Stirling University Press, Stirling.

McCrone, D., 1992, *Understanding Scotland*, Routledge, London.

Massey, D., 1993, Power-geometry and a progressive sense of place, in Bird, J. *et al.* (eds), *Mapping the futures: local cultures, global change*, Routledge, London, pp. 59–69.

Probyn, E., 1990, Travels in the postmodern: making sense of the local, in Nicholson, L. (ed.), *Feminism/postmodernism*, Routledge, New York, pp. 176–89.

Robins, K., 1991, Tradition and translation: national culture in its global context, in Corner, J., Harvey, S. (eds), *Enterprise and heritage: crosscurrents of national culture*, Routledge, London, pp. 21–44.

Rose, G., 1992, Geography as a science of observation: the landscape, the gaze and masculinity, in Driver, F., Rose, G. (eds), *Nature and science: essays in the history of geographical knowledge*, Historical Geography Research Series, No. 28, pp. 8–18.

Said, E., 1990, Narrative and geography, *New Left Review*, March.

Samuel, R., Thompson, P., 1990, *The myths we live by*, Routledge, London.

Scottish Tourist Board, 1990, *Tourism in Scotland*, STB, Edinburgh.

Scottish Tourist Board, 1991, *Visitor attractions survey*, STB, Edinburgh.

Short, J., 1981, *Imagined country*, Routledge, London.

Trevor-Roper, H., 1987, The invention of tradition; the Highland tradition of Scotland, in Hobsbawm, E., Ranger, T. (eds), *The invention of tradition*, Cambridge University Press, Cambridge, pp. 15–41.

Urry, J., 1990, *The tourist gaze*, Routledge, London.

Uzzell, D., 1989, The hot interpretation of war and conflict, in Uzzell, D. (ed.), *Heritage interpretation* vol. 1, Belhaven, London, pp. 33–47.

Walby, S., 1992, Woman and nation, *International Journal of Comparative Sociology*, 33(1–2): 81–99.

Womack, P., 1989, *Improvement and romance: constructing the myth of the Highlands*, Macmillan, London.

Yuval-Davies, N., Anthias, F., 1989, *Woman-nation-state*, Macmillan, London.

9
A note on women travellers

Derek Hall and Vivian Kinnaird

> . . . these women in the nineteenth and early twentieth centuries took for themselves the identities of 'adventurer' and 'explorer'. Both labels were thoroughly masculinized. Masculinity and exploration had been as tightly woven together as masculinity and soldiering. These audacious women challenged that ideological assumption, but they have left us with a bundle of contradictions. (Enloe, 1989, p. 23)

INTRODUCTION

By way almost as an endpiece, this short chapter reflects on the role and depiction of women travellers and their discourses within and on foreign cultures and landscapes. Although analysis of women travellers and their power relations is not a central characteristic of this book, it is nonetheless an area of some considerable interest. This review can no more than offer a gesture in the direction of this discourse.

Recognition of the gendered nature of the motivations, acts and aspirations of travelling (as opposed to touring) has seen lately a proliferation both of anthologies of women travellers (particularly those of the Victorian era (e.g. Middleton, 1965; Allen, 1983; Olds, 1985; Davies et al., 1986; Russell, 1986; Aitken, 1987; Birkett, 1989; Keay, 1989; Smith, 1989; Tinling, 1989; Davies and Jansz, 1990; Robinson, 1990; Melchett, 1991), and of contemporary guides specifically designed for women who travel (e.g. Davies *et al.*, 1986; Moss and Moss, 1987; Davies and Jansz, 1990; Ferrari, 1991; McCarthy, 1992; Zepatos, 1992; Barnard, 1993; Belford, 1993; Cullen, 1993). This in itself reflects the gendered nature of publishing and the perceptions of publishers, lately responding to the recognition of women's place in the history of science and discovery (e.g. Keller, 1985; Siegel and Finley, 1985; Babcock and Parezo, 1988; Phillips, 1990), not least in the history of geography (e.g. Berman, 1974; Bronson, 1975; Stoddart, 1986, 1991; Domosh, 1991a, 1991b), and of the market niches arising from a previous neglect of the needs of women travellers, itself resulting from the gendered nature of market evaluations.

But this belated development has led to something of a bookshelf ghettoisation: guides for women are often found on the travel bookshop shelf next to those for 'other' 'minority' and 'specialist' groups such as vegetarians (Sanger, 1987; Bowler, 1990), the disabled (Abbott and Tyrrell, 1990; Stanford, 1990; Walsh, 1991; see also Kanga, 1991), the retired (Lees and Lees, 1988), gays (Van Gelder and Brandt, 1992), and those travelling with children (Wheeler, 1985).

TRAVELLERS AND WRITING: WRITERS AND TRAVELLING

In making the contentious distinction between 'travellers' and 'tourists', we recognise in the former those people who have specifically chosen, or who have had no option but, to travel on their own (or with a small number of people – not a 'group'), and to do that in an individual, 'basic' or even 'eccentric' manner.

We distinguish further between travellers who write and

(a) good travel writers, such as Jan Morris and Mary McCarthy (1959, 1961);

(b) 'place' writers and novelists such as Nadine Gordimer (1979), using South Africa, and Irini Spanidou (1987), in the context of post-war Greece, both exploring female experiences within a strong sense of geographical identity; and

(c) novelists who use travel as a central theme or framework for their work (e.g. Arnot Robertson, 1931; or Agatha Christie's *Murder on the Orient Express*).

By definition, we are concerned with those travellers who have committed their exploits, thoughts, feelings and motivations to paper. But what of the travellers who never write? How far have gender, class, race and sexual orientation circumscribed the literary expression of the art of travel? In the history of travel, just as in histories of a broader nature, how far have the writings of men, drawn from particular backgrounds and outlooks, and underpinned by an imperial imperative, foreclosed the construction of travel as a meta-thesis of individual expression and self-identity?

Women travellers overcoming the male and the domestic

The transformation of the spatial mobility of women, from subservience to male aspirations and employment demands to the independence of women travellers, may be traced to the eighteenth century, and was implicitly very class-specific. Ironically, the modern pioneering spirit of women travellers began after Lady Mary Wortley Montagu (Halsband, 1965–7), decided to follow her husband on his appointment as British Ambassador to Turkey in 1716, thereby rendering London's chattering classes lost for words at such a precedent. Initially acquiescing in the role of an 'accompanist', once alone, however, she let her curiosity whet an appetite for travel.

The contemporary emphasis of aloneness as a female travel trait is particularly noticeable in publishers' hypes, acknowledging the lack of a need for men, but at the same time, perhaps being written by men in their own self-image, sounding almost incredulous that women would wish to be, and could survive, in such a condition. Emily Lowe (1859) would have had none of it. Describing herself proudly as an 'unprotected female', she maintained that men were only good for carrying luggage. For her, travelling with her mother and being treated with unremitting courtesy wherever they went, avoided the unnecessary passions and crises of (masculine) pride which travelling with adult males was likely to provoke. In sympathy with such sentiments, Mabel Crawford's (1863) *Through Algeria* was prefaced by a seven page 'Plea for lady tourists', in which she argued passionately against the injustices of a world that deemed women only fit to travel if accompanied by 'a gentleman'.

Progress was not easy: Esmé Scott-Stevenson (1879, 1881, 1883) for example, felt impelled to dedicate all three of her books to her husband, as peace-offerings for not having told him she was going into print: he was a man with an Important Position who could not afford to have a wife making a fool of herself (Robinson, 1990, p. 223). Subsequently, however, her discourses on Cyprus, Armenia and Turkey became standard texts.

Travel writers

Indulging women to be able to travel of their own volition was one thing. To then permit them to further encroach on the male domain by actually pursuing gainful employment through such travelling was quite another. Not until the mid-nineteenth century did women begin to earn a living by recounting their travels in published form. Louisa Costello (1840, 1842, 1844, 1846) is recognised as the first professional woman travel writer. To successfully extend the boundaries of women's activity space – both literally and metaphorically – required women to better men. Louisa Costello was not merely a successful author, but was also an accomplished artist and an experienced and imaginative traveller (Robinson, 1990, p. 177).

Paradoxically, also from the mid-nineteenth century, when the upper classes of Europe would gather in fashionable watering holes or on lower Alpine slopes, a glut of lightweight 'lady tourists'' illustrated writings appeared in print. The tendency in such texts to self-deprecating humour is ascribed by Mills (1991) to the fact that these particular female writers could less easily adopt the narrative voice of the *Boy's Own* adventure hero than could men (McKenna, 1992).

In recent years, the distinction between the writer who travels, for whom the final written word is the goal, and the traveller who writes, for whom the journey is the end in itself, has become particularly blurred as travel for writers has become more ubiquitous and as travellers have felt the need to write in order to help finance their travel. Both travellers who write and travel writers tend to alternate their writing and travelling, cultivating an audience of armchair travellers while encouraging the more active to follow in their footsteps. Jan Morris (e.g. 1972, 1976, 1980, 1984, 1992), may be regarded as a very good travel writer rather than a traveller, even though she has travelled further than most of those who would see themselves in the latter category. The role of women travel writers in setting agendas for the tourism experience should not be underestimated. Of some considerable note in this respect is Rose Macaulay, whose only true travel book, *Fabled shore: from the Pyrenees to Portugal* (1949), is claimed to have been at least partly responsible for the subsequent tourist development of the Iberian coastline, one of the most notable aspects of post-war European tourism,

> Which must make it one of the most successful – or most disastrous – travel books ever published. (Robinson, 1990, p. 95)

Travelling, writing and underpinning: gender, race and class

Among other groups of travelling women whose writings have been acknowledged, Robinson (1990) identifies 'diplomatic appendages' of empire, those travelling by default or caught up in wars, sieges and the like, reluctant travellers and women who travelled and stayed rather than returning home. Much has been made of the problematic role played by Victorian women travellers within empire (e.g. in Africa: Birkett, 1986; Frank, 1986a; 1986b; Oliver, 1982; Stevenson, 1982; Russell, 1986; Chaudhuri and Strobel, 1990; Strobel, 1991; Romero, 1992). As Blake (1990, p. 347) points out, at one end of a positional spectrum Lady Florence Douglas Dixie appears to have recognised and acknowledged the almost systemic connections between restrictions on women's rights in Britain and British imperialism overseas (Stevenson, 1982), while at the other end, Daisy Chown (1927) reiterates without question both imperial attitudes towards Africans and popular stereotypes of independent women. Paradoxically, travellers to Africa such as Mary Hall (1907) and Mary Kingsley (1897, 1899), mixed

> ... in varying proportions, endorsements of empire and accounts of personal experience that undercut it. (Blake, 1990, p. 348)

The extent to which the presence of colonial women was responsible for increasing the social distance between coloniser and colonised and thereby worsening race relations, has been long debated (Callan and Ardener, 1984; Strobel, 1987, 1991; Birkett, 1989). In acknowledging themselves to have been 'colonised' by gender, at least some women travellers recognised their own embodiment of the power and prestige of the ruling group and opposed colonisation based on race (Blake, 1990), addressing the racial status underpinning their own freedom of movement as Europeans within the imperium (Callaway, 1987).

However, at least in the case of Mary Hall's (1907) rejection of racial superiority as a source of power because of its inseparability from gender superiority, her passage from the Cape to Cairo nonetheless succumbed to an adoption of the authority of class:

> Her relations with the chief and other African royalty are reciprocal; with her servants and porters, maternal. (Blake, 1990, p. 353)

Proud of our routes

Then there are those women who have written about their attempts to trace their roots through geographical endeavour: retracing routes taken by their forebears to establish a personal cultural and spatial point of reference. Doris Lessing's (1957) return to Rhodesia, Esther Cheo Ying's (1980) going back to a transformed China, and Maya Angelou's (1987) root-tracing journey to Ghana are notable examples of this genre. Of particular pertinence to the contemporary British experience is Zenga Longmore's (1989) exploration of her Caribbean ancestry, which is suitably prefaced with a 'Farewell to Brixton'. Awareness of identity and the sense of both time and place are central to such travel and the literature it yields.

Media reconstruction(s)

In passing, we note and question the role of the latter day media in reconstructing women and their images. One extreme example has been the transformation of Hannah Hauxwell from an eccentric rustic, introspectively experiencing the expanse of the Yorkshire Dales, to a fêted travelling media star bedecked with Ascot hats and crinolin, all the while being ghost-written (by a man) (Hauxwell and Cockcroft, 1989, 1990, 1991a, 1991b, 1993). Muriel Gray's media image and exploits provide an interesting counterpoint to those of Hannah Hauxwell, although thus far she has only transferred some of her mountaineering experiences to the literature of travel (Gray, 1991).

THE WOMAN TRAVELLER CONSTRUCTED AS ROLE MODEL

In attaching importance to the role of women travellers in establishing new frameworks for the behaviour 'norms' and activity spaces of women, we confront the problem of the extent to which the media, publishers and travellers' own biographers have (re-)constructed them as role models. By definition, earlier travellers, of whatever gender, were far from representative of any but their privileged class group: they appeared to have time, connections, (financial) resources and a drive which most could not call upon. When Victorian women not only travelled but used that travelling as a means to an end – whether scientific, artistic or of a more prosaic nature – they were doubly removed, from other women and from societal norms, for seeking fulfilment in life other than with family and fireside.

In the portrayal of women travellers' discourses, publishers' rhetoric has tended to emphasise the 'individuality' of their authors' personal characteristics and the 'uniqueness' of their exploits, thereby exacerbating the problem of the credibility of the traveller as a role model:

> She married when she was sixteen and for seven years managed a sugar plantation in the Venezuelan Andes. Since 1981 she has moved between Norfolk, Scotland, Bristol, the Italian Riviera, Siena, London and Paris. (St Aubin de Terán, 1989, p. i)

Although privileged upbringing, unusual social tastes and extraordinary strength of character have tended to be reflected in
both female and male travellers, the 'ideals of feminine self-
sacrifice and duty' (Callaway, 1990, p. 405) imposed on women
and particularly youngest daughters, the roles of nurse and
carer for sick relatives, particularly parents. The deaths of such
loved ones released wives and daughters who may have long
been constrained by the confinement of their charges' infirmity
(Birkett, 1986). Emily Beaufort (1861, 1864), for example, began
travelling only following the death of her father, and Isabella
Bird (1880, 1883, 1891, 1894, 1899) was well into her forties when
she began travelling in earnest after the deaths of the parents for
whom, as youngest daughter, she had been designated to care.

Combining privilege and adversity, Alexandra David-Neel
(1927, 1936), the first European woman to enter Lhasa, ran away
from her unhappy home several times as a child, and her marriage lasted just five days. Yet, in addition to her travelling, she
was able to maintain a career as *première chanteuse* at the Opéra-
Comique in Paris together with serious study of theosophy and
Buddhism at the Sorbonne (Robinson, 1990, p. 9).

Certainly, changes in personal circumstance, whether a broken
romance or marriage, death of a close relative or sudden inheritance, have often appeared to provide the releasing mechanism
enabling women to embark on concerted travelling. Margaret
Fountaine, for example (1980, 1986), the daughter of a Norfolk
parson, came into an inheritance at the age of twenty-seven, in
1889, sufficient for her to indulge her passions for travel and
collecting butterflies. Although women travellers as sex objects is
not an agenda explicitly addressed by publishers and biographers, Margaret Fountaine's claimed additional passion for 'Un-
suitable Attachments' (sic) (Robinson, 1990, p. 132) does seem to
have marked her for some sensationalist attention from her
(posthumous) publishers, somewhat overshadowing her achieve-
ments in the art of travel and in scientific discovery:

> . . . in addition to her fabulous butterfly collection – she netted, among
> others, an Egyptian ship's officer, an aristocratic Hungarian, a Sicilian
> butterfly-hunter and a married Syrian dragoman with whom she spent
> twenty-eight years enjoying great happiness. (Fountaine, 1980, 1982 pa-
> perback issue, back cover)

Re-gendered travellers

We note two elements of this process. The 'renaming' and even 're-gendering' of women travellers as 'honorary men' by their hosts sometimes acted as a mechanism of accommodation within the structure and function of the host society. Particularly in relation to nineteenth century women travellers, however, we would question the extent to which such 're-gendering' reinforced the 'masculinisation' of their role as perceived by Western society.

Secondly, has the re-gendering of James/Jan Morris influenced the perceptions and direction of that travelling writer? She would argue that from an early age particular gender orientations were already in place to confound outward biological indicators (Morris, 1974, 1989). As a consequence, processes of ageing and experience would be seen to be of infinitely greater significance than her 1972 'gender rôle change' (Robinson, 1990, p. 189) operation. Her publishers would appear largely to concur with this sentiment, now referring exclusively to *her* exploits in books which *he* wrote (e.g. Morris, 1969 (1985 paperback version), back cover). Yet, as a man, James was able to ride with the Sultan of Oman (Morris, 1957) and intimately converse with New York longshoremen (Morris, 1969) in situations where, as Jan, she would be unable to do so. Conversely, Jan is able to gain access to male-proscribed situations to which James would not have been privy.

Gendered travellers in gendered places?

An essential ingredient of the recent 'marketing' of women travellers is the commoditisation of exoticism: marginal voices in marginal texts succumbing to, for example, the lure of high and mystical places. Most notable among such lures has been Tibet, not least for the forbidden (and forbidding?) nature of its capital (Annie Taylor, 1894; Susie Carson Rijnhart, 1901; Carey, 1902; Jenkins, 1909; Audrey Harris, 1939; Dervla Murphy, 1966; Christina Dodwell, 1985; Margaret Fountaine, 1980, 1986; Hadfield and Hadfield, 1988; Catriona Bass, 1990; Gill Marais, 1991). Most notable within this genre has been the portrayal of Alexandra

David-Neel (1927, 1936), who, precisely because she was forbidden on pain of death to do such a thing, set out in 1923 to become the first European woman to reach the sacred Tibetan capital. Such travel was undertaken in the face of both environmental adversity and male ridicule, at least from the traveller's own countrymen. Indeed, in her Foucauldian analysis of women's travel writing and colonialism, Sara Mills (1991) highlights the incredulous reception which David-Neel's first account of her Tibetan exploits received from Western (male) audiences as typical of the way in which women's texts were invalidated or questioned.

'Little Tibet' (Kashmir), as the northern extremity of British India, has provided a similar if less dramatic, exotic foregrounding to women travellers' discourses (Harriet Aynsley, 1879; Isabella Bird, 1894; Marion Doughty, 1902; Ella Maillart, 1937; Caroline Noble, 1987; Brigid Keenan, 1990; Helen Norberg-Hodge, 1992). Reinforcing the exotic has been the portrayal of women on the edge of empire as 'eccentric' and 'imperial': when Jane Duncan (1906) travelled in Kashmir and Tibet for half a year, much publicity was given to the fact that her eighty-pound 'Cabul' tent was replete with brass bedstead and separate 'bathroom' (Robinson, 1990, p. 43). Both Bhutan (Katie Hickman, 1987) and Nepal (Ella Maillart, 1955; Murphy, 1967; Elaine Brook, 1986, 1987; Monica Connell, 1991), despite the latter's notoriety as the terminus of the hippy trail, have provided contexts of high mystical places through which women travellers have pursued their discourses.

The Arab and wider Islamic world, while presenting insurmountable proscriptions for women travellers, has also allowed them into situations from which men would be barred (e.g. see the writings of Nawal el Saadawi, 1980, 1991). Legacies of empire in the Middle East, together with the region's latent volatility and strongly permeating mystique of 'otherness', have acted as a potent catalyst for women travellers' writings, the most prolific being those of Freya Stark (1934, 1936, 1937, 1940, 1956, 1958, 1959, 1966, 1970; also, for example, Crawford, 1863; Maillart, 1947). (For more recent discourses see Christina Dodwell (1987), Bettina Selby (1988, 1993), Kathleen Jamie (1992) and Sylvia Kennedy (1992)). Closer to home, overcoming the prescriptions and constraints of the Muslim Balkans has been a source of inspiration for a number of women travellers (Allcock and Young, 1991; Finder, 1991). Most notably, the writings of Edith Durham (1904, 1905, 1909, 1914, 1920, 1925, 1928) still provide some of the most important and colourful records of pre-independence Albania and adjacent lands (Hill, 1991; Hodgson, 1991; Hall, 1994).

Gendered travellers in gendered mode?

The gendering of travel mode has resonated particularly around women travellers' accounts. Publishers highlight the 'un-feminine' (bicycles, horses, camels, canoes, mountaineering), and yet tend to de-emphasise women's 'progressive' harnessing of technology (Christina Dodwell's (1989) exploits with a micro-light across West Africa appears to be an exception, but these appeal to audiences of exotica).

The 'lungs, wind and limbs' syndrome has some pedigree. Miss Erskine's (1885, 1896, 1897) Lady's Safety Cycle, soon evolved into an acceptable form of transport and exercise. From the evangelist Lucy Broad (1909) to Josie Dew (1992: adorned with a front cover photograph of the author executing a hand-stand, legs akimbo, by her trusty steed, in the Faroe Islands), the bicycle has become a well accepted instrument of movement and relaxation, as well as an ecological symbol, through which women travellers have expressed identity (e.g. Dervla Murphy, 1965; Christian Miller, 1980; Bettina Selby, 1984, 1985, 1988, 1993; Georgina Harding, 1990; Anne Mustoe, 1992). Sailing has also developed as a framework for discourse in which women have been to the forefront, most notably Ann Davison (1951, 1956, 1962, 1964), Clare Francis (1977, 1978), and Rosie Swale (1974, 1986). On a somewhat different level, Ella Maillart (1942) and Freya Stark (1956) also became closely associated with travel on water, albeit of a more leisurely nature.

The Ladies' Alpine Club was founded in 1907 to foster and encourage the art and science of mountaineering, and the Pinnacle Club, its rock-climbing equivalent, was established in 1921. Of all the 'unfeminine' activities related to travel, arguably mountaineering has developed furthest, inspired by such women as Dorothy Pilley (1935), the outstanding woman mountaineer of the 1920s, Gwen Moffat (1961), Britain's first qualified female climbing guide, Janet Adam Smith (1946) and Nea Morin (1968), two of Britain's best women mountaineers.

ANTHROPOLOGISTS AND EXPLORERS

Of contemporary women travellers who write, two approaches to their art can perhaps be discerned, echoing the outlook of earlier years. For 'anthropologists' and 'explorers' alike there is inevitably a strong element of self-discovery in the art of travel, but the major contrast between the two is that 'explorers' lead, make waves, do extrovert things, draw attention to themselves, explore travel itself and its relationship with its physical and cultural context. By contrast, 'anthropologists', as participant-observers, try to meld into the background, not always suc-cessfully, as this reflective piece reveals:

> The lobby of my hotel was filled with the most beautiful women I have ever seen . . . These were the women of Leningrad who emerged from their stale desk jobs or secretary pools every Friday night to service the Finnish men . . . these . . . women . . . sat like mannequins, lips perfectly glossed, eyelashes thick as horse hair, curled to perfection, cheeks with just the right blush . . . Their dead eyes gazed at me as I entered their midst dressed in jeans, bulky shirt. I thought about turning back, but it became a matter of pride. Instead I traversed the obstacle course set up by their legs which stretched across the room . . . I looked across for sympathetic eyes and found none. Just blank stares and suspicious looks. They must have been having a slow night . . . they wanted to know what I was doing there, intruding upon their terrain. I sat nursing my vodka, staring into its cold glass. (Morris, 1993, pp. 180–2)

Inevitably, it is the 'explorers', such as Dervla Murphy (1965, 1966, 1967, 1968, 1976, 1977, 1978, 1979, 1983, 1985, 1989) who, with their higher profile, challenge both women and men in their 'mould-breaking' self-images. Christina Dodwell is one of the more notable current members of this 'school'. Her travel-ling started in 1975 when, aged twenty-four, she forsook a series of unfulfilling jobs to answer an advertisement for a travel com-panion. Although never having carried a rucksack before, the outcome of that response was to see her embarking on a three-year journey across Africa (Dodwell, 1979) by any means available:

> She walked; she rode horses, camels and zebroids; she cadged lifts on anything with a wheel or two and even spent several weeks paddling along the Congo in a dug-out canoe. (Robinson, 1990, p. 90)

Further journeys of exploring both new environments – Papua New Guinea, China, Turkey, Kamchatka – and ways of traversing those environments, ranging from reindeer and dog sleds, through white-water rafting, to microlight flying (Dodwell, 1983, 1984, 1985, 1987, 1989, 1993) followed, such that she could be hailed as

> . . . one of those intrepid British female explorers in the great tradition that stretches from Mary Kingsley to Freya Stark (*Daily Express*, quoted on the front cover of Dodwell, 1989 paperback).

Indeed,

> I identify with a tradition of British women explorers, including the Victorian Mary Kingsley, who fell through a hut's thatched roof saying, 'it's only me'. (*Guardian Weekend*, 26 June 1993, p. 62)

Appearing on both UK television and radio, having taken sound recording equipment on her last foray at least (Dodwell, 1993), Christina Dodwell appears to have developed a style which not only her readers but also the media have been able to adopt, and perhaps adapt.

> Readers of her earlier books know that combination of feminine common sense and a certain carelessness as to her own safety or comfort . . . she keeps her eyes open, her good humour intact. (*Sunday Times*, quoted in the endpaper of Dodwell, 1993)

QUESTIONS

As indicated in Cynthia Enloe's quotation heading this chapter, any assessment of the role of women travellers is fogged with contradictions, and a number of paradoxes remain to be unravelled:

(i) the extent to which the ambiguous and ambivalent relationship between Victorian women travellers and imperial race, class and gender relationships is embodied in women travellers of the late twentieth century, reinforcing global inequalities and insidiously promoting cultural imperialism;

(ii) the degree to which, in their attitudes, modes of travel, travelling environments and subsequent discourses, women travellers may be distinguished from men travellers;

(iii) this raises the question as to whether women travellers are spiritually closer to their male counterparts than to other women;

(iv) the extent to which social construction and media reconstruction foreground discourse and foreclose debate;

(v) the (lost) value of the unwritten literature of women travellers (and tourists), which remains unwritten because of class, race and gender constraints.

REFERENCES

Abbott, S., Tyrrell, M.A., 1990, *The world wheelchair traveller*, Automobile Association/Spinal Injuries Association, Basingstoke.

Adam Smith, J., 1946, *Mountaineering holidays*, J.M. Dent, London.

Aitken, M., 1987, *A girdle round the earth: adventuresses abroad*, Constable, London.

Allcock, J.B., Young, A., 1991, *Black lambs and grey falcons: women travellers in the Balkans*, Bradford University Press, Bradford.

Allen, A., 1983, *Travelling ladies: Victorian adventuresses*, Jupiter, London.

Angelou, M., 1987, *All God's children need travelling shoes*, Virago, London.

Arnot Robertson, E., 1931, *Four frightened people*, Jonathan Cape, London. Republished 1982 by Virago, London.

Aynsley, H., 1879, *Our visit to Hindostan, Kashmir, and Ladakh*, Wm Allen, London.

Babcock, B.A., Parezo, N.J., 1988, *Daughters of the desert: women anthropologists and the Native American Southwest, 1880–1980*, University of New Mexico Press, Albuquerque.

Barnard, J., 1993, *The woman's travel guide: New York*, Virago, London.

Bass, C., 1990, *Inside the treasure house: a time in Tibet*, Victor Gollancz, London.

Beaufort, E., 1861, *Egyptian sepulchres and Syrian shrines*, Longman, London, 2 vols.

Beaufort, E., 1864, *The eastern shores of the Adriatic in 1863; with a visit to Montenegro*, Richard Bentley, London.

Belford, R., 1993, *The woman's travel guide: Rome*, Virago, London.

Berman, M., 1974, Sex discrimination and geography: the case of Ellen Churchill Semple, *Professional Geographer*, **26**: 8–11.

Bird, I.L., 1880, *Unbeaten tracks in Japan*, John Murray, London, 2 vols.

Bird, I.L., 1883, *The Golden Chersonese and the way thither*, John Murray, London.

Bird, I.L., 1891, *Journeys in Persia and Kurdistan*, John Murray, London, 2 vols.

Bird, I.L., 1894, *Among the Tibetans*, Religious Tract Society, London.

Bird, I.L., 1899, *The Yangtse Valley and beyond*, John Murray, London.

Birkett, D., 1986, The invalid at home, the Samson abroad, *Women's Review*, **6**: 18–19.

Birkett, D., 1989, *Spinsters abroad: Victorian lady explorers*, Basil Blackwell, Oxford.

Blake, S.L., 1990, A woman's trek: what difference does gender make? *Women's Studies International Forum*, **13**(4): 347–55.

Bowler, J., 1990, *The vegetarian travel guide 1991*, The Vegetarian Society UK, Altrincham, Cheshire.

Broad, L., 1909, *A woman's wanderings the world over*, Headley Bros., London.

Bronson, J.A.C., 1975, A further note on sex discrimination and geography: some thoughts on Ellen Churchill Semple, *Professional Geographer*, **15**: 102–9.

Brook, E., 1986, *The windhorse*, Cape, London.

Brook, E., 1987, *Land of the snow lion*, Cape, London.

Bulstrode, B., 1920, *A tour in Mongolia*, Methuen, London.

Callan, H., Ardener, S. (eds), 1984, *The incorporated wife*, Croom Helm, London.

Callaway, H., 1987, *Gender, culture and empire: European women in colonial Nigeria*, University of Illinois Press, Urbana.

Callaway, H., 1990, Book reviews: *A voyager out; Spinsters abroad*, *Women's Studies International Forum*, **13**(4): 405.

Carey, W., 1902, *Travel and adventure in Tibet: including the diary of Miss Annie R. Taylor's remarkable journey from Tau-Chau to Ta-Chien-Lu through the heart of the forbidden land*, Hodder and Stoughton, London.

Chaudhuri, N., Strobel, M., 1990, Western women and imperialism: introduction, *Women's Studies International Forum*, **13**(4): 289–93.

Chown, D., 1927, *Wayfaring in Africa: a woman's wanderings from the Cape to Cairo*, Heath Cranton, London.

Connell, M., 1991, *Against a peacock sky*, Viking, London.

Costello, L., 1840, *A summer amongst the bocages and the vines*, R. Bentley, London, 2 vols.

Costello, L., 1842, *A pilgrimage to Auvergne, from Picardy to Le Velay*, R. Bentley, London, 2 vols.

Costello, L., 1844, *Béarn and the Pyrenees: a legendary tour to the country of Henri Quatre*, R. Bentley, London, 2 vols.

Costello, L., 1846, *A tour to and from Venice, by the Vaudois and the Tyrol*, John Ollivier, London.

Crawford, M.S., 1863, *Through Algeria*, R. Bentley, London.

Cullen, C., 1993, *The woman's travel guide: Paris*, Virago, London.

David-Neel, A., 1927, *My journey to Lhasa: the personal story of the only white woman who succeeded in entering the forbidden city*, Heinemann, London.

David-Neel, A., 1936, *Tibetan journey*, John Lane, London.

Davies, M., Longrigg, L., Montefiore, L., Jansz, N. (eds), 1986, *Half the earth: women's experience of travel worldwide*, Pandora, London.

Davies, M., Jansz, N. (eds), 1990, *Women travel: adventures, advice and experience*, Harrap Columbus, London.

Davison, A., 1951, *Last voyage*, Davies, London.

Davison, A., 1956, *My ship is so small*, Davies, London.

Davison, A., 1962, *By Gemini: a coastwise cruise from Miami to Miami*, Davies, London.

Davison, A., 1964, *Florida junket: the story of a shoestring cruise*, Davies, London.

Dew, J., 1992, *The wind in my wheels*, Little Brown and Company, London.

Dodwell, C., 1979, *Travels with fortune: an African adventure*, W.H. Allen, London.

Dodwell, C., 1983, *In Papua New Guinea*, Oxford Illustrated Press, Yeovil.

Dodwell, C., 1984, *The explorer's handbook*, Hodder and Stoughton, London.

Dodwell, C., 1985, *A traveller in China*, Hodder and Stoughton, London.

Dodwell, C., 1987, *A traveller on horseback in Eastern Turkey and Iran*, Hodder and Stoughton, London.

Dodwell, C., 1989, *Travels with Pegasus: a microlight journey across West Africa*, Hodder and Stoughton, London.

Dodwell, C., 1993, *Beyond Siberia*, Hodder and Stoughton, London.

Domosh, M., 1991a, Towards a feminist historiography of geography, *Transactions of the Institute of British Geographers (New Series)*, **16**(1): 95–104.

Domosh, M., 1991b, Beyond the frontiers of geographical knowledge, *Transactions of the Institute of British Geographers (New Series)*, **16**(4): 488–90.

Doughty, M., 1902, *Afoot through the Kashmir Valley*, Sands, London.

Duncan, J.E., 1906, *A summer ride through Western Tibet*, Smith, Elder, London.

Durham, M.E., 1904, *Through the lands of the Serb*, Edward Arnold, London.

Durham, M.E., 1905, *The burden of the Balkans*, Edward Arnold, London.

Durham, M.E., 1909, *High Albania*, Edward Arnold, London.

Durham, M.E., 1914, *The struggle for Scutari (Turk, Slav and Albanian)*, Edward Arnold, London.

Durham, M.E., 1920, *Twenty years of the Balkan tangle*, George Allen and Unwin, London.

Durham, M.E., 1925, *The Sarajevo crime*, George Allen and Unwin, London.

Durham, M.E., 1928, *Some tribal origins, laws and customs of the Balkans*, George Allen and Unwin, London.

el Saadawi, N., 1980, *The hidden face of Eve*, Zed Books, London.

el Saadawi, N., 1991, *My travels around the world*, Methuen, London.

Enloe, C., 1989, *Bananas, beaches and bases: making feminist sense of international politics*, Pandora, London.

Erskine, F.J., 1885, *Tricycling for ladies: or, hints on the choice and management of tricycles with suggestions on dress, riding and touring*, Illiffe, London.

Erskine, F.J., 1896, *Bicycling for ladies*, Illiffe, London.

Erskine, F.J., 1897, *Lady cycling*, W. Scott, London.

Ferrari, M. (ed.), 1991, *International places of interest to women*, Ferarri, Phoenix, Arizona.

Finder, J., 1991, Women travellers in the Balkans: a bibliographical guide, in Allcock, J.B., Young, A., 1991, *Black lambs and grey falcons: women travellers in the Balkans*, Bradford University Press, Bradford, pp. 192–201.

Fountaine, M., 1980, *Love among the butterflies: the travels and adventures of a Victorian lady*, Collins, London. Republished 1982 by Penguin, London, with the new sub-title, *The diaries of a wayward, determined and passionate Victorian lady*.

Fountaine, M., 1986, *Butterflies and late loves: the further travels and adventures of a Victorian lady*, Collins, London.

Francis, C., 1977, *Come hell or high water*, Pelham, London.

Francis, C., 1978, *Come wind or weather*, Pelham, London.

Frank, K., 1986a, *A voyager out: the life of Mary Kingsley*, Houghton Mifflin, Boston.

Frank, K., 1986b, Voyages out: nineteenth century women travelers in Africa, in Sharistanian, J. (ed.), *Gender, ideology and action: historical perspectives on women's public lives*, Greenwood, Westport CT, pp. 67–93.

Gordimer, N., 1979, *Burger's daughter*, Jonathan Cape, London.

Gray, M., 1991, *The first fifty: Munro-bagging without a beard*, Mainstream, Glasgow.

Hadfield, C., Hadfield, J., 1988, *A winter in Tibet*, Impact, London.

Hall, D.R., 1994, *Albania: development and change*, Pinter, London.

Hall, M., 1907, *A woman's trek from the Cape to Cairo*, Methuen, London.

Halsband, R. (ed.), 1965–7, *The complete letters of Lady Mary Wortley Montagu*, Clarendon Press, Oxford, 3 vols.

Harding, G., 1990, *In another Europe*, Hodder and Stoughton, London.

Harris, A., 1939, *Eastern vistas*, Collins, London.

Hauxwell, H., Cockcroft, B., 1989, *Seasons of my life: the story of a solitary Daleswoman*, Century Hutchinson, London.

Hauxwell, H., Cockcroft, B., 1990, *Daughter of the Dales: the world of Hannah Hauxwell*, Century, London.

Hauxwell, H., Cockcroft, B., 1991a, *Hannah the complete story*, Century, London.

Hauxwell, H., Cockcroft, B., 1991b, *Innocent abroad*, Random House, London.

Hauxwell, H., Cockcroft, B., 1993, *Hannah's North Country*, Century, London.

Hickman, K., 1987, *Dreams of the peaceful dragon: a journey into Bhutan*, Victor Gollancz, London.

Hill, J., 1991, Edith Durham as a collector, in Allcock, J.B., Young, A., 1991, *Black lambs and grey falcons: women travellers in the Balkans*, Bradford University Press, Bradford, pp. 29–34.

Hodgson, J., 1991, Edith Durham, traveller and publicist, in Allcock, J.B., Young, A., 1991, *Black lambs and grey falcons: women travellers in the Balkans*, Bradford University Press, Bradford, pp. 8–28.

Jamie, K., 1992, *The golden peak: travels in Northern Pakistan*, Virago, London.

Jenkins, Lady (C.M.), 1909, *Sport and travel in both Tibets*, Blades, East and Blades, London.

Kanga, F., 1991, *Heaven on wheels*, Bloomsbury, London.

Keay, J., 1989, *With passport & parasol: the adventures of seven Victorian ladies*, BBC Books, London.

Keenan, B., 1990, *Travels in Kashmir*, Oxford University Press, Oxford, New York, Delhi.

Keller, E.F., 1985, *Reflections on gendered science*, Yale University Press, New Haven.

Kennedy, S., 1992, *See Ouarzazate and die: travels through Morocco*, Scribners, London.

Kingsley, M., 1897, *Travels in West Africa: Congo Français, Corisco and Cameroons*, Macmillan, London.

Kingsley, M., 1899, *West African studies*, Macmillan, London.

Lees, D., Lees, M., 1988, *Travel in retirement*, Christopher Helm, London.

Lessing, D., 1957, *Going home*, Michael Joseph, London.

Longmore, Z., 1989, *Tap-taps to Trinidad: a journey through the Caribbean*, Hodder and Stoughton, London.

Lowe, E., 1859, *Unprotected females in Sicily, Calabria, and on the top of Mount Ætna*, Routledge, Warnes and Routledge, London.

Macaulay, R., 1949, *Fabled shore: from the Pyrenees to Portugal*, Hamish Hamilton, London.

McCarthy, Á., 1992, *Get up and go: a travel survival kit for women*, Attic Press, Dublin.

McCarthy, M., 1959, *The stones of Florence*, Heinemann, London.

McCarthy, M., 1961, *Venice observed*, Heinemann, London.

McKenna, B., 1992, Insightful travellers on imperial roads, *The Higher*, 13 March.

Maillart, E.K., 1937, *Forbidden journey: from Peking to Kashmir*, Heinemann, London.

Maillart, E.K., 1942, *Gypsy afloat*, Heinemann, London.

Maillart, E.K., 1947, *The cruel way*, Heinemann, London. Reprinted, 1986 by Virago, London.

Maillart, E.K., 1955, *The land of the Sherpas*, Hodder and Stoughton, London.

Marais, G., 1991, *Right over the mountain*, Element, Shaftsbury.

Melchett, S., 1991, *Passionate guests: five modern women travellers*, Heinemann, London.

Middleton, D., 1965, *Victorian lady travellers*, John Murray, London.

Miller, C., 1980, *Daisy, Daisy: a journey across America on a bicycle*, Routledge and Kegan Paul, London.

Mills, S., 1991, *Discourses of difference: an analysis of women's travel writing and colonialism*, Routledge, London.

Moffat, G., 1961, *Space below my feet*, Hodder and Stoughton, London.

Morin, N., 1968, *A woman's reach: mountaineering memoirs*, Eyre and Spottiswoode, London.

Morris, J., 1957, *Sultan in Oman*, Faber, London.

Morris, J., 1969, *The great port*, Oxford University Press, Oxford.

Morris, J., 1972, *Places*, Faber, London.

Morris, J., 1974, *Conundrum*, Faber, London.

Morris, J., 1976, *Travels*, Faber, London.

Morris, J., 1980, *Destinations*, Oxford University Press, Oxford.

Morris, J., 1984, *Journeys*, Oxford University Press, Oxford.

Morris, J., 1989, *Pleasures of a tangled life*, Barrie and Jenkins, London.

Morris, J., 1992, *Locations*, Oxford University Press, Oxford.

Morris, M., 1988, *Nothing to declare: memoirs of a woman travelling alone*, Hamish Hamilton, London.

Morris, M., 1993, *Wall to wall: a woman's travels from Beijing to Berlin*, Flamingo, London.

Moss, M., Moss, G., 1987, *Handbook for women travellers*, Judy Piatkus, London.

Murphy, D., 1965, *Full tilt: Ireland to India with a bicycle*, John Murray, London.

Murphy, D., 1966, *Tibetan foothold*, John Murray, London.

Murphy, D., 1967, *The waiting land: a spell in Nepal*, John Murray, London.

Murphy, D., 1968, *In Ethiopia with a mule*, John Murray, London.

Murphy, D., 1976, *On a shoestring to Coorg: an experience of South India*, John Murray, London.

Murphy, D., 1977, *Where the Indus is young: a winter in Baltistan*, John Murray, London.

Murphy, D., 1978, *A place apart*, John Murray, London.

Murphy, D., 1979, *Wheels within wheels*, John Murray, London.

Murphy, D., 1983, *Eight feet in the Andes*, John Murray, London.

Murphy, D., 1985, *Muddling through in Madagascar*, John Murray, London.

Murphy, D., 1989, *Cameroon with Egbert*, John Murray, London.

Mustoe, A., 1992, *A bike ride: 12,000 miles around the world*, Virgin, London.

Noble, C., 1987, *Over the high passes: a year in the Himalayas*, Collins, London.

Norberg-Hodge, H., 1992, *Ancient futures: learning from Ladakh*, Rider Books, London.

Olds, E.F., 1985, *Women of the four winds*, Houghton Mifflin, Boston.

Oliver, C., 1982, *Western women in colonial Africa*, Greenwood, Westport CT.

Phillips, P., 1990, *The scientific lady: a social history of women's scientific interests, 1520–1918*, Weidenfeld and Nicolson, London.

Pilley, D., 1935, *Climbing days*, G. Bell, London.

Rijnhart, S.C., 1901, *With the Tibetans in tent and temple*, Oliphant, Anderson and Ferrier, Edinburgh.

Robinson, J., 1990, *Wayward women: a guide to women travellers*, Oxford University Press, Oxford.

Romero, P.W. (ed.), 1992, *Women's voices on Africa: a century of travel writings*, Markus Wiener, Princeton and New York.

Russell, M., 1986, *The blessings of a good thick skirt: women travellers and their world*, Collins, London.

St Aubin de Terán, L., 1989, *Off the rails: memoirs of a train addict*, Bloomsbury, London.

Sanger, A., 1987, *The vegetarian traveller*, Thorsons, London.

Scott-Stevenson, E., 1879, *Our home in Cyprus*, Chapman and Hall, London.

Scott-Stevenson, E., 1881, *Our ride through Asia Minor*, Chapman and Hall, London.

Scott-Stevenson, E., 1883, *On summer seas*, Chapman and Hall, London.

Selby, B., 1984, *Riding the mountains down*, Victor Gollancz, London.

Selby, B., 1985, *Riding to Jerusalem*, Sidgwick and Jackson, London.

Selby, B., 1988, *Riding the desert trail: by bicycle to the source of the Nile*, Chatto and Windus, London.

Selby, B., 1993, *Beyond Ararat: a journey through Eastern Turkey*, John Murray, London.

Siegel, P.J., Finley, K.T., 1985, *Women in the scientific search: an American bibliography, 1724–1979*, Scarecrow Press, Metuchen NJ.

Smith, C., 1989, *Off the beaten track: women adventurers and mountaineers in western Canada*, Coyote Books, Lake Louise, Alberta.

Spanidou, I., 1987, *God's snake*, Secker and Warburg, London.

Stanford, J. (ed.), 1990, *Holidays and travel abroad 1990/91: a guide for disabled people*, The Royal Association for Disability and Rehabilitation, London.

Stark, F., 1934, *The valleys of the assassins, and other Persian travels*, John Murray. Reprinted 1991 by Arrow, London.

Stark, F., 1936, *The southern gates of Arabia: a journey in the Hadhramaut*, John Murray, London.

Stark, F., 1937, *Baghdad sketches*, John Murray, London. Reprinted 1992 by The Marlboro Press, Marlboro Vermont.

Stark, F., 1940, *A winter in Arabia*, John Murray, London.

Stark, F., 1956, *The Lycian shore: along the coast of Turkey by yacht*, John Murray, London.

Stark, F., 1958, *Alexander's path from Caria to Cilicia*, John Murray, London.

Stark, F., 1959, *Riding to the Tigris*, John Murray, London.

Stark, F., 1966, *Rome on the Euphrates: the story of a frontier*, John Murray, London.

Stark, F., 1970, *The minaret of Djam: an excursion in Afghanistan*, John Murray, London.

Stevenson, C.B., 1982, *Victorian women travel writers in Africa*, Twayne, Boston.

Stoddart, D.R., 1986, *On geography and its history*, Basil Blackwell, Oxford.

Stoddart, D.R., 1991, Do we need a feminist historiography of geography – and if we do, what should it be? *Transactions of the Institute of British Geographers (New Series)*, **16**(4): 484–7.

Strobel, M., 1987, Gender and race in the nineteenth- and twentieth-century British Empire, in Bridenthal, R., Koonz, C., Stuard, S.M. (eds), *Becoming visible*, Houghton Mifflin, Boston, pp. 375–96.

Strobel, M., 1991, *European women in British Africa and Asia*, Indiana University Press, Bloomington.

Swale, R., 1974, *Children of Cape Horn*, Paul Elek, London.

Swale, R., 1986, *Back to Cape Horn*, Collins, London.

Taylor, A., 1894, *The origin of the Tibetan Pioneer Mission, together with some facts about Tibet*, Morgan and Scott, London.

Tinling, M., 1989, *Women into the unknown: a sourcebook on women explorers and travellers*, Greenwood Press, New York.

Van Gelder, L., Brandt, P.R., 1992, *Are you two . . . together?*, Virago, London.

Walsh, A. (ed.), 1991, *Nothing ventured: disabled people travel the world*, Harrap Columbus, London.

Wheeler, M., 1985, *Travel with children*, Lonely Planet, Hawthorn, Victoria, Australia.

Ying, E.C., 1980, *Black Country to Red China*, Century Hutchinson, London.

Zepatos, T., 1992, *A journey of one's own: uncommon advice for the independent woman traveler*, The Eighth Motivation Press, Portland, Oregon.

10
Conclusion: the way forward

Vivian Kinnaird and Derek Hall

GENDERED TOURISM

One aim of this volume has been to draw on a range of contributions in order to prompt further discussion and debate on the
gendered nature of tourism-related activities and processes.
There is no doubt that consideration of the social construction of
tourism is a major focus of discussion within the tourism literature. Analysing tourism's role in capital accumulation, and in
creating the social meaning of places is significant, and highlights relationships of power and control at a number of levels.
Within an international economic framework, these relationships are configured by the income-earning potential that the
tourism industry brings, particularly to large, multinational
companies which are involved in many horizontally and ver-
tically structured aspects of tourism provision. They are responsible for setting a tourism agenda which locates destinations
within a complex international political and economic environment that is largely controlled by their own financial interests.

Yet, discussions of power relationships must also focus on the
national scale and at regional and local levels, where the interface between host and guest takes place. Nationally, differences
between class, race and ethnicity may underpin the types of
tourism-related activity offered and the ways in which tourism
is promoted and experienced by different groups. We cite the

examples of British 'royalty', whose justification as an institution is partially due to their popularity with tourists, or the promotion of 'ethnic tourism' by governments eager to reveal the uniqueness of aspects of their societies, such as the indigenous Indian populations of Central and South America. In Chapter 6, Peggy Fairbairn-Dunlop concludes by stating that Samoan women have been able to 'capitalise on the opportunities [tourism] offers because their rights have been safeguarded by customary norms'. Thus, the uniqueness of Samoan customs and traditions serves to offer tourists a chance to gaze on Samoan 'otherness' which includes the articulation of 'traditional' Samoan gender roles and relations.

Similarly, issues of race and ethnicity are evident in the promotion of sex tourism in South-east Asia, where the majority of sex tourism workers are members of ethnic minorities who have not, historically, held power or influence in national decision-making. Michael Hall (Chapter 7) notes the significance of economic marginality and racial inequality as factors which enable the perpetuation of a prevailing indigenous set of gender relations. These in turn allow the maintenance of sex tourism and the view that the image of the passive, subservient woman is representative of east Asian women.

The way in which gender roles and relations are represented in the process of tourism development is another aspect of political power sharing which is readily seen at the local level. The differential experiences of women and men, and their social interaction with others as either hosts or guests, is dependent upon the particular construction of gender relations in any society and how these are changing over time. Examples of women's role and position in tourism-related employment (including the sex tourism industry), in representing 'culture' and 'tradition', and in their motivations for engaging in tourism-related activity (as either hosts or guests) attest to this claim. The involvement of women in new tourism enterprises in Ireland (Chapter 3) is accepted in a society where, historically, women's work has been intensely controlled. The view of women in their role as wife, mother and the carer of others has remained dominant in Irish society. Consequently, the extension of this role into providing lodgings for tourists is acceptable. This type of activity does not challenge prevailing notions of gender roles and relations.

The contributions to this book represent various gender perspectives of tourism and tourism development. They provide strong arguments for the value of utilising gender as an organising social framework for an analysis of tourism development processes. They highlight the ways in which societal constructs and practices cut across conventional categories of social analysis, particularly analyses of tourism. Consequently, it is difficult to look at the economic 'impacts' or tourism without an integrated discussion of their social and political implications. Similarly, environmental issues can be analysed as highly politicised, social and economic concerns which pay attention to differing perceptions of the environment and the ways in which they change over time.

In the light of the case studies and related discussions, we can suggest that analyses of tourism development need to take into consideration the following:

1. *Gendered tourists*:
We need to pay attention to the ways in which we assume a homogeneous notion of leisure and motivation for the participation in tourism-related activities. Critical social scientists have already reminded us that the idea of a work/leisure dichotomy in contemporary modern society is problematic. The motivations behind travel are constructed out of the social realities of the lives of those who participate in tourism-related activity. By definition, this implies that these motivations are gendered. Women's and men's differential experience of various recreational activities and the socialisation of girls and boys to enjoy and participate in gender-specific activities have an influence on motivation and behaviour.

The different way in which male and female travellers are viewed by their societies is of importance too. Men who travel alone (or with other groups of men) may often be perceived as either being involved in some type of adventure-seeking activity, such as mountain climbing or expeditions undertaken for scientific interest, or are participating in sex tourism. Lone women travellers are often perceived as participating in something that is abnormal within the context of their position in society. At the same time, however, they are also heralded as very brave, ambitious people who exemplify the heights to which women can rise in achieving that which is normally expected of men, as noted in our discussion of women travellers in Chapter 9. The recent media hype of the first British woman to climb Mount Everest says as much about British society's expectations of women's participation in mountain climbing as it does about the climber's personal feat. She may have been Britain's first woman climber, but many women from around the world have preceded her ascent of the mountain.

Society's expectations of men's and women's involvement in tourism-related activity is mediated by the way in which tourism is promoted as a (heterosexual) couple's or family's annual pursuit. Packages are sold relying on at least two participants, and the 'honeymoon' images of many resorts reinforce specific types of gender relationships at home. However, challenges to this notion are now being heard. For example, the BBC *Holiday* magazine has been running a campaign to highlight the high cost of the single person supplement.

2. *Gendered hosts*:
As we have seen in many of the chapters in this volume, the gendering of tourism employment and the tourism-related activities of hosts reveal the heterogeneity of the individuals that comprise the host society. In the Caribbean (Chapter 5), for example, women and men are involved in different types of tourism service provision. Women are more apt to be working as chambermaids or as kitchen help. Men are often more directly involved with the guests as waiters and bartenders. Their hospitality is a large part of the 'good time' atmosphere of the beachfront resorts and hotels.

We need to pay particular attention to who is doing the work that is needed to provide tourists with the services they desire, and consequently, to the way in which patterns of patriarchal power relations are articulated and perhaps reinforced, as suggested by Hennessy in Chapter 2. These are reflected through an analysis of the opportunities available for women and men in tourism development and how they are part of historically constructed social practices and prejudices regarding women's and men's roles. Thus, when we write about and discuss 'hosts', we need to be asking who exactly is the object of our attention.

3. *Gendered tourism marketing*:
The promotion of tourism and the myths and fantasies of 'places over there' is dependent upon specific notions of gender, sexuality and gender relations. As mentioned above, a prescribed assumption regarding gender relations is articulated through the promotion of 'couples-only' clubs and resorts. However, women are often used in the promotion of the exoticised nature of a place. Sexual imagery, when used to depict the desirability of places in such a way, says a great deal about the gendered nature of the marketing agents and their fantasies. Although the promotion of Club 18–30 holidays is a rare example of the encouragement of single people to travel, it is packaged with overt sexual overtones which reinforce heterosexuality. As a result, the sexualised myths and fantasies extolled in the tourism promotion literature lead to the construction of these ideas in the hearts and minds of tourists.

4. *Gendered tourism objects*:
Due to the ways in which tourism is marketed and the stereotyped, perceived needs of men and women in a mythical homogeneous society, many aspects of tourism become masculinised or feminised. Stereotyped, gender-specific leisure activities may mean that different landscapes take on a gendered perception. For example, the rough rugged natural environment of wild national parks, Arctic tundra or high mountains are there to be 'conquered', usually by men. Similarly, family-oriented entertainment or 'shopping' as a leisure pursuit are often marketed toward women in their role as carers of the family.

   The (re)presentation of objects of the tourist's gaze can also be viewed as the configuration of gendered society. For example, Tim Edensor and Uma Kothari (Chapter 8) described the way in which Stirling's tourism attractions are a white, male representation of Stirling's heritage embodied in Scottish nationalism. The significance of Stirling Castle and the conquests of Robert the Bruce are the central focus of tourism promotion in the region. This raises questions for the way in which women interpret the old Scottish military myths, as they are presented at the Museum of the Argyll and Sutherland Highlanders, and their exclusion as participants in the history of Scotland, as presented at the Hall of Heroes. Their conclusions point to the need for an appreciation for a plurality of heritages 'that express different identities and operate within different networks'.

FUTURE RESEARCH AGENDAS

It is clear that the contributions to this book do not cover all gender perspectives on the processes of tourism development. However, the issues raised here do point to future research agendas that will move us closer to a greater understanding of the social complexities of tourism-related activity.

First, there is a need for more empirical, case study analyses which are attentive to the inter-relationships that occur within the process of tourism development. We have stressed the fact that tourism is best understood through the inter-relatedness of the social, economic, political, environmental and cultural aspects of societies. Yet, empirical evidence tends to avoid this inter-relatedness, finding it perhaps simpler to focus on one aspect. This is problematic within a gendered analytical framework.

Secondly, we need to address, both theoretically and empirically, studies of the social construction of the environment, the way in which women and men perceive and value the environment in different spatial contexts. Of particular interest are the ways in which women and men have been socialised with respect to their use of the environment. In geography and urban planning, for example, there have been discussions of women's use and perception of space, particularly urban space, and the social construction of the fear of certain spaces.

Thirdly, we need to take a look at intra-gender differences and the construction of power relationships among men and among women. How does the intersection of class, race, ethnicity and sexuality create intra-gender relationships, and how are these articulated as part of tourism practices?

Fourthly, we need to be careful that when we look at gender perspectives of tourism development, we are not only looking at the role, status and position of women within the tourism process and the relationships that occur between hosts and guests, but that we view the societal change that is occurring for both hosts and guests through a recognition of the dynamic nature of these roles and positions and through an analysis of changing gender relations. How gender relations are altered as a result of increased family income, for example, or the ways in which women and men (re)present their gender relations as part of a cultural showpiece are important issues. The transformation of the role of women and men in any form of tourism-related labour, whether it is formal or informal, will alter their perceptions and understandings of prevailing gender relations, modifying the latter as a consequence.

Finally, we have not covered issues relating to the role and position of women and men within alternative tourism, eco-tourism, and sustainable tourism. Nor have we paid adequate attention to differences in gender roles and changing gender relations within specific types of tourism market; for example, the differences articulated through mass-tourism in Greece, Spain or Barbados and through ethnic tourism or special-interest tourism. What are the effects of different types of tourism development on gender roles and gender relations and how do societies, appreciated for their uniqueness and traditions, articulate gender relations through their re-presentation of their culture?

The issues raised in this volume further the discussion of tourism's relationship with different societies and places. The profound social implications of processes of tourism development demand an analytical framework which is attentive to differences within societies. A gender-focused framework moves us towards this goal and suggests an agenda for further debate.

Index